Rick Paulos

PROGRAMMING LANGUAGE/ONE

With Structured Programming

Rick Faulds

PROGRAMMING LANGUAGE / ONE

With Structured Programming

THIRD EDITION

Frank Bates

American Micro-Systems, Inc.
Santa Clara, California

Mary L. Douglas

Applied Physics Laboratory
The Johns Hopkins University

Prentice-Hall, Inc.

Englewood Cliffs, New Jersey

Library of Congress Cataloging in Publication Data

BATES, FRANK
    Programming language/one.

    Includes index.
      1.–PL/I (Computer program language) I.–Douglas,
Mary L., joint author. II.–Title.
QA76.73.P25B37   1975   001.6′424   75-2113
ISBN 0-13-730457-9
ISBN 0-13-730473-0 pbk.

© 1975, 1970, 1967, Prentice-Hall, Inc.
Englewood Cliffs, N. J.

10 9 8 7 6

Printed in the United States of America

PRENTICE-HALL INTERNATIONAL, INC., *London*
PRENTICE-HALL OF AUSTRALIA, PTY. LTD., *Sydney*
PRENTICE-HALL OF CANADA, LTD., *Toronto*
PRENTICE-HALL OF INDIA PRIVATE LIMITED, *New Delhi*
PRENTICE-HALL OF JAPAN, INC., *Tokyo*
PRENTICE-HALL OF SOUTHEAST ASIA (PTE.) LTD., *Singapore*

CONTENTS

PREFACE TO THE THIRD EDITION   vii

LIST OF PROGRAM EXAMPLES   x

Chapter 1   BASIC PRINCIPLES   1

      2   LOGICAL PROGRAM STRUCTURE   18

      3   ATTRIBUTES   49

      4   ARRAYS (TABLES)   69

      5   STRUCTURES   96

      6   INPUT/OUTPUT   110

      7   PROCEDURES   144

      8   BLOCK STRUCTURE   165

      9   TESTING AND DEBUGGING   172

      10   CHARACTER MANIPULATION   190

      11   ADDITIONAL INPUT/OUTPUT FACILITIES   202

      12   STORAGE MANAGEMENT   227

Appendix A CHARACTER SETS AND OPERATORS 248

   B ABBREVIATIONS FOR KEYWORDS 252

   C BUILT-IN FUNCTIONS 254

   D CONDITIONS 262

   E PICTURE AND FORMAT SPECIFICATIONS 266

      ANSWERS TO EXERCISES 273

      INDEX 327

PREFACE TO THE THIRD EDITION

The purpose of this edition, as of the previous two, is to explain some of the techniques for using computers and the implementation of those techniques in the programming language PL/I. Since publication of the first edition in 1967 and the second edition in 1970, developments have occurred both in computer programming in general and in PL/I in particular. The third edition represents a major revision to the second edition to reflect those developments.

A number of improvements have been made in the third edition in response to suggestions from users of the second edition. In particular, Chapter 1 has been revised substantially. The book should now be of benefit to a wider range of beginning students.

A major development in expanding the use of PL/I is the ANSI Standard PL/I. The third edition has been modified wherever necessary to reflect accurately this standard. At the time of publication of this edition the proposed standard BASIS–11 was used.

The book has been kept independent of a specific implementation of PL/I in order to make it versatile. In the recent past, a number of PL/I dialects have developed. In particular, the Cornell University compiler, PL/C, is in wide use. Notes have been added to the end of appropriate chapters referencing PL/C implementation deviation from the PL/I standard.

The usefulness of the concept of "structured" programming is becoming ever more evident and is treated in this third edition in two ways. The philosophy and the benefits derived are discussed explicitly in Chapter 9 together with the application of the technique and the resulting contribution to the debugging effort and correctness of programs. Since the subject of structured programming is the basis for several complete texts, cited in the bibliography, its inclusion here is an effort to illustrate the basic attitude and approach to constructing correct and easily debugged programs. If this book is used as an introduction to programming as well as PL/I, we feel that by seeing examples of structured programs the student will learn to program by using structured techniques from the beginning. If the user already is versed in programming of some other programming language, we feel that by the illustrations in Chapter 4 and Chapter 9 the student will learn how to change to structured approach.

Nearly two-thirds of the examples and solutions to exercises presented at the end of each chapter have been reprogrammed to incorporate structured programming techniques. The intent remains to make the book as accurate and correct as possible. As in the first two editions, all of the program examples have been tested on a computer (an IBM System/360) and the program listings and results, where shown, are reproduced directly from the printed pages produced by the computer. The programs shown at the back of the book as solutions to the exercises have been similarly tested. Thus, the programs included here are not programs that should work; they are programs that do work, and will work for the user if they are reproduced exactly as they appear here.*

PL/I was originally developed jointly by IBM and the two organizations composed of major users of IBM equipment, SHARE and GUIDE. Now other manufacturers in addition to IBM such as Honeywell, Digital Equipment Corporation, Control Data Corporation, and General Electric have been involved in the development of PL/I through the ANSI standards committee. PL/I combines many of the features of other programming languages into a single language of more general utility. Consequently, once one has learned to use PL/I effectively, he will find it easy to become proficient in other lan-

---

*System control statements applicable to the particular computer system installation must, of course, be included.

guages. Similarly, one who is familiar with other languages such as FORTRAN, ALGOL, and COBOL will find it easy to become proficient in PL/I.

We are indebted to Michael Marcotty of General Motors for his valuable assistance in preparing this edition. In particular, his help with Chapter 9 and, as Chairman of the PL/I ANSI Standards Committee 1971–1974, his comments and notations in advance of formal publication of the standard are most appreciated as they have ensured both accurate and timely inclusion here.

The third edition of this book would not have been possible without the first two editions, and we wish to note the fundamental contributions and assistance given by The Johns Hopkins University Applied Physics Laboratory. Many individuals provided technical support, reviewed the text, and offered constructive suggestions for our first two editions. Notable among these are Mr. Jack Pendray of the ASSIST Corporation, William T. Altmann, formerly of IBM; George S. Brown and Carl Papa of IBM; Philip H. Dorn, Conrad H. Weisert, and Herb Van Brink then active in SHARE; and Dr. R. P. Rich of the Applied Physics Laboratory.

We wish to remember Dr. George E. Forsythe, who was our editor for the first two editions, for his enthusiasm, advice, and encouragement.

F. B., M. L. D.

LIST OF PROGRAM EXAMPLES

1.	Compute Age	2
2.	Maximum Age	14
3.	Statement Labels and Transfers	22
4.	Decisions (Conditional Transfers)	27
5.	Decisions (Computational Alternatives)	31
6.	Decisions (Either-Or)	34
7.	DO Groups	43
8.	Character String Data	60
9.	LENGTH of Character String Data	61
10.	Label Variables	66
11.	Array Declaration and Use	70
12.	Descriptive Use of Array Bounds	72
13.	Indexing	73
14.	Multi-Dimensional Arrays	76
15.	Array Expressions	77
16.	Indexing With a DO Loop	80
17.	Behavior of Control Variable	83
18.	DO WHILE Looping	84
19.	Alternate Method of DO WHILE Looping	85
20.	Nested DO Loops	85

21.	Inefficient Use of Inner Loop	86
22.	Efficient Use of Inner Loop	87
23.	Use of Structures	103
24.	Output Without PUT Options	131
25.	Output With PUT Options	131
26.	Repetitive List Specifications	133
27.	Computation in Output List	135
28.	Prepare and Print a Table	135
29.	The STRING Option	138
30.	Use of Remote Format Specifications	140
31.	Function Subprogram	145
32.	Name, Value Parameters	147
33.	Quadratic Roots by Subroutine	149
34.	Subroutine and Function Combined	150
35.	Arrays as Arguments to Subprogram	151
36.	Structures as Arguments to Subprogram	152
37.	Recursion	163
38.	Use of BEGIN Blocks	168
39.	Use of ON Statement	177
40.	CHECK Prefix—General Principle	187
41.	CHECK as a Diagnostic Aid	188
42.	Typical String Assignment Statements	191
43.	Applications of SUBSTR	195
44.	SUBSTR as Pseudo-Variable	197
45.	Concatenation	198
46.	Analysis of Text	200
47.	Use of a Non-Standard File	205
48.	Inefficient Use of Files	212
49.	Efficient Use of Files	213
50.	Build a New File From an Existing File	213
51.	BASED Variables in Input/Output	216
52.	Multiple Record Formats	218
53.	Direct Access Files (Keyed)	220

54. Creating a Keyed Direct Access File   222

55. Updating a File   224

56. Updating a DIRECT File   225

57. Building a Linked List   234

58. Maintaining a Linked List   236

59. Arrays of Linked Lists   239

60. AREA Variables and Applications   243

PROGRAMMING LANGUAGE/ONE

With Structured Programming

BASIC PRINCIPLES

Electronic data processing machines (computers) are devices which perform various operations based on instructions which they have been given by the people who use them. The process of specifying a set of instructions for a computer is called programming, and the set itself is called a program.

There are two steps involved in preparing a program for a computer. First, the individual preparing the program—the programmer—must know what instructions to specify, and the sequence in which to specify them. Second, he must be able to communicate his specifications to the computer. Communication is accomplished by means of a programming "language" which the programmer writes, and the computer "reads" to decide what to do.

There are many programming languages in use today. Some are designed for very specialized applications and some are designed for more general use. PL/I is a language in the latter category.

For a first example of a PL/I program we will discuss a simple program to compute your age. That is, given the month and year in which you were born and the current month and year the program will determine the elapsed time in years and fractions. The method we will use is

1. Subtract your year of birth from the current year to find the difference in years.

2. Add to that the difference between the current month and your month of birth (divided by 12 to put it in terms of years).

A PL/I program is made up of one or more procedures, which in turn are made up of statements. A PL/I statement is very much like a declarative or imperative sentence in English, in that it either states a property of the program or tells the computer to perform some operation or sequence of operations. For instance, one of the statements in our program states the symbols that we will use (for example, YEAR and AGE); another statement tells the computer to find the difference between the years.

The computation of your age—the steps listed above—is the heart of the program, but there are two other things our program must do. First we must give numeric values to the current date and your birth date. Second, we must include some means of getting the results out of the computer. These functions are performed by GET and PUT statements, respectively.

The program uses five variables, which we choose to name BIRTHYR, BIRTHMO, YEAR, MONTH, and AGE. Subject to rules described later in this chapter, we may choose any names we like for variables. It's a good idea to select names suggestive of the uses to which the variables are being put. Our program would give the same answers if its five variables were named DISTANCE, NETPAY, BBZ3, JOEBLOW, and ELEPHANTS, but the purpose of the program would be obscured.

Now, see if you can read the program. Ignore the first two lines, and the last line.

```
AGES: PROCEDURE OPTIONS (MAIN) ;
        /* EXAMPLE NO. 1 - COMPUTE AGE ; */

        DECLARE (BIRTHMO, BIRTHYR, MONTH, YEAR, AGE)   FLOAT;

        GET LIST (BIRTHMO, BIRTHYR, MONTH, YEAR) ;

        AGE = YEAR - BIRTHYR + (MONTH - BIRTHMO) / 12 ;

        PUT LIST (BIRTHMO, BIRTHYR, MONTH, YEAR, AGE) ;

    END AGES ;
```

Every PL/I statement ends with a semicolon, just as every English sentence ends with a period. In our example, each statement occupies one line. This format is purely for the sake of readability, and does not affect the meaning of the program. A long statement might extend over several lines, or several short statements might be placed on a single line.

Before we look at a PL/I program in more detail, you should observe a few general principles about solving problems. First, it is important to have a very precise description of the problem to be solved or the job to be performed. Simple problems, such as the first example, are easily defined. Others, e.g., payroll systems, may be very complex and difficult to define.

Once the problem is understood, a method must be devised to solve it. There may be many methods for solving a given problem and some may be better than others. For instance, in the first example, we converted the difference in months to a fraction of a year. It would have been just as easy to compute your age in months and then divide by twelve to get the desired result.

How does one select a particular method, i.e., logical process, to perform a given task? You might select one method to solve a problem using pencil and paper, and a different method to solve the same problem by computer. Generally, when using a computer, you will be interested in selecting the method which gives the most accurate results in the least time. To accomplish this, it is always good practice to analyze the problem to try to find the "simplest" method of solving it. One measure of "simplicity" is often the number of arithmetic operations required: the fewer, the better.

When you have defined the problem and selected a logical process to solve it, the next step is to write a computer program that tells the computer what you want it to do.

Thus, there are three general steps to solving a problem by means of a computer:

1. Define the problem.

2. Analyze the problem to develop the simplest logical process which leads to the solution.

3. Write a program which directs the computer to follow the process.

AGES: PROCEDURE OPTIONS (MAIN) ;

This is a <u>PROCEDURE statement</u>. It and the statements which follow form a procedure who name is AGES. Every PL/I program is either a single procedure like this example, or a collection of procedures. As we shall see later, the words PROCEDURE, OPTIONS, and MAIN have special significance.

/* EXAMPLE NO. 1 – COMPUTE AGE */

This is a comment. It is not really a statement and it is not terminated by a semicolon. The general form of a comment is

/* <u>anything</u> */

where <u>anything</u> is a message of any length that does not contain the character pair */. No blank spaces may separate the / and the * at either end of the comment.

Comments may appear almost anywhere in a program and are ignored by the computer. They are used to aid a human reader in understanding the operation of a program. As a general rule, the more comments you use in a program, the better.

DECLARE (BIRTHMO, BIRTHYR, MONTH, YEAR, AGE) FLOAT ;

This is a <u>DECLARE statement</u>. In it we list the names of all the variables used in the program. The word FLOAT tells the range of values the variables may assume. DECLARE statements can be quite complicated, as Chapter 3 will show. For the moment, we can give them the general form

DECLARE (<u>variable names separated by commas</u>) FLOAT ;

It is not always necessary to list all variables in a DECLARE statement, but we recommend that you do so. It is easier to remember to put them in DECLARE statements than it is to remember when they may be left out.

$$GET \ LIST \,(\, BIRTHMO, \ BIRTHYR, \ MONTH, \ YEAR \,) \,;$$

This GET statement takes four numbers in sequence from the input data° and assigns them to the variables BIRTHMO, BIRTHYR, MONTH, and YEAR, respectively.

$$AGE = YEAR - BIRTHYR + (\, MONTH - BIRTHMO \,) \,/\, 12 \,;$$

This assignment statement computes the age and gives this value to the variable AGE.

AN ASSIGNMENT STATEMENT IS NOT AN EQUATION, EVEN THOUGH IT LOOKS LIKE ONE. It states an action for the computer to perform, and not a condition of equality of the two sides. The expression on the right-hand side of the assignment operator (=) corresponds to the method defined starting on page 1.

$$PUT \ LIST \,(\, BIRTHMO, \ BIRTHYR, \ MONTH, \ YEAR, \ AGE \,) \,;$$

This PUT statement prints the input data (BIRTHMO, BIRTHYR, MONTH, and YEAR), and the result of our computation (AGE). Why print the input data? There are a couple of reasons. First, it enables us to associate the answers with the proper input values. This is especially important when a program produces several hundred or thousand lines of answers rather than just one. Second, by printing the input data we can check that the numbers we read in were really the numbers we intended to read in. In a program with complicated input data it is very easy to have a few numbers missing or out of order.

The form of PUT statement we are using prints values to as many decimal places as the computer uses in doing the computation—usually between six and sixteen decimal places.

°"Input data" in general means data that can be accessed by a GET statement. The sources of input data differ among computer installations.

END AGES ;

This <u>END statement</u> marks the end of procedure AGES and the end of our program.

Identifiers are used to name things in PL/I. In Example No. 1 we used identifiers to name variables, such as BIRTHMO and AGE; and to name the program, AGES, itself. Identifiers are used to name many other PL/I entities as well.

An identifier is a combination of letters, numbers, and underscores. The first character of an identifier must be a letter.° An identifier may not contain blanks.

These are identifiers:

    X

    A1

    VERYLONGIDENTIFIER

    W6IPB

    $_INCOME

    NET_COST

These are not identifiers:

    RATE OF PAY   (contains blanks)

    4F   (starts with a number)

    F.I.C.A.   (. is neither a letter nor a number)

°The characters $, @, and # are considered to be letters in PL/I.

Some of the identifiers used in the example program have special meanings because of the way they are used. These identifiers are called keywords. Keywords are used as names for kinds of statements, such as DECLARE; names of other program components, such as PROCEDURE; and for other purposes. As we shall see later, a given identifier may or may not be a keyword; whether it is or not depends on how it is used in a program.

The keywords used in Example No. 1 are:

PROCEDURE   GET

OPTIONS   LIST

MAIN   PUT

DECLARE   END

FLOAT

Arithmetic Expressions

As the assignment statement in Example No. 1 shows, arithmetic expressions in PL/I differ somewhat from the way they are usually written in algebra. Most of the differences are caused by the limitations of the computer equipment used for reading and printing. For instance, the numerator and denominator of a fraction must be written on the same line, separated by a /.

Arithmetic expressions are made up of operators, operands, and parentheses. In the expressions

$$A + B - 3 \text{ and } (A - B)/3$$

the operators are $+$, $-$, and /. The operands are A, B, and 3.

The conventional operators are

7

Operator	Meaning	Example
$+$	Addition	$a + b$
$-$	Subtraction or negation	$x - y$ $-b$
$\times$ or $\cdot$ or nothing	Multiplication	$r \times t \quad m \cdot q \quad 4ac$
$/$ or ——— or $\div$	Division	$\text{mi/hr} \quad \dfrac{a+b}{c-d}$ $p \div q$
superscript	Exponentiation	$c^2 \, 2^n$

The corresponding PL/I operators are

Operator	Meaning	Example
$+$	Addition	A + B
$-$	Subtraction or negation	X − Y −B
*	Multiplication	R*T M*Q 4*A*C
/	Division	MI/HR (A+B)/(C−D) P/Q
**	Exponentiation	C**2 2**N

The multiplication operator * may never be omitted, as in MN for M*N. The computer must be able to distinguish betwen the identifier 'MN' and the expresion 'M times N'. The multiplication operator must appear even when you would not expect ambiguity by leaving it out. For example, (A+B)C is illegal; the expression must be written (A+B)*C.

The <u>strength</u> of arithmetic operators determines the order in which operations are performed. Multiplication, for instance, is stronger than addition, so in the expression

$$A + B * C$$

the multiplication is done before the addition.

Strengths of Arithmetic Operators

Strongest:	** exponentiation	− negation (leading −)
Next strongest:	* multiplication	/ division
Weakest:	+ addition	− subtraction

Exponentiation and negation have equal strength, as do multiplication and division, and addition and subtraction.

Parentheses may always be used to change the order in which operations are performed.

What about the order for operations of equal strength? The rules vary for different cases. For multiplication and division, or addition and subtraction, the <u>leftmost</u> operation is done first. Thus,

$$A - B + C \text{ means } (A - B) + C \qquad \text{not} \qquad A - (B + C)$$

and

$$P / Q*R \text{ means } (P/Q)*R \qquad \text{not} \qquad P / (Q*R).$$

For exponentiation and negation, the <u>rightmost</u> operation is done first. Thus,

$$B ** POW1 ** POW2 \text{ means } B ** (POW1 ** POW2)$$

and

$$-A ** B \text{ means } -(A ** B)$$

and

$$A ** -B \text{ means } A ** (-B)$$

Because division and exponentiation must be written on one line in PL/I, without use of "built-up" fractions, an expression may need some extra parentheses. For instance,

$$\frac{a+b}{x+\dfrac{y}{z}} \qquad \text{becomes} \qquad (A + B) / (X + Y / Z)$$

$$x^{n-1} \qquad \text{becomes} \qquad X ** (N - 1)$$

Always use enough parentheses to make your meaning clear. When in doubt, add parentheses. They never hurt.

An expression may consist of a single operand, such as

A or B or C or −3.7 or 6

A constant is a particular form of expression. All constants are expressions but not all expressions are constants.

There are several different kinds of constants in PL/I. The only ones we will use for a while are decimal numbers. A constant may be written as an integer, with or without a sign, as

+1   0   −300000000   3244111   72037

It may be written with a decimal point, as

1.99   3.141159   −.001   007.   −1.0   0.95

It must, however, be a single number. 1/2 is an expression, but it is not a constant.

A third way of writing constants, called scientific notation, is frequently used in technical work. In scientific notation, a number is written as a decimal fraction (usually between 1 and 10), followed by 10 to some power. For example,

300000000 is written in scientific notation as 3.0×10^{8}

−.00000065 is written in scientific notation as -6.5×10^{-7}

10

The power of 10 counts the number of places the decimal point must be shifted left in the original number of order to write it in scientific notation.

Scientific notation can be used in PL/I. The letter E replaces the '$\times 10$' and the power of 10 follows the E. The power of 10 must be an integer constant.

$$3.0 \times 10^8 \quad \text{is written in PL/I as} \quad 3.0E8$$

$$-6.5 \times 10^{-7} \quad \text{is written in PL/I as} \quad -6.5E-7$$

The E may be read as "times ten-to-the". These constants all have the same value:

4.76E−2   47.600E−3   47.6E−3   0.0476E0   .0000476E3

Most computers will accept constants in the range 1E−35 to 1E35 in absolute value, and zero. Many computers will accept a much wider range.

It is important to remember two facts about arithmetic in a computer. First, a computer holds numeric values only to a fixed number of places, usually the equivalent of between 6 and 16 decimal places. (The number of digits is called the precision of a number.) For instance, a computation involving numbers of 12-digit precision will produce a result of 12-digit precision, and any low-order digits to the right of the twelfth will usually be discarded.

The second important fact is that most computers do not use base ten—that is, decimal—arithmetic internally. They may use base two, base sixteen, or some other base. This fact would be of little importance to most programmers, except for one thing: accuracy. There are fractions which, in the base-ten number system, repeat indefinitely. An example is the fraction 1/3, which is .3333... . In the same way, many fractions which can be expressed exactly in the base-ten system may turn out to be repeating fractions in the number system used by the computer. For this reason, a number like 0.1 (base-ten) cannot be represented exactly in a base two computer, no matter how many digits there are.° The inaccuracy, however slight, may lead to trouble, as we will see in Chapter 4.

° $\frac{1}{10}$ base ten = (0. 0001100110011...) base two

Example No. 1 used an assignment to give value to the variable AGE. Assignment statements have the general form

variable name = expression ;

where

variable name is the name of a variable, i.e., an identifier, and

expression is any expression. °

THE = DOES NOT REPRESENT EQUALITY. It states that the variable to its left is to be given the value of the expression on its right. That is, it states an action to be performed, and not a condition of equality. Put another way, it states that the value of the expression on the right is to be assigned to the variable whose name appears on the left. The = in an assignment statement is thus called the assignment operator.

The following sequence of assignment statements will give you a better idea of how they work:

X = 3 ;   (the variable X takes on the value 3)

Y = −4 ;   (Y takes on the value −4)

Z = X + Y ;   (Z takes on the value −1)

X = X + 1 ;   (X takes on the value 4)

The last statement in the sequence illustrates an important fact about assignment statements: the expression on the right of the assignment operator is evaluated fully before the assignment is made to the variable on the left. Before the last statement in the sequence is executed, X has the

---

°The notation used here (lower case letters with an underscore) means that a specific variable name or expression is not required, i.e, that any variable name or expression may appear. The items that are not underscored must appear. Thus, the general form of the assignment statement should be read, "a variable name followed by = followed by an expression followed by ;".

value 3 (which it was given by the first of the four statements), and that is the value which is used in evaluating the expression $X + 1$. The result (4) is then assigned to the variable on the left, which happens to be X. The net effect of the statement, then, is to increase the value of X by one. (The effect would have been the same if the expression had been $1 + X$ instead of $X + 1$.)

What will be the value of the variable VAR (an identifier chosen arbitrarily for purposes of the example) after these statements are executed in sequence?

$$VAR = 4 ;$$

$$VAR = VAR * (VAR - 1) + VAR/(VAR - 2);$$

$$VAR = VAR + 3;$$

(Answer: 17)

It is frequently convenient to assign the same value to more than one variable. This can be done in PL/I by means of a <u>multiple assignment</u> statement. The general form of a multiple assignment statement is

$$\underline{variable}_1 , \underline{variable}_2 , \quad . \ . \ . \ . \ , \underline{variable}_n = \underline{expression} ;$$

which should be read, "any number of variable names separated by commas followed by = followed by an expression followed by ;". For example, the statement

$$X, Y = 0 ;$$

sets the variables X and Y to zero.

The assignment statement is the fundamental operational statement in PL/I as well as in all programming languages, because it is the only way of saving a computed value. The most important thing to note about the assignment statement is that the value of the expression on the <u>right</u> of the assignment operator is assigned to the variable on the <u>left</u>. <u>THE ONLY THING THAT MAY APPEAR TO THE LEFT OF THE ASSIGNMENT OPERATOR IS THE NAME OF A VARIABLE,</u> or, in the case of multiple assignment, a list of variables.

Expressions may sometimes involve functions which are built into PL/I to perform operations which would be difficult or laborious for programmers to describe. Functions usually represent small "built-in" programs.

To illustrate how a function might be used, we will discuss a program which reads three numbers representing ages and prints the largest.

```
MAXAGE:   PROCEDURE OPTIONS(MAIN) ;

          /* EXAMPLE NO. 2   FIND THE MAXIMUM AGE */

          DECLARE (PERSON1, PERSON2, PERSCN3, OLDEST) FLOAT ;

          GET LIST (PERSON1, PERSON2, EERSCN3) ;

          OLDEST = MAX (PERSON1, PERSON2, PERSON3) ;

          PUT LIST (PERSON1, PERSON2, PERSON3, OLDEST) ;

     END MAXAGE ;
```

The identifier MAX in Example 2 is the name of a function.

A function may or may not have arguments, which are values upon which the function is to operate. In Example No. 2, for instance, PERSON1, PERSON2, and PERSON3 are arguments of the MAX function.

A function is used by writing its name followed by its arguments, if any, enclosed in parentheses. The functions we will use for the present all have numerical arguments, which may be variables, constants, or expressions. Some functions require several arguments, some require only one, and others require none. Some functions may have a variable number of arguments. Some typical PL/I functions are shown on the next page. A more complete list appears in Appendix C.

Function	No. of Arguments	Value	Example of Use
SQRT (X)	1	$\sqrt{X}$	SQRT (A**2 + B**2)
DATE	none	a number representing today's month, day, and year.	DATE
MAX(A,B,C)	two or more	value of largest argument	MAX (X + Y, X/Y, 0)

Alternative Form of DECLARE Statement

Examples 1 and 2 in this chapter use DECLARE statements of the form

DECLARE (variable names separated by commas) FLOAT ;

and it has been noted that the word FLOAT tells the range of values each of the variables may assume. In this form of DECLARE statement the word FLOAT is said to be factored because it applies to each of the identifiers between the parentheses. The factored form used in Example 1 is

DECLARE (BIRTHMO, BIRTHYR, MONTH, YEAR, AGE) FLOAT ;

Alternatively, and equivalently, the word FLOAT may be attributed individually to each of the identifiers being declared. The equivalent non-factored form for Example 1 would be

DECLARE BIRTHMO   FLOAT,
          BIRTHYR   FLOAT,
          MONTH   FLOAT,
          YEAR   FLOAT,
          AGE   FLOAT;

In general, the non-factored DECLARE statement has the form

DECLARE variable FLOAT, variable FLOAT, . . . variable FLOAT ;

Each "variable FLOAT" pair is separated from the other by a comma, because each pair is a single element in a list.

Although factoring contributes to brevity, it may also impair readability. Use of the non-factored form, although extending program length, makes the program easier to read and modify. As shown in Chapter 3, moreover, FLOAT is only one of a wealth of words which may be attributed to variables. Because most programs will not use FLOAT exclusively, there may be advantages to specifying the appropriate word for each variable, i.e., using the non-factored form.

Notes

Some implementations, such as PL/C, may restrict the use of certain identifiers so that they are always keywords. The use of factoring of attributes may also be restricted.

EXERCISES

1.1   Which of the following are identifiers?

A*B	IBM
A__B	VARIABLE
TIME	S360
PL/I	X1Y2
$__AMOUNT	(TEMP)
ACCOUNT-NUMBER	

1.2 Write the PL/I equivalent of the following expressions. (Example: the PL/I equivalent of a+b is A+B)

$$x^3$$
$$(x-1)(x+1)$$
$$x^2 + 2x + 1$$
$$\sqrt{a^2 + b^2}$$
$$\frac{a + b + c}{3}$$

1.3 Write a PL/I program which reads two numbers representing the lengths of the legs of a right triangle and computes the hypotenuse by means of the Pythagorean Theorem,

$$\text{hypotenuse} = \sqrt{leg_1^2 + leg_2^2}$$

1.4 Write a PL/I program which reads a number representing an employee's gross earnings and prints two values based on the earnings: a value equal to 22% of the gross pay (representing taxes), and the employee's net earnings.

1.5 Same as exercise 1.4, but use each of the following methods:
   a. Determine taxes as 22% of gross pay, and net pay as 78% of gross pay.
   b. Determine net pay as 78% of gross pay, and then determine the tax by subtracting the net pay from gross pay.
   c. Determine taxes as 22% of gross pay, and then determine net pay by subtracting the taxes from gross pay.
   In each case, the sum of the two numbers (taxes and net pay) should equal the gross pay. Can you think of any reason why they might not?

1.6 Write a PL/I program to solve the quadratic equation, which is given by:

$$root1 = \frac{-b + \sqrt{b^2 - 4ac}}{2a}$$

$$root2 = \frac{-b - \sqrt{b^2 - 4ac}}{2a}$$

1.7 Interest on a sum of money is componded annually by the following

$$P*(1 + i)^n$$

where P is the original sum of money, i.e., the principal; i is the annual interest rate; and n is the number of years.
     Write a PL/I program which reads three numbers corresponding to P, i, and n, and prints the resulting value.

Chapter 2

LOGICAL PROGRAM STRUCTURE

Chapter 1 discussed this PL/I program, to compute a person's age:

```
AGES: PROCEDURE OPTIONS (MAIN) ;
      /* EXAMPLE NO. 1 - COMPUTE AGE */

      DECLARE (BIRTHMO, BIRTHYR, MONTH, YEAR, AGE)   FLOAT;

      GET LIST (BIRTHMO, BIRTHYR, MONTH, YEAR) ;

      AGE = YEAR - BIRTHYR + (MONTH - BIRTHMO) / 12 ;

      PUT LIST (BIRTHMO, BIRTHYR, MONTH, YEAR, AGE) ;

   END AGES ;
```

Before the program can be executed on the computer, it must be translated into the computer's internal language. The translation is performed by another program called a compiler which reads the PL/I program (just as the example program reads values for the variables BIRTHMO, BIRTHYR, MONTH, and YEAR) and converts the PL/I statements into the proper computer instructions. The machine-language equivalent, or object program, is then executed to perform the operations specified in the original, or source program. Every PL/I program is thus processed in two phases: a compilation phase, and an execution phase. The entire process is illustrated on the following page. It is extremely important to maintain the distinction of the two phases.

18

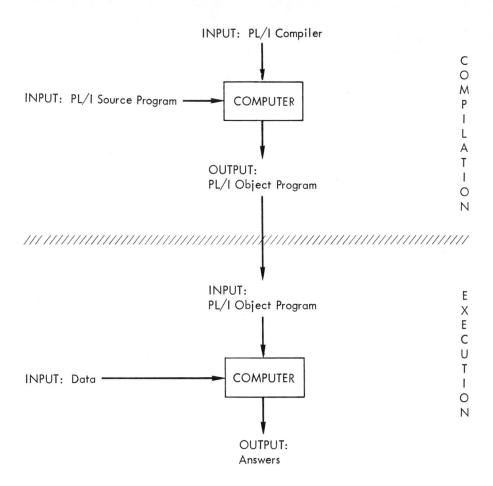

INPUT: PL/I Compiler

INPUT: PL/I Source Program ⟶ COMPUTER

COMPILATION

OUTPUT:
PL/I Object Program

INPUT:
PL/I Object Program

EXECUTION

INPUT: Data ⟶ COMPUTER

OUTPUT:
Answers

Some of the statements in our program tell the compiler what instructions to generate for use during the execution phase. These are called executable statements. The GET statement, the assignment statement, and the PUT statement are the executable statements in the program. These PL/I statements are translated by the compiler into computer instructions which are to be executed.

The PROCEDURE, DECLARE, and END statements in our program tell the compiler how to generate instructions for the executable statements. These statements are called non-executable statements, or declarations.

The PROCEDURE statement

AGES: PROCEDURE OPTIONS(MAIN);

serves to begin a logical entity called a procedure. All subsequent PL/I statements are considered by the compiler to be contained in this procedure. After the PUT statement has been compiled, the compiler sees the statement

END AGES ;

which signifies the end of the procedure. In our example, the END statement also signifies the ·end of the program. After it has been compiled, the execution phase can begin.

The DECLARE statement tells the compiler something about the properties of the variables to be used in the program. The DECLARE statement is discussed at length in Chapter 3.

The sequence in which operations are executed is called the logical sequence and normally corresponds to the physical sequence of left to right, top to bottom in the source program. The logical sequence determines whether or not a program will operate correctly.

We can diagram the logic of our program by means of a flow chart which shows the required steps and their sequence. Three steps are required:

1. establish the dates,

2. compute the age, and

3. print the results.

These three steps could be implemented in any programming language to solve this problem. Thus, we can consider programs in general as logical constructions which are implemented by means of programming languages.

The flow chart on the following page is a logical diagram of the process of computing a person's age. To the right of the chart is the implementation of this process in PL/I.

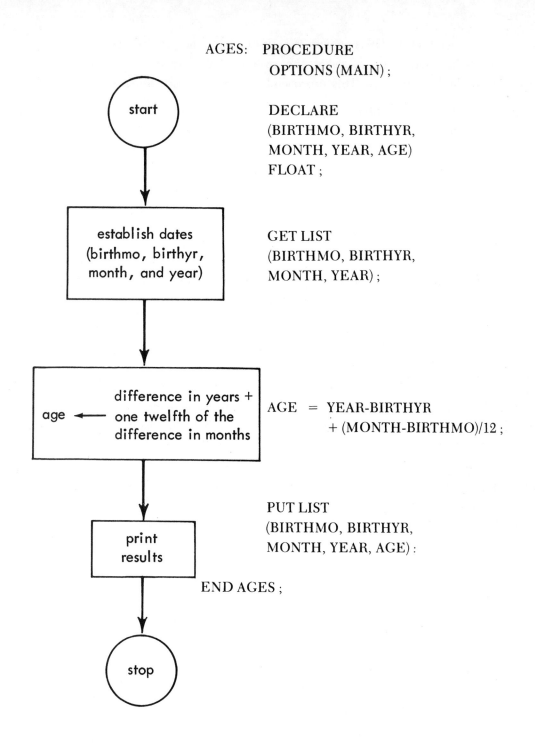

AGES: PROCEDURE
       OPTIONS (MAIN) ;

       DECLARE
       (BIRTHMO, BIRTHYR,
       MONTH, YEAR, AGE)
       FLOAT ;

       GET LIST
       (BIRTHMO, BIRTHYR,
       MONTH, YEAR) ;

AGE = YEAR-BIRTHYR
        + (MONTH-BIRTHMO)/12 ;

       PUT LIST
       (BIRTHMO, BIRTHYR,
       MONTH, YEAR, AGE) :

       END AGES ;

As procedure AGES is now written, it can solve the problem only once. Every time we want to solve the problem, it may be necessary to recompile the program.° This approach has two real disadvantages:

1. It does not utilize the computer efficiently. The compilation phase may take several seconds, while the execution phase may take only a few thousandths of a second. This means that most of the cost (and time) of running the program is incurred by the non-productive compilation phase, while only a small fraction is directly connected with the productive work of solving the problem.

2. The time and effort required to prepare the program, submit it for processing on the computer, and receive results would probably be far greater than the time and effort required to solve the problem by hand.

Both of these disadvantages can be overcome by modifying the program so that it will compute the ages of a number of people, rather than just one person. In other words, we want to write a PL/I program to implement the logical construction (flow chart) shown on the following page. The PL/I implementation of the process is shown on page 24.

The new program (Example No. 3) is very similar to the original program (Example No. 1). The GET statement has been given the name START, and a GO TO statement has been inserted following the PUT statement.

°The necessity for recompiling depends on the particular computer and compiler in use.

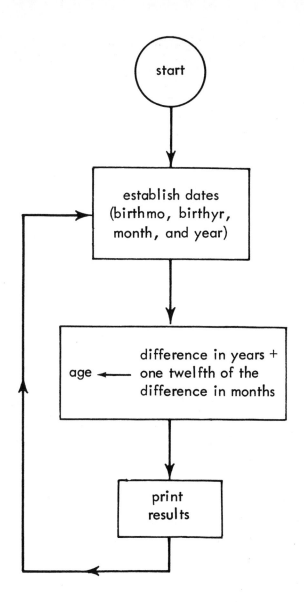

The name START in Example No. 3 is a <u>statement label</u>, or, simply, a
<u>label</u>. Labels are used to name statements in <u>PL/I</u>.

```
AGES: PROCEDURE OPTIONS (MAIN) ;
          /* EXAMPLE NO. 3 - COMPUTE AGE
             FOR AN ARBITRARY NUMBER OF CASES.   */

          DECLARE (BIRTHMO, BIRTHYR, MONTH, YEAR, AGE) FLOAT ;

START:    /* EVERY SOLUTION STARTS HERE.  */
          GET LIST (BIRTHMO, BIRTHYR, MONTH, YEAR) ;
          AGE = YEAR - BIRTHYR + (MONTH - BIRTHMO) / 12 ;
          PUT LIST (BIRTHMO, BIRTHYR, MONTH, YEAR, AGE) ;
          GO TO START  ;

       END AGES ;
```

Labels have the general form

name :

where <u>name</u> is an identifier, i.e., a combination of letters, numbers, and
underscore (break characters), the first character of which is a letter. The
colon following the name tells the compiler that the name is being <u>defined</u>
as a label. There may be any number of blanks (or no blanks) between the
name and the colon.

A statement label is associated with the statement which physically
follows it. In Example No. 3, the label START is the name of the GET
statement. There is no significance in the fact that the label is on a
different line from the GET statement which it names. The only
restriction is that the named statement must be the first statement
following the label. As long as that restriction is satisfied, physical
placement is arbitrary. As a general rule, it is a good idea to place labels so
that they can be readily discerned by someone reading the program.

Labels are usually used for documentation purposes to indicate the
logical segments of the program to a human reader. However, labels can
also be employed to name statements so that control can be transferred to
them during execution.

The GO TO statement used in Example No. 3 is used to alter the sequence of execution (not compilation). The general form of a GO TO statement is

GO TO label;

where label is a statement label which is defined in the program.

GO TO statements are sometimes called "transfers". They may transfer control "forward" or "backward". In Example No. 3 the transfer is "backward", i.e., in the direction opposite to normal program flow.

Use of the GO TO statement is not the only way to control sequence of execution, since the desired process can often be obtained by constructing the program in a particular way. In large programs, the GO TO statement may be a source of difficulty when trying to understand the logical sequence of operations.

In Example No. 3 the END statement cannot be executed. After the PUT statement is executed, control passes to the next statement in sequence. That statement is the GO TO statement which tells the computer to break the sequence and take its next instruction from a specified place, namely, the label START. After transferring to START (more precisely, to the statement labeled START), control resumes in the normal sequence from that point and continues until the normal sequence is again broken by the GO TO statement. The process continues as long as there are data to be read into the computer. After the last results have been printed, the program will return to the GET statement as usual, but upon sensing no more data, the computer will terminate program execution.

There are several ways in which we can modify our program so that it can decide for itself when it has processed the last set of data. For example, month of birth cannot reasonably be less than 1 or more than 12.

We can use this fact as the basis for a <u>decision</u>, and implement the construction shown below.

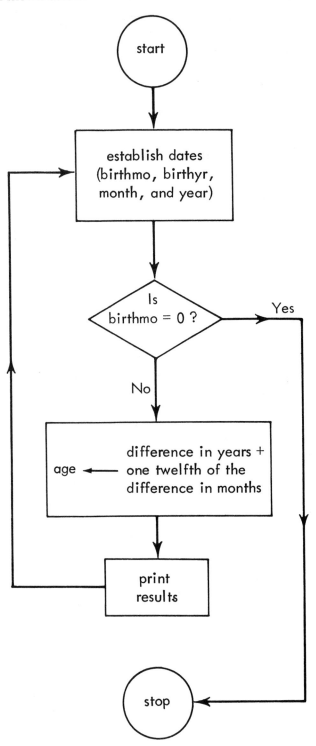

The diamond-shaped block in the flow chart on the following page is called a <u>decision block</u> (rectangular blocks are called <u>process blocks</u>), and indicates that a decision is to be made. In this case, the decision is to terminate program execution if the value read in for BIRTHMO is zero.

Now, here is the PL/I implementation of the process:

```
AGES: PROCEDURE OPTIONS (MAIN) ;
          /* EXAMPLE NO. 4 - COMPUTE AGE
             FOR AN ARBITRARY NUMBER OF CASES
             AND TERMINATE WHEN BIRTHMO IS
             LESS THAN 1                        */

          DECLARE   BIRTHMO   FLOAT,
                    BIRTHYR   FLOAT,
                    MONTH     FLOAT,
                    YEAR      FLOAT,
                    AGE       FLOAT ;

START:    /* EVERY SOLUTION STARTS HERE.  */
          GET LIST (BIRTHMO, BIRTHYR, MONTH, YEAR) ;
          IF BIRTHMO < 1 THEN GO TO FINISH ;

          AGE = YEAR - BIRTHYR + (MONTH - BIRTHMO) / 12 ;
          PUT LIST (BIRTHMO, BIRTHYR, MONTH, YEAR, AGE) ;
          GO TO START  ;

 FINISH:  END AGES ;
```

There are two differences between Example No. 4 and the previous examples: an <u>IF</u> statement has been inserted following the GET statement, and a label (FINISH) has been placed on the END statement.

After each set of data has been read in, the value of the variable BIRTHMO is tested. If BIRTHMO is equal to zero, control is transferred to the label FINISH, i.e., to the END statement, and execution is terminated.

What happens if BIRTHMO is not equal to zero? The GO TO statement is not executed; it is skipped, and execution proceeds to the calculation of the age. The remainder of the computation follows, and eventually the GO TO statement following the PUT statement will be executed, transferring control back to the label START. The next set of data will be read in as usual, the value of BIRTHMO will be tested, and control may or may not be transferred to FINISH, depending on its value.

The statement

IF BIRTHMO = 0 THEN GO TO FINISH ;

is a <u>conditional</u> transfer statement. The transfer may or may not occur, depending on a specific condition, namely, that the value of the variable BIRTHMO is zero. If BIRTHMO is equal to zero, the condition is "true", and the transfer will occur. Otherwise, the condition is "false", and the transfer will not occur.

IF statements have the general form

IF <u>condition</u> THEN <u>statement</u> ;

where <u>condition</u> describes the condition that must exist in order for <u>statement</u> to be executed. If the prescribed condition does not exist, the statement is simply skipped.

In Example No. 4, the condition is that BIRTHMO is equal to zero, written in PL/I as BIRTHMO=0. The statement is GO TO FINISH.

The same effect can be achieved by the statement

IF BIRTHMO = 0 THEN STOP ;

This is an example of how program structuring may be used to advantage in describing the desired process. STOP in the context is a keyword, which has the expected effect.

A condition is specified in PL/I by two expressions separated by a <u>comparison operator</u>.° In Example No. 4, the expressions are BIRTHMO and the constant zero; the comparison operator is the equals sign (=), which specifies the relationship that must exist between the two expressions in order for the condition to be true.

THE EQUALS SIGN USED AS A COMPARISON OPERATOR HAS AN ENTIRELY DIFFERENT MEANING FROM THAT WHICH IT

° Also called a <u>relational operator</u>.

HAS WHEN USED AS AN ASSIGNMENT OPERATOR. The meaning of the symbol = is determined by the compiler from the context in which it appears in the PL/I program. It is very important to remember that in PL/I the symbol = has two distinct meanings; its meaning at any particular appearance in a PL/I program is determined by context.*

There is one set of comparison operators in PL/I, but their representation varies among computer installations. The symbols used in this book are listed below. An alternative set appears in Appendix A.

Condition	True if . . .
A ¬< B	A is not less than B
A < B	A is less than B
A < = B	A is less than or equal to B
A = B	A is equal to B
A ¬ = B	A is not equal to B
A > = B	A is greater than or equal to B
A > B	A is greater than B
A ¬ > B	A is not greater than B

Some conditions are equivalent. For example, the condition A<B is equivalent to B>A; A=B is equivalent to A−B=0; and A¬<B is equivalent to A>=B.

Simple conditions can be combined into more complex conditions by means of logical operators. (These operators are more accurately described as "bit-string operators" but for the moment we will use them in a "logical" sense, to determine the truth or falsity of conditions.) As with comparison operators, the representation of the logical operators varies among computer installations. The symbols used in this book are listed below. An alternative set appears in Appendix A.

---

*In some programming languages the symbol = is used exclusively as a comparison operator. In these languages, the assignment operation is specified by symbols which are much more descriptive of the operation. Two of the more common assignment operators are ← and :=. Note that we have used the symbol ← in the flow charts appearing in this book.

Symbol	Meaning
¬	NOT
&	AND
|	OR

As an example, <u>statement</u> in the following IF statement will be executed if the expression A is equal to 3 and expression B is greater than expression C:

IF A=3 & B>C THEN <u>statement</u> ;

We might want to execute <u>statement</u> if and only if that condition were not true. In that case, the PL/I statement would be

IF ¬ (A=3 & B>C) THEN <u>statement</u> ;

The parentheses specify that the symbol ¬ applies to the entire condition. In other words, if the condition (A=3 & B>C) is <u>not</u> true, then <u>statement</u> will be executed.

It must be emphasized that logical operators are used to combine <u>conditions</u>. Sometimes, this is a very easy point to overlook. For example, if A and B are expressions and it is desired to execute a statement if either or both are equal to zero, you might be tempted to write

IF A\|B=0 THEN <u>statement</u> ;

which is incorrect. The correct statement is

IF A=0 \| B=0 THEN <u>statement</u> ;

An easy way to avoid such problems is to parenthesize each of the conditions to be combined. For example, the following IF statement could be used to execute a statement if the value of expression Y lies between the value of expression X and the value of expression Z (in mathematical terms, if x<y<z):

IF (X<Y) & (Y<Z) THEN <u>statement</u> ;

Logical operators in PL/I have the following strengths:

Strengths of Logical Operators

Strongest:	¬	"not"	(logical negation)
Next strongest:	&	"and"	(conjunction)
Weakest:	|	"or"	(disjunction)

As with arithmetic expressions, parentheses may be used in logical expressions to prescribe the order in which operations are to be performed.

The following program example reads three numbers denoting the lengths of the sides of a triangle, and sets the variable TYPE to 1 if the triangle is isosceles (two sides equal) or equilateral (all three sides equal). If the triangle is neither isosceles nor equilateral, the program sets TYPE to 0.

```
TRIANGL: PROCEDURE OPTIONS (MAIN) ;

         /* EXAMPLE NO. 5
            GIVEN SIDES OF A TRIANGLE:
            IF ISOSCELES OR EQUILATERAL, PRINT 1;
            ELSE PRINT 0. */

         DECLARE (TYPE, SIDE1, SIDE2, SIDE3) FLOAT ;

START:   GET LIST(SIDE1, SIDE2, SIDE3) ;
         IF SIDE1=0 THEN STOP ;

         /* ASSUME TRIANGLE IS NEITHER ISOSCELES NOR
            EQUILATERAL. */
            TYPE = 0;
         /* SET TYPE TO 1 IF NECESSARY. */
         IF (SIDE1=SIDE2) | (SIDE1=SIDE3) | (SIDE2=SIDE3)
            THEN TYPE = 1 ;

         /* PRINT DATA AND RESULTS. */
         PUT LIST(SIDE1, SIDE2, SIDE3, TYPE) ;
         GO TO START ; /* PROCESS NEXT CASE. */
      END TRIANGL ;
```

An IF statement of the form

IF <u>condition</u> **THEN** <u>statement</u> ;

can be illustrated by the following flow chart. <u>Statement</u> will be executed if <u>condition</u> is true, and not otherwise.

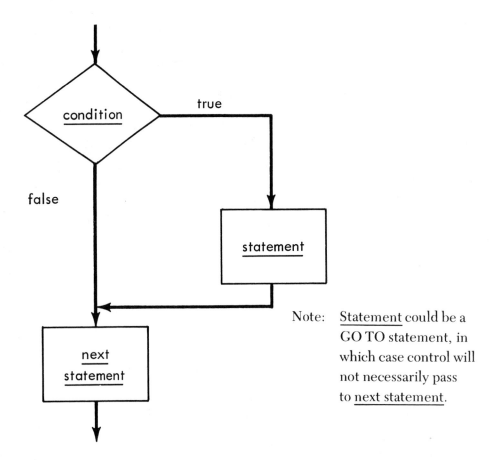

Note: <u>Statement</u> could be a GO TO statement, in which case control will not necessarily pass to <u>next statement</u>.

IF <u>condition</u> **THEN** <u>statement</u> ;

<u>next statement</u> ;

If your program requires a logical construction like that illustrated above, then you would use an **IF** statement of the form shown beneath the flow chart.

In addition to deciding whether or not to execute a given statement, the **IF** statement can be used to decide which one of two alternative statements is to be executed, i.e., to implement the logical construction shown below. The IF statement required for the implementation is shown beneath the flow chart.

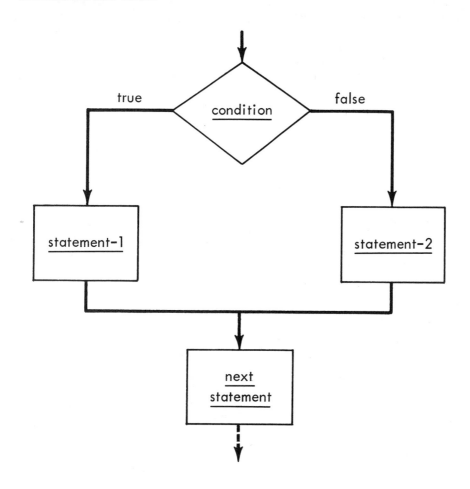

IF condition THEN statement-1 ;

ELSE statement-2 ;

next statement ;

This form of the IF statement specifies that if the condition is true when it is evaluated, statement-1 is to be executed. Otherwise, statement-2 is to be executed. One or the other will be executed; the two are mutually exclusive.

The following program reads two numbers and prints them out such that the larger of the two numbers is printed first.

```
SORT: PROCEDURE OPTIONS (MAIN) ;

          /* EXAMPLE NO. 6
             GIVEN TWO NUMBERS, PLACE THE LARGER IN
             'BIG' AND THE SMALLER IN 'SMALL'. */

          DECLARE (X, Y,  /* THE TWO NUMBERS */
                   BIG, SMALL) FLOAT ;

START:    GET LIST(X, Y) ;

          IF X>Y THEN BIG = X ;
                 ELSE BIG = Y ;

          IF X>Y THEN SMALL = Y ;
                 ELSE SMALL = X ;

          PUT LIST(X, Y, BIG, SMALL) ;
          GO TO START ;
        END SORT ;
```

The "ELSE-form" of the IF statement can be expanded to govern execution of any number of alternative statements, rather than just two. The flow chart on the following page illustrates one such construction, and the IF statement which follows it illustrates its implementation in PL/I.

The indentation used in the IF statement is intended to emphasize the logical construction implemented by the statement.

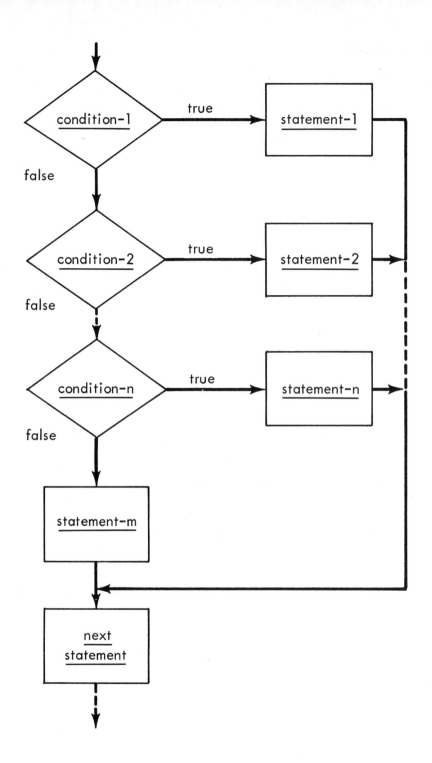

```
IF condition-1

    THEN statement-1 ;

    ELSE  IF condition-2

        THEN statement-2 ;

        ELSE .
                .
            ELSE  IF condition-n

                THEN statement-n ;

                ELSE statement-m ;
```

next statement ;

One way to analyze a relatively complex IF statement like this is to examine it from bottom to top, step-by-step:

1. Under what conditions will statement-m be executed? (What happens if condition-n is true?)

2. Under what conditions will condition-n be evaluated? Answer: if condition-2 is false. If it is true, statement-2 will be executed instead; the IF-ELSE construction always presents mutually exclusive alternatives.

3. Under what conditions will condition-2 be evaluated?

It is worth noting in passing that the first condition found to be true causes the corresponding statement to be executed; the ELSE-path is not taken, and consequently any conditions which lie in that ELSE-path are not evaluated.

This statement could be used to place the largest of three values, A, B, and C, into BIG:

```
IF  (A>B)  &  (A>C)
    THEN BIG = A ;
    ELSE IF B>C
            THEN BIG = B ;
            ELSE BIG = C ;
```

The following flow chart is similar, but not identical, to the preceding one. Here, it is possible for none of the alternatives to be executed.

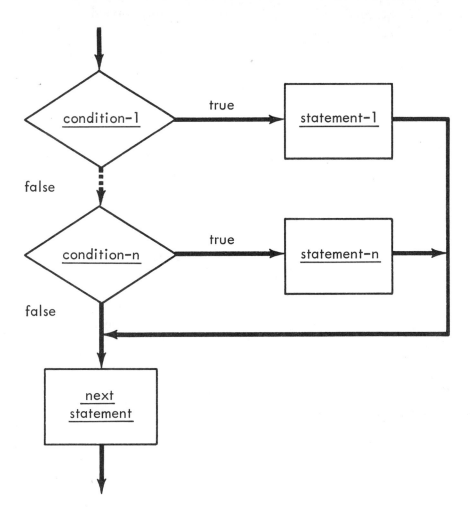

IF <u>condition-1</u> THEN <u>statement-1</u> ;

.

.

.

     ELSE IF <u>condition-n</u> THEN <u>statement-n</u> ;

<u>next statement</u> ;

The statement on page 37 differs from the previous one in that it specifies no alternative (ELSE) for the last IF statement contained in it. If, in the above statement, condition-n is not true, statement-n is skipped; in any case control then passes to next statement.

The following statements could be used as part of a payroll program to compute federal income tax to be withheld. It is assumed that the most common withholding figure is 20%, so the figure is initially set to 0.20 and modified only if necessary.

```
TAX = 0.20 ;

IF PAY>1400
   THEN TAX = 0.30 ; .
   ELSE IF PAY>1200
             THEN TAX = 0.25 ;
             ELSE IF PAY>1000
                       THEN TAX = 0.23 ;
```

You may have noticed from the preceding illustrations that ELSE, if used, specifies an alternative path to be taken if the last preceding condition is false. In PL/I, that is in fact the rule:

ELSE, if used, specifies an alternative path for the last preceding IF for which an ELSE path is not already specified.

The following flow chart and statement illustrate the rule.

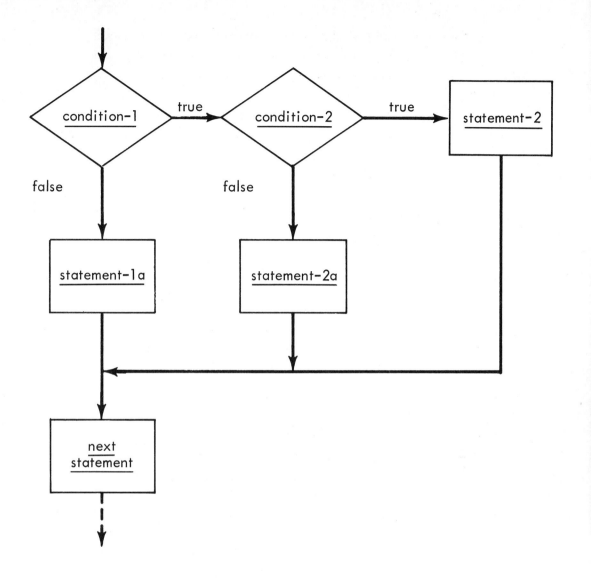

IF <u>condition-1</u>

   THEN IF <u>condition-2</u>

            THEN <u>statement-2</u> ;

            ELSE <u>statement-2a</u> ;

   ELSE <u>statement-1a</u> ;

<u>next statement</u> ;

A typical application of this kind of IF statement might be as follows. Assume an employer allows his employees a certain number (S) of "sick days" per year. Employees who have a perfect attendance record receive an extra day of vacation, but those who were absent more than the allowable number of sick days are docked the excess. The employer could use the following statement to compute the number of vacation days due an employee:

```
IF ABSENCES < S
   THEN IF ABSENCES = 0
           THEN VACATION = VACATION + 1 ;
       ELSE ;
   ELSE VACATION = VACATION - (ABSENCES - S) ;
```

The construction

ELSE ;

appearing in the preceding IF statement is an example of a null statement. It specifies that if the last preceding condition is false then no operations are to be performed. A null ELSE path is needed here so that the following ELSE will be taken as the alternative for the first IF. Remember that ELSE, if used, is always associated with the last preceding IF for which an ELSE path was not specified. In other words, if we need an ELSE path for an outer IF, we must first have ELSE paths for all of the inner IFs. As in the preceding statement, some of these paths may be null paths.

The construction

(a)   IF condition THEN statement ;

ELSE ;

is equivalent to the construction

(b)   IF <u>condition</u> THEN <u>statement</u> ;

which is the first kind of IF statement discussed in this chapter. Indeed, form (a) can be used anywhere that form (b) could be used and the operation of the program would be the same. The converse, however, is not true. Form (a) <u>must</u> be used when an IF statement is "nested" within another IF statement and it is necessary to specify an ELSE path for one of the outer IFs.

The IF statements used so far have been used to decide whether or not a single statement is to be executed, or which one of a set of alternative single statements is to be executed. Often, you will find it necessary—or convenient—for an IF statement to govern the execution (or non-execution) of a group of statements, rather than just one.

A group of statements is begun in PL/I by the <u>DO statement</u>, which has the form

DO ;

and is terminated by an END statement.* The DO statement, the END statement, and any statements in between comprise a <u>DO group</u>. As shown in the following example, a DO group behaves much like a single statement.

Example No. 6 (page 34) read two numbers and placed the larger in BIG and the smaller in SMALL by using two IF statements. By using an IF statement to govern the execution of more than one statement we can do the same thing by implementing the construction shown on the next page.

---

*The DO statement can be used in a different form to specify that the group of statements is to be executed repeatedly. This use of the DO statement is described in Chapter 4.

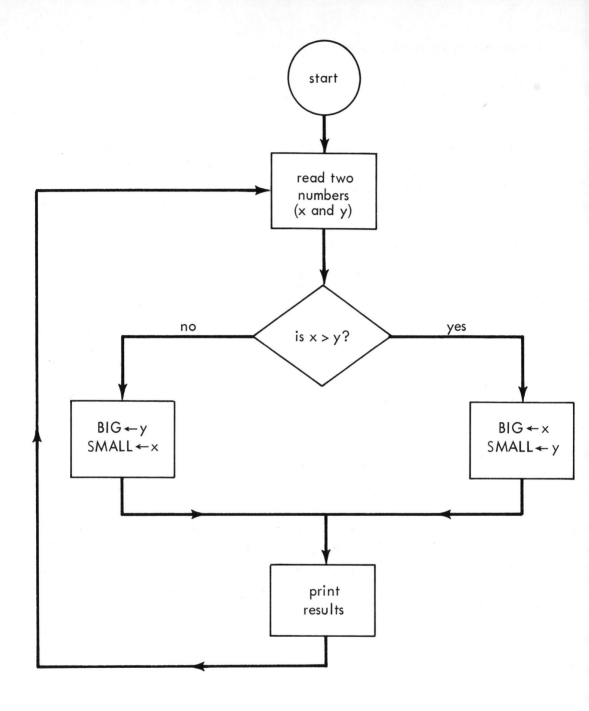

The PL/I program to implement the construction uses a DO group in each branch of the IF statement:

```
SORT: PROCEDURE OPTIONS (MAIN) ;

        /* EXAMPLE NO. 7
           GIVEN TWO NUMBERS, PLACE THE LARGER IN
           'BIG' AND THE SMALLER IN 'SMALL'. */

        DECLARE (X, Y, BIG, SMALL) FLOAT ;
START:  GET LIST(X, Y) ;

        IF X>Y THEN
            DO ;
                BIG = X ;
                SMALL = Y ;
            END ;

        ELSE
            DO ;
                BIG = Y ;
                SMALL = X ;
            END ;

        PUT LIST(X, Y, BIG, SMALL) ;
        GO TO START ;
    END SORT ;
```

The DO statement, which in the present context is a non-executable statement, serves to begin a logical entity, just as does the procedure declaration in the first line of the example. In the present case, the DO groups are logical entities (groups) "nested" within another logical entity (the procedure, SORT).

In order for the DO groups to be <u>executed</u> as logical entities, the compiler must be told when to end them; that is the function of the END statements. The END statements in the DO groups in Example No. 7 serve to terminate only the DO groups; they do not terminate the larger entity, the procedure. Two general rules are

1. Every logical entity must be terminated by an END statement.

2. An END statement matches the last previous DO or PROCEDURE statement.

There may be any number of statements in a DO group, but the principle is always the same: the group is executed or skipped as a whole. A DO group containing a single statement behaves in exactly the same way as would the statement by itself.

Some of the statements in a DO group may be IF statements, and the statements governed by the conditions in those IF statements may also be DO groups.

Note the indentation used in Example No. 7. The particular indentation in the example is used to emphasize the logical structure of the program, to make it easier to read and understand what it is supposed to do. The same results would be obtained if the statement had been written

```
IF X >Y THEN DO;BIG=X;SMALL=Y;END;ELSE DO;BIG=Y;SMALL=X;END;
```

but the logical structure of the program would have been obscured.

Most cases of improper results can be traced to errors in logical program structure. Almost every program has such "bugs" which must be located and fixed before the program can be used successfully. You will find it extremely helpful to emphasize the logical structure of your programs wherever possible in order to simplify the inevitable problem of finding logical errors or oversights ("debugging"). The indentation used in Example No. 7, for instance, shows at a glance that the DO groups are associated with a particular decision. That same glance can determine the contents, or scope of the groups.

This chapter has introduced the concept of a computer program as a logical construction. PL/I is one particular language used to communicate with the computer, just as English is one particular language used to communicate with people. There is not necessarily any correlation between the physical appearance of a PL/I program and the logical construction it represents, but it is essential to remember that it is the logical construction that determines whether a program will produce the desired results.

IF (decision) statements and DO groups are two of the most powerful constructions in PL/I. They can be used to express complicated logical constructions very simply.

There are three basic forms of the IF statement. When you set out to solve a problem on a computer you will first formulate the logical construction representing the solution, and then write the appropriate statements to express that construction to the computer. The form of IF statements you use should be the one that makes for the simplest program; there is no generally "preferable" form.

The algebra of logic, known as Boolean algebra, is concerned with two values: "true" and "false". In PL/I, "true" is represented as the quantity 1 (one) and "false" is represented as the quantity 0 (zero). Every condition in PL/I yields one of these values when it is evaluated.

Because the values resulting from the evaluation of conditions (logical expressions) are numeric (0 or 1), logical expressions can be used in arithmetic expressions.° For example, a company preparing monthly statements for its customers may wish to indicate a balance due for those accounts in which current charges exceed the current amount in the account; otherwise, the statements are to show a balance due of zero. The following statement might appear in the PL/I program used to prepare the statements:

```
BALANCE_DUE = (CHARGES>DEPOSITS) * (CHARGES-DEPOSITS)  ;
```

This statement is an assignment statement which assigns a value to the variable named BALANCE__DUE. As in all assignment statements, the expression to the right of the assignment operator (=) is evaluated before the assignment is made. In this case, there are two expressions to the right of the assignment operator: a logical expression, or condition (CHARGES>DEPOSITS), and an arithmetic expression (CHARGES − DEPOSITS). The asterisk, of course, specifies that the values of the two expressions are to be multiplied together.

The logical expression (CHARGES>DEPOSITS) yields a value of 0 or 1; the value is 1 if CHARGES has a value greater than that of DEPOSITS.

°Thus, conditions are not at all restricted to use with IF statements.

Otherwise, the value is 0. In other words, the expression has a value of 1 if there is a balance due, else 0.

The entire expression on the right side of the assignment operator then evaluates to either

$$0*(CHARGES-DEPOSITS) \quad \text{or zero}$$

or

$$1*(CHARGES-DEPOSITS) \quad \text{or the amount due,}$$

and the resulting value is then assigned to the variable named BALANCE_DUE.

EXERCISES

2.1 The variable named DISC in the program below is not really necessary, because it could be replaced by the expression B**2 − 4*A*C at each appearance. Furthermore, if DISC were not used, an assignment statement would be eliminated from the program, thus making the program physically shorter. What advantages, if any, are gained by using this "extra" variable in the program?

```
QUAD: PROCEDURE OPTIONS (MAIN) ;
            /* COMPUTE QUADRATIC ROOTS FOR ARBITRARY
               NUMBER OF CASES. */

            DECLARE (A, B, C, ROOT1, ROOT2, DISC) FLOAT ;

    START:  /* EVERY SOLUTION STARTS HERE. */
            GET LIST(A, B, C) ;
            DISC = SQRT(B**2 - 4*A*C) ;
            ROOT1 = (-B + DISC) / (A+A) ;
            ROOT2 = (-B - DISC) / (A+A) ;
            PUT LIST(A, B, C, ROOT1, ROOT2) ;
            GO TO START ;
        END QUAD ;
```

2.2   Given the following three sets of data

1)	A = 10	B = 5	C = 0
2)	A = 0	B = 10	C = 5
3)	A = 5	B = 0	C = 10

For each of these cases, what value will be printed by each of the two PUT statements below.

1)
```
IF  A>B  THEN  R  =  1  ;
IF  B>C  THEN  R  =  2  ;
IF  A>C  THEN  R  =  3  ;

PUT  LIST( R )  ;
```
3, 2, 1

2)
```
        IF  A>B  THEN  R  =  1  ;
ELSF IF  B>C  THEN  R  =  2  ;
ELSE IF  A>C  THEN  R  =  3  ;

        PUT  LIST( R )  ;
```
1, 2, 1

27 Sep 79

2.3   Write a PL/I program which reads three numbers and prints results as follows:

0   if the numbers do not represent the sides of a triangle.

1   if they represent the sides of a triangle which is neither isosceles nor equilateral.

2   if they represent the sides of an isosceles triangle.

3   if they represent the sides of an equilateral triangle.

Write the program so that it will process an arbitrary number of sets of three numbers, and will terminate upon reading a set of three numbers, all of which are 0. (Assume that all non-zero data will be positive.)

2.4   Modify the program written for exercise 2.3 so that it will print the following additional values:

4   if the triangle is a right triangle, but is not isosceles.

5   if the triangle is a right isosceles triangle.

(Hint: First, find the longest side, then determine if its square is equal to the sum of the squares of the other two sides.)

2.5 The equals sign (=) has two different meanings in PL/I. It can specify assignment, and it can specify the relationship that must exist between two expressions in order for a condition to be true. Is the statement

$$A \ = \ B \ = \ C \ ;$$

a legal PL/I statement? If so, what will happen when it is executed?

Chapter 3

ATTRIBUTES

In the program examples in previous chapters all data items have been arithmetic (numeric) but PL/I permits other kinds of data as well; for example, strings of alphabetic characters.

There are three kinds of data with which we will be concerned throughout this book:

1. Arithmetic data,

2. String data, and

3. Label data.

The characteristics of data are called <u>attributes</u>. Attributes may be specified explicitly by including them in DECLARE statements, or "by default" by omitting them from DECLARE statements.

In all cases, data items may be constants, or variables. Constants are specified by writing their <u>values</u> each time they are to be used. The form in which they are written determines their attributes.

Variables are used by writing their <u>names</u> each time they are to be used. The attributes of variables are specified in DECLARE statements before the names are used. The declared attributes remain the same throughout the program.

Certain attributes are applicable only to certain kinds of data. For example, we can specify the precision of arithmetic data, and the length of a character string, i.e., how many characters it contains, but it is meaningless to specify the "precision" of a character string.

The general form of a DECLARE statement is

DECLARE <u>name</u> <u>attributes</u> ;

where <u>name</u> is an identifier and <u>attributes</u> specify its characteristics.

Usually, several identifiers will have the same attributes. In such cases, the attributes can be "factored."

The general form of a DECLARE statement with factored attributes is

DECLARE (<u>name-1</u>, <u>name-2</u>, . . .) <u>attributes</u>;

which is similar to the first form, except that the names are separated by commas and the list is enclosed in parentheses.

Arithmetic Data

Arithmetic data items have numeric values. The range of values that an item can assume and the form in which these values are maintained inside the computer can be specified in a DECLARE statement.

In order to understand the range of values that an arithmetic data item can assume, it may be helpful to think of an item as a box into which a specified number of digits can be placed. Suppose, for example, that each arithmetic data item can hold six decimal digits.[*] The range of numeric values that each item can assume then depends on the position of the decimal point.

---

[*]In the computer, the item might have a sign (+ or −), too.

Range	Arithmetic Data Item (6 digits)

0 to 999999
in steps of 1

0 to 9999.99
in steps of 0.01

0 to .999999
in steps of .000001

The range of values, as well as the resolution (the smallest detectable difference between two values) depends entirely upon the position of the decimal point. If the position is specified, the data item is called a fixed-point quantity. For example, if the item is to be used in calculations involving dollars and cents, it would be specified as fixed-point with two digits to the right of the decimal point (as in the second illustration above).

When the decimal point is at the right-hand end of the data item, as in the first illustration, the item is called an integer. Integers are a special case of fixed-point numbers; the value of an integer is always a whole number.

The general form of specifying the characteristics of a fixed-point arithmetic data item is

$$\text{DECLARE} \ \underline{\text{name}} \ \text{FIXED} \, (\underline{p}, \underline{q}) \, ;$$

where

>   name is the name of the item (an identifier),
>
>   p is the number of digits in the item ("the size of the box"), and
>
>   q is the number of digits to the right of the decimal point.
>
>   p is called the precision attribute.

The three illustrations on page 51 reflect the following three DECLARE statements:

DECLARE name FIXED (6, 0) ;

DECLARE name FIXED (6, 2) ;

DECLARE name FIXED (6, 6) ;

The first DECLARE statement declares name to be an integer. When declaring an integer, the number of digits to the right of the decimal point (always zero) need not be specified. The statement could have been written

DECLARE name FIXED (6) ;

In the case of integers, it is not even necessary to specify the number of digits unless there is some particular reason for doing so. Thus, the statement could be shortened to

DECLARE name FIXED ;

and the number of digits would depend on the particular computer in use.

The second and third DECLARE statements declare name to be a fixed-point item other than an integer, because they specify that 2 and 6 digits, respectively, are to follow the decimal point. If the number of digits following the decimal point is specified, the number of digits in the entire item must also be specified.

The smallest absolute value, except for zero, that a six-digit data item may assume is 0.000001, and the largest is 999999. However, as the illustrations on page 51 show, this range cannot be realized if the position of the decimal point is fixed. For small numbers, the decimal point must be toward the left-hand end of the number; for large numbers, it must be toward the right. In order to maximize the range of values the item can assume, the decimal point must be permitted to "float."

The general form of specifying a floating-point item is

$$\text{DECLARE } \underline{\text{name}} \text{ FLOAT} (\underline{\text{p}});$$

where

> $\underline{\text{name}}$ is the name of the item (an identifier), and
>
> $\underline{\text{p}}$ is the number of digits.

As in the case of fixed-point items, it is not necessary to specify the number of digits unless there is some particular reason for doing so. When the number of digits is not specified, i.e., given a DECLARE statement of the form

$$\text{DECLARE } \underline{\text{name}} \text{ FLOAT};$$

the number of digits would be determined by the particular computer in use, typically between six and sixteen.

FLOAT and FIXED are called scale attributes. Every arithmetic data item must have one or the other of these attributes. FIXED specifies that the decimal point is to be fixed at some specified position in the item. FLOAT specifies that the decimal point is to be moved automatically by the computer so that the item can assume the widest possible range of values.

For illustrative purposes, it has been assumed that arithmetic data items contain decimal digits, and that the FIXED, FLOAT, and precision attributes apply to the positioning of a decimal point. In most computers, numeric values are represented internally to some base other than decimal (base ten), usually binary (base two).° The base of arithmetic data items is specified in DECLARE statements by means of a base attribute. The two base attributes in PL/I are BINARY and DECIMAL. When numeric values are in binary form, the scale and precision attributes apply to the positioning of a binary point.

°An excellent explanation of non-decimal number systems and arithmetic can be found in An Introduction to Digital Computing by Bruce Arden, Addison-Wesley, 1963, Chapter 7.

Examples

DECLARE (A, B, C) FIXED DECIMAL (4, 2) ;

specifies that the variables A, B, and C are decimal arithmetic data items which can contain numbers of the form

dd.dd

where d represents a decimal digit (0 through 9).

DECLARE (X, Y) FIXED BINARY (5,1) ;

specifies that the variables X and Y are binary arithmetic data items which can contain numbers of the form

bbbb.b

where b represents a binary digit (0 or 1).

You can think of the base attributes (DECIMAL and BINARY) as modifiers of the corresponding precision attribute: they tell whether the precision attribute specifies the number of decimal or the number of binary digits in the item.

In many cases you will not be concerned with the bases of the quantities used in computation. Two plus two equals four, regardless of the base in which the quantities are represented. Thus, a DECLARE statement of the form

DECLARE name FLOAT ;

or

DECLARE name FIXED ;

may be quite satisfactory for your purposes.° However, if you find it necessary to specify a precision attribute, you should also specify a base attribute to tell the computer whether the precision attribute means binary digits (bits) or decimal digits. For example, if an arithmetic data

---

°In general, the computation will proceed somewhat faster when the BINARY base is specified.

item is to be used in calculations involving dollars and cents, it is important for the item to have two <u>decimal</u> digits to the right of the <u>decimal</u> point, and you would need a DECLARE statement of the form

DECLARE <u>name</u> FIXED DECIMAL (<u>n</u>, 2) ;

where <u>n</u> is an integer constant which you would specify, based on the largest value that <u>name</u> can assume, i.e., the maximum number of digits that it must hold.

Chapter 1 indicated that it is not always necessary to list the names of variables in DECLARE statements (although it is good practice to do so). When arithmetic variables which are used in a program do not appear in a DECLARE statement, they are "declared by default" to have certain attributes. The specific attributes assigned depend upon the particular compiler being used, and the rules in effect in each case may be both unique and complex. As a practical matter, for instance, the same program could produce different results when presented to different compilers if the identifiers assumed different default attributes. It is really much easier to specify all of the attributes for items as it is to remember what happens when some of them are omitted. When in doubt, declare!

The PICTURE attribute is another way to specify the form of arithmetic data items. The PICTURE attribute defines the form of arithmetic items by means of a symbolic representation or "picture" of their contents.

The PICTURE attribute consists of a string of "specification characters," each of which specifies the permissible contents of a digit position in the associated item(s). The present discussion will be limited to a description of only a few of these specification characters, and will show only how various item characteristics can be specified either by scale, base, and precision attributes; or by the PICTURE attribute.

Note: The PICTURE attribute cannot be used in conjunction with scale, base, and/or precision attributes.

The general form of a DECLARE statement with a PICTURE specification is

DECLARE name PICTURE 'specifications' ;

where

name is the name of the item (an identifier), and specifications is a string of characters enclosed in a pair of single quote marks.

The specification character '9' specifies that the corresponding position in the item can contain a decimal digit. The character 'V' is used to indicate that a decimal point should be assumed to appear between the digits to either side of the 'V'.

The following pairs of DECLARE statements are equivalent:

DECLARE name FIXED DECIMAL (10) ;

DECLARE name PICTURE '9999999999' ;

DECLARE name FIXED DECIMAL (5,2) ;

DECLARE name PICTURE '999V99' ;

The character 'F' is used to modify the position of the decimal point. The parenthesized number following the 'F' specifies the number of positions the decimal point should be shifted to the left (a negative number specifies a shift to the right) from its assumed position. The following four DECLARE statements are equivalent:

DECLARE name FIXED DECIMAL (5,2) ;

DECLARE name PICTURE '999V99' ;

DECLARE name PICTURE '99999F(2)' ;

DECLARE name PICTURE 'V99999F(−3)' ;

There are, of course, many other ways in which a PICTURE specification could be written to specify the same form of the data.

A "replication factor" can be used to specify a PICTURE. A replication factor is a decimal integer constant enclosed in parentheses preceding the

PICTURE character that is to be repeated. The following three DECLARE statements are equivalent:

DECLARE name FIXED DECIMAL (16,3) ;

DECLARE name PICTURE '9999999999999V999' ;

DECLARE name PICTURE '(16)9F(3)' ;

PICTURE specifications may also be used to specify the form in which the values of arithmetic data items are to be edited for printing. The use of PICTURE for this purpose is discussed in Chapter 6, Input/Output.

It is important to note that a PICTURE specification may not contain more than one 'V' or 'F'.

Equivalent characteristics for arithmetic data items can be specified either by the scale, base, and precision attributes; or by a PICTURE specification. When specified by means of a PICTURE specification, however, computation will proceed much more slowly than it would if the individual attributes were explicitly specified. For this reason, it is far better to use the scale, base, and precision attributes when declaring arithmetic data items.

String Data

String data items are constants or variables whose "value" is a string of characters or a string of bits. A character string can contain any characters, including alphabetic, numeric, and special characters. A bit string can contain only the binary digits 0 and 1.

Character strings have two attributes: the CHARACTER attribute, which specifies a character string; and a length attribute, which specifies the number of characters in the string.

The general form of a character string constant is

'string'

where string is a sequence of characters. The quote marks bracketing the string specify a character string; the number of characters between the quote marks specifies its length. If a string is to <u>contain</u> a quote mark, that quote mark is written as two consecutive quote marks within the string.°

The '' string (two consecutive quote marks) is the <u>null string</u>; its length is zero.

<u>Examples</u>

```
'THIS IS A STRING OF LENGTH 29'

'DUNN & BRADSTREET'

'/* THIS ISN''T A COMMENT */'

'12345.67'
```

One of the most important points to note is that blanks are significant in character string constants. Blanks are considered to be characters like any other. In fact, a character string can consist of nothing but blanks, if desired. In that case, it would be written as two quote marks, separated by the appropriate number of blank spaces.

Another way to write a character string constant is to precede the constant with a replication factor. As mentioned in the discussion of the PICTURE attribute, a replication factor is a decimal integer constant enclosed within parentheses. The notation

```
(10)' '
```

specifies a character string constant containing ten blanks.

Use of (120)'*' certainly is easier to write and to read than counting the

---

°Thus, '''' is a character string constant of length 1; it contains a single quote mark. The first and last quote marks delimit the string, and the two central quote marks represent the <u>contained</u> quote mark.

number of asterisks in the string. The following constants are identical in value:

```
'ABCABCABC'

(3) 'ABC'
```

Character string contants can be used in PUT statements to print out alphameric information. For instance, to indicate that the end of the program was reached, the following statement might be placed just before the END statement:

```
PUT LIST( 'END OF JOB' ) ;
```

Character string variables must appear in a DECLARE statement. (Otherwise, they may be declared by default to be arithmetic by many compilers.) The general form of specifying a character string variable is

DECLARE name CHARACTER (length) ;

where

name is the name of the variable (an identifier), and

length is the number of characters that name will contain.

Input data items to be assigned to variables with the CHARACTER attribute must be bracketed by quote marks, i.e., they must be character string constants.

The PL/I program on the following page will read four-letter groups of characters from the input medium, count the number of times the group "PL/I" appears, and will print that number upon reading the four-letter group "STOP".

```
COUNT:      PROCEDURE OPTIONS (MAIN) ;
            /* EXAMPLE NO. 8
                READ FOUR-CHARACTER GROUPS AND COUNT THE
                NUMBER OF APPEARANCES OF 'PL/I'. PRINT
                RESULTS UPON READING THE GROUP 'STOP'. */

            DECLARE GROUP CHARACTER(4),
                APPEARANCES FIXED ;

            APPEARANCES = 0 ;  /* INITIALIZE THE COUNT. */
START:      GET LIST( GROUP ) ;
            IF GROUP ¬= 'STOP'
                THEN DO ;
                    /* NOTE THAT THE CHARACTER
                        STRING 'STOP' AND A
                        STOP STATEMENT ARE UNRELATED. */
                    IF GROUP='PL/I' THEN
                    APPEARANCES = APPEARANCES + 1 ;
                    GO TO START ;
                    END ;

            PUT LIST( '''PL/I'' APPEARED ',
                APPEARANCES, ' TIMES.' ) ;
        END COUNT ;
```

Sometimes, the length of a character string variable will not be known because it will change from time to time. For instance, when processing a mailing list, the character strings representing names and addresses may be of varying lengths. A character string variable may be given the VARYING attribute in a DECLARE statement, in which case the length specification specifies the maximum length of the string. The statement

```
DECLARE ( NAME, ADDRESS ) CHARACTER ( 20 ) VARYING ;
```

specifies that NAME and ADDRESS are character strings of varying length, each containing at most 20 characters.

When working with character strings of varying length, it is frequently useful to know how many characters are in the string at any given time. PL/I contains a built-in function, LENGTH, which returns an integer value which is the number of characters in the string. The following program will read an arbitrary number of words (character string constants) from the input medium and print only those consisting of five characters. The program will terminate when it reads a one-character string containing a zero.

```
PRINT5:     PROCEDURE OPTIONS (MAIN) ;
            /* EXAMPLE NO. 9
               READ CHARACTER GROUPS AND PRINT ONLY THE
               FIVE-CHARACTER GROUPS. TERMINATE UPON
               READING A ONE-CHARACTER STRING CONSISTING
               OF A ZERO. */

            DECLARE STRING CHARACTER(20) VARYING,
                    CHARS FIXED ;
            /* GROUPS CAN CONTAIN UP TO 20 CHARACTERS. */
START:      GET LIST( STRING ) ;
            CHARS = LENGTH( STRING ) ;
            IF (CHARS=1) & (STRING='0')
                THEN STOP ;

            IF CHARS=5 THEN PUT LIST( STRING ) ;

            GO TO START ;

          END PRINT5 ;
```

The two IF statements in Example No. 9 could have been written

```
IF (LENGTH(STRING) =1) & (STRING ='0') THEN STOP ;

IF LENGTH(STRING) =5 THEN PUT LIST( STRING ) ;
```

but by using the fixed-point variable CHARS, we avoid computing the string length more than once.

The number of characters in a string is always an integer, that is, a string always contains a whole number of characters. Although this may be obvious, you will find it worthwhile to remember where integers must appear, and where they may or may not appear. The result of the LENGTH function is always an integer.

The PICTURE attribute may be used instead of the CHARACTER attribute to specify a character string variable. If PICTURE is used, neither the CHARACTER nor the VARYING attribute may appear.

The specification characters used to describe character string variables are:

A   specifies an alphabetic character, or blank

X   specifies any character

The specification character '9' specifies that the corresponding position may contain any decimal digit (as it does when used in a PICTURE for arithmetic variables), or blank.

In order for a PICTURE specification to specify a character string variable, at least one of the specification characters must be 'A' or 'X'.

PICTURE cannot be used to specify a string of varying length.

In addition to character string data, PL/I programs can operate on bit string data. A bit is a single binary digit (0 or 1). A bit string is a sequence of binary digits; the number of digits in the string is the length of the string.

Bit string data, like all other kinds of data in PL/I, can be constant or variable. Bit string constants have the general form

$$\text{'bit string'B}$$

where bit string is a sequence of binary digits (0's and/or 1's). The "B" following the terminal quote mark specifies that the string is a bit string; if it were omitted, the string would appear to be a character string constant consisting of alphabetic 0's and 1's rather than binary 0's and 1's. No blanks may appear between the ' and the B.

A bit string constant may also be specified as a bit string preceded by a replication factor. The following constants are identical:

$$\text{'100 100 100' B}$$

$$\text{(3) '100' B}$$

Bit string variables must appear in a DECLARE statement with the BIT attribute, e.g.,

$$\text{DECLARE \underline{name} BIT (\underline{length});}$$

where length specifies the length of the string in bits. Note that when a name in a DECLARE statement has the CHARACTER attribute the length specification refers to characters; when it has the BIT attribute, the length specification refers to bits. The CHARACTER and BIT attributes are mutually exclusive.

Bit string variables may also have the VARYING attribute, in which case the length specification states the maximum number of bits which the variable may contain.

The LENGTH function may be used with bit string data, just as with character string data, but it returns the length of the string in bits instead of in characters. The number of bits in a string must always, of course, be an integer.

Bit strings of length 1 are particularly important. Such a string can contain a single binary digit, i.e., a single 1 or a single 0. Thus, a bit string of length 1 can be used to represent a "true" or a "false" condition, i.e., either of the two possible logical values.

The similarity of conditions (Chapter 2) and bit strings of length 1 should be apparent. In fact, when the computer evaluates a condition, the result is a bit string of length 1; this bit string is then tested and the truth or falsity of the original condition is determined by the outcome of the test. Thus, we can substitute a bit string of length 1 for a condition in an IF statement. The general form of such an IF statement is

IF b THEN statement ;

where b is either a condition, as in Chapter 2, or a bit string constant or variable (normally the latter) of length 1. If b is a condition, it is converted to a one-bit string by the computer; if b is a one-bit string originally, it is tested directly.

Whenever a condition is evaluated during execution the outcome is expressed as a bit string of length 1.

A bit string of length 1 has a numeric value of 0 or 1 corresponding to its logical value of false or true, respectively. It follows, then, that a one-bit string can be used in either or both logical and arithmetic operations. For example, the statement

$$X = (A > B) + (C = D) ;$$

will assign a value of 0, 1, or 2 to the variable X. Each of the expressions (A>B) and (C=D) will have a logical value of true or false, i.e., 1 or 0. These values, which are also numeric, are added—an arithmetic operation—to give one of the three possible numeric results.

What values can be assigned to X in this statement? (Recall that the symbol | means "or".)

$$X = (A > B) \mid (C = D) ;$$

Bit string variables of length 1 are sometimes called "Boolean variables" because they always carry one of the two possible logical, or "Boolean" values: true, or false. Similarly, the two bit string constants of length 1 ('1'B and '0'B) are sometimes called "Boolean constants".

The "not" operator (¬) applied to a one-bit string specifies that its value is to be reversed, i.e., subtracted from 1. It does not specify that a positive numeric value is to be made negative (or a negative made positive). "Positive" and "negative" are meaningless in a logical sense; only "true" and "false" have meaning. If a condition is "not true" (¬ '1'B), it is "false" ('0'B). Conversely, if a condition is "not false" it is "true."

To summarize, there are two kinds of string data in PL/I: character strings, and bit strings. Character strings are used most frequently to manipulate alphabetic data, while bit strings are used most frequently in logical operation. Bit strings in general are of little interest except in more advanced applications, but one-bit strings have application in even the simplest logical operations.

There is a set of string operators in PL/I which are used to operate directly on character and bit string data. These operators and their uses are discussed in Chapter 10, Character Manipulation.

Label data are constants or variables which assume labels as their values. Labels, as you know, are used to name PL/I statements. When it has been necessary in the examples to transfer to a statement labeled name, the appropriate PL/I statement has been of the form GO TO name, i.e., the statement label has appeared explicitly in a GO TO statement. Statement labels which are explicitly specified in places other than their definition are called label constants.

A label variable is an identifier which appears in a DECLARE statement with the LABEL attribute. The LABEL attribute specifies that the associated variable(s) may take on statement labels as values. The general forms of declaration and assignment of labels as values are, respectively

$$\text{DECLARE name LABEL};$$

and

$$\text{name} = \text{label};$$

The following program example, which uses label variables, might be used by a national magazine to print a list of those subscribers who live in a particular geographical region. It is assumed that the data for each subscriber consists of three parts: ZIP code, name, and address; and that the geographical region in question is defined by a "key" ZIP code.

The program reads a subscriber's ZIP code. If it matches the "key" ZIP code, then the name and address are printed; if not, then the name and address are ignored, and the next ZIP code is read. Each subscriber is processed in the same way. The program terminates upon reading a ZIP code of 00000, or, simply, 0.

```
SUBLIST: PROCEDURE OPTIONS (MAIN) ;
         /* EXAMPLE NO. 10
            SUBSET MAILING LIST. */

            DECLARE (KEYZIP, ZIP) FIXED(5),
                    (NAME, ADDRESS) CHARACTER(20) VARYING,
                    SWITCH LABEL ;

            GET LIST( KEYZIP ) ; /* READ KEY ZIP CODE. */
NEWSUB:     GET LIST( ZIP ) ; /* SUBSCRIBER'S ZIP CODE. */
            IF ZIP ¬= 0
              THEN DO ;
                    IF ZIP¬=KEYZIP THEN SWITCH = NEWSUB ;
                                   ELSE SWITCH = PRINT ;
                    GET LIST( NAME, ADDRESS ) ;

                    GO TO SWITCH ;   /* THIS CAUSES A TRANSFER
                                        EITHER TO NEWSUB OR TO
                                        PRINT, DEPENDING ON
                                        LAST ZIP CODE. */

PRINT:              PUT LIST( NAME, ADDRESS, ZIP ) ;
                    GO TO NEWSUB ; /* PROCESS NEXT
                                      SUBSCRIBER.    */
                    END ;

         END SUBLIST ;
```

Initialization

A very common programming error is to refer to variables before they have been assigned values, i.e., initialized. All three kinds of data (arithmetic, string, and label) can be set to initial values by means of the INITIAL attribute in DECLARE statements. The general form of a DECLARE statement with the INITIAL attribute is

DECLARE name attributes INITIAL (value);

where attributes may be any appropriate combination of attributes discussed previously, and value is a constant of the appropriate data type.

The following DECLARE statement is a hypothetical statement used to illustrate the proper use of the INITIAL attribute.

```
DECLARE   A FIXED               INITIAL ( 0 ),
          B BIT( 1)             INITIAL ( '1'B ),
          C CHARACTER(1C)       INITIAL ( (10)' ' ),
          D LABEL               INITIAL ( LB ) ;
```

The INITIAL attribute serves a number of useful functions. Most importantly, it simplifies initialization; if it is not used, initialization must be accomplished by assignment statements or some other means which contribute bulk to programs. Another advantage is that it enables one to see at a glance the initial values with which a program is working.

Notes on Chapter 3

1. When specifying fixed-point arithmetic variables, the decimal (or binary) point need not lie within the variable. For example, the statement

$$\text{DECLARE } \underline{\text{name}} \text{ FIXED DECIMAL}(3, 4);$$

specifies that $\underline{\text{name}}$ can assume values in the range 0 to 0.0999 (resolution = 0.0001). As another example,

$$\text{DECLARE } \underline{\text{name}} \text{ FIXED DECIMAL}(2, -1);$$

specifies that $\underline{\text{name}}$ can assume values in the range 0 to 990 (resolution = 10).

2. One attribute not discussed in this chapter is the $\underline{\text{mode}}$ attribute, which is of interest to scientific programmers. Arithmetic variables may be declared to be of REAL or COMPLEX mode by inclusion of the appropriate attribute in a DECLARE statement. If the mode is not specified, it is assumed to be REAL.

3. In some implementations such as PL/C replication factors may not be used to specify string constants.

EXERCISES

3.1 What are the range of values and resolution of each of the identifiers in this DECLARE statement:

```
DECLARE   A DECIMAL FIXED(5),
          B DECIMAL FLOAT(5),
          C DECIMAL FIXED(5,2),
          D BINARY  FIXED(3)  ;
```

3.2 What are the attributes of the following constants:

```
123              -3.75
'CAT'            0.03
'''CAUSE'        .03
```

3.3 The IF statements in Examples 9 and 10 (pages 61, 66) could be transposed within the respective programs without affecting program operation. Can you think of any reason why they were written in the sequence shown?

3.4 What will be the output of the program shown below?

```
ODD:      PROCEDURE OPTIONS (MAIN) ;

          DECLARE   X BIT(1) INITIAL ( '0'B ),
                    Y FIXED INITIAL ( 0 ),
                    Z LABEL  INITIAL ( START ) ;

START:    X = ¬X ;
          Y = Y + 1 ;

          IF  X  THEN PUT LIST ( Y ) ;
          ELSE PUT LIST( -Y ) ;

          IF  Y=10  THEN Z = STOP ;

          GO TO Z ;

STOP:     END ODD ;
```

Chapter 4

ARRAYS (TABLES)

It is frequently convenient to collect a number of simple variables into a list or table and use a single name to refer collectively to the list or table. Lists or tables are called arrays in PL/I.

As an illustration of the use of an array, we might want to make up a list of four kinds of automobiles and refer to the entire list by the identifier CARS. Such a list can be visualized like this:

CARS   (1) | FORD |
                  (2) | CHEVY |
                  (3) | OLDS |
                  (4) | VOLKSWAGEN |

In this illustration, CARS is the name of a four-element array. The individual elements are numbered 1, 2, 3, and 4. The contents of each element is a character string representing the name of an automobile. The following program example declares CARS to be a four-element array, and then places the appropriate automobile names into the array.

```
LIST_CARS:   PROCEDURE OPTIONS (MAIN)  ;
                  /* EXAMPLE NO. 11
                     DECLARE A FOUR-ELEMENT ARRAY AND PLACE
                     NAMES OF AUTOMOBILES IN THE ELEMENTS. */

                  DECLARE CARS(4) CHARACTER(10)  ;

                  CARS(1) = 'FORD' ;
                  CARS(2) = 'CHEVY' ;
                  CARS(3) = 'OLDS' ;
                  CARS(4) = 'VOLKSWAGEN' ;
                  PUT LIST (CARS)  ;

              END LIST_CARS ;
```

The statement

```
          DECLARE CARS(4) CHARACTER(10)  ;
```

declares the name CARS to be the name of a four-element array. The entire array, that is, each element of the array, has the CHARACTER attribute and a length attribute of 10. These attributes should be familiar from the preceding chapter.

The 4 in parentheses is called the <u>dimension attribute</u> and means that CARS is the name of a list having a "dimension" or "length" of four.

The general form of an array declaration is

DECLARE <u>name</u> (<u>dimension</u>) <u>other attributes</u> ;

where <u>other attributes</u> are as described in the preceding chapter. When an attribute, e.g., FIXED, is applied to an array declaration, it refers to all of the elements in the array. Thus, we can think of an array as a collection of homogeneous information, i.e., data having the same attributes.

The array CARS as declared in Example No. 11 can contain up to four data items. If we needed a longer list, we would have to rewrite the DECLARE statement to increase the dimension attribute. Similarly, if any of the items in the list were to contain more than ten characters, the length specification on the CHARACTER attribute would have to be increased.

The construction DECLARE CARS(4) tells the computer that CARS is the name of a four-element array, but it also tells the computer something else, namely, that the first element of the array has the number 1 and the last has the number 4. These numbers, which identify specific elements, are called subscripts.

Both of the following arrays have four elements. In illustration (a) the elements are referenced by subscript values 1, 2, 3, and 4; in illustration (b) the elements are referenced by subscript values 0, 1, 2, and 3. The corresponding DECLARE statements are shown above the illustrations.

DECLARE A(4) ;   DECLARE B(0:3) ;

A (1) _____   B (0) _____
   (2) _____   (1) _____
   (3) _____   (2) _____
   (4) _____   (3) _____

           (a)   (b)

In illustration (a) the subscript 1 refers to the first element of array A, while in illustration (b) the subscript 1 refers to the second element of array B. The subscript value which refers to the first element of an array is called the lower bound; the value which refers to the last element is called the upper bound. Both bounds can be specified in a DECLARE statement:

DECLARE name (lower bound : upper bound) ;

If the lower bound (and the colon) are omitted, the lower bound is assumed to be 1. Thus,

DECLARE name (10) ;

is equivalent to

$$\text{DECLARE } \underline{name} \ (1{:}10) \ ;$$

The upper bound must be greater than or equal to the lower bound and both bounds must, at this stage of the discussion, be decimal integer constants. Except for these restrictions, the subscript bounds can be any numbers you care to choose. (Either or both can even be negative.)

Suppose the XYZ Company wishes to perform some analysis of sales figures for the years 1973 to 1975, based on the sales data for each of the three years. For this example, assume that the only results desired are (1) total sales, and (2) average sales. The program might look like this:

```
XYZ_3:    PROCEDURE OPTIONS (MAIN) ;
          /* EXAMPLE NO.  12
             XYZ COMPANY, SALES ANALYSIS, 1973-75. */

          DECLARE (SALES(1973:1975), TOTAL, AVG)
                                DECIMAL FIXED(10,2) ;

          GET LIST(SALES(1973), SALES(1974), SALES(1975)) ;
          TOTAL = SALES(1973) + SALES(1974) + SALES(1975) ;
          AVG = TOTAL/3 ;
          PUT LIST( TOTAL, AVG ) ;
        END XYZ_3 ;
```

The array SALES was declared in the example to have bounds of 1973 and 1975, because these bounds simplify reference to the array. For example, to obtain sales for the year 1973, we refer simply to SALES (1973).

The attributes DECIMAL FIXED (10,2) as used in Example No. 12 apply to the array SALES as well as to the two simple variables, TOTAL and AVG.

The range of values of subscripts are established by the dimension attribute in DECLARE statements, and subscripts outside this range are meaningless. In Example No. 12, for instance, it would be meaningless to try to reference SALES (1979) because the upper subscript bound on the array SALES is declared to be 1975.

Zero is frequently a very convenient lower bound. For example, when working with a polynomial of the form

$$a_0 + a_1x + a_2x^2 + \ldots$$

it is convenient to hold the coefficients, a_i, in an array. (In the notation a_i, i is called a subscript and it is therefore very consistent to place the i'th coefficient in the i'th element of the array.)

An individual array element has precisely the same properties as a simple variable. It can be assigned a value, e.g., SALES (1973) could have appeared to the left of an assignment operator in Example No. 12; and it can have only one value at a time. In order to use an array element as a variable, however, the subscript must be specified. Individual array elements are thus called <u>subscripted variables</u>.

The subscript(s) used in an array declaration must, at this stage of the discussion, be decimal integer constants, but the subscripts used to reference elements of arrays may be any expressions which have values within the specified subscript range. The process of referencing elements of arrays is called <u>indexing</u>, and the constant, variable, or other expression used as a subscript is sometimes called the <u>index</u>. In Example No. 13, below, the variable I is used as an index.

```
POW2: PROCEDURE OPTIONS (MAIN) ;
          /* EXAMPLE NO. 13
             FILL AN ARRAY WITH POWERS OF TWO, SUCH THAT
             A(0)=2**0, A(1)=2**1, ... */

          DECLARE A(0:10) FIXED INITIAL (1),
                  I FIXED INITIAL (1) ;

LOOP:     A(I) = A(I-1) + A(I-1) ;
          PUT LIST (A(I)) ;
          I = I + 1 ;
          IF I<=10 THEN GO TO LOOP ;

      END POW2 ;
```

The initial value of array elements can be specified by the INITIAL attribute. In the case of arrays, the INITIAL attribute can specify a number of initial values to initialize a corresponding number of array elements. The first element in the array (the element having the lowest subscript) is set to the first initial value, the second is set to the second initial value, etc., until the list of initial values is exhausted. The statement

```
DECLARE A(10) FIXED INITIAL ( 0, -5, 3 ) ;
```

would set the first three elements of A to 0, −5, and 3, respectively; the values of the next seven elements of A are said to be <u>undefined</u>.°

In Example No. 13, only one initial value is specified for A. This value is placed in the first element of the array A, i.e., A(0).

Another way to specify a list of initial values for an array is replication. The statement

```
DECLARE A (0:10) INITIAL ( (11)0 ) ;
```

specifies that the entire array A is to be initialized to 0. (Note that A has eleven elements.)

What are the subscript bounds, number of elements, and initial values in each of these arrays?

```
DECLARE  A (5),
         B (-3:3) INITIAL( (3)-1 ),
         C (10) INITIAL( (2)1, (3)2 ) ;
```

Answers: (? = "undefined")

	Bounds	No. elements	Values
A	1, 5	5	?, ?, ?, ?, ?
B	−3, 3	7	−1, −1, −1, ?, ?, ?, ?
C	1, 10	10	1, 1, 2, 2, 2, ?, ?, ?, ?, ?

Arrays can be organized in various ways to make them most convenient to use. In Example No. 12, page 72, the subscripts were

---

°Unless explicitly specified by the INITIAL attribute or a GET or assignment statement, you should <u>never</u> assume that an array element or a simple variable has a particular value.

chosen to reflect the various years in question; to refer to sales in the year 1973, we referred to SALES (1973). In this case, the choice of subscripts helped to make the array most convenient to use.

Suppose now, we want to represent a checkerboard in the computer. We could do this by declaring an array of 64 elements, each element corresponding to one of the squares on the checkerboard, but it would be much more convenient to visualize the array like this:

	1	2	3	4	5	6	7	8
1	1,1	1,2						
2	2,1							
3								
4								
5								
6								
7								7,8
8							8,7	8,8

Each element of the board has two indices: the first specifies the row, and the second specifies the column. Conceptually, the checkerboard is not a list of 64 elements; instead, it is a square, having two dimensions ("horizontal" and "vertical"). It has eight squares in each dimension.

What we must do now is specify to the compiler by means of a DECLARE statement that we want to think of this array as an 8 by 8 matrix; not as a list of 64 elements. The appropriate DECLARE statement is

DECLARE CHECKERBOARD(8,8) ;

This DECLARE statement declares a two-dimensional array; the upper subscript bounds for each dimension are separated by a comma. (The lower bounds are 1 in each dimension.) The first dimension indicates the number of rows; the second indicates the number of columns.

Lower, as well as upper bounds may be specified for either or both dimensions. The DECLARE statements below are all equivalent.

```
DECLARE CHECKERBOARD( 8,8 ) ;
DECLARE CHECKERBOARD( 1:8,8 ) ;
DECLARE CHECKERBOARD( 8,1:8 ) ;
DECLARE CHECKERBOARD( 1:8,1:8 ) ;
```

Arrays in PL/I may have any number of dimensions. Although the arrays used so far in this chapter have had physical representations (a list, a checkerboard), there are no such representations for arrays of more than three dimensions. Nevertheless, n-dimensional arrays do have their uses. A four-dimensional array might be used, for example, to maintain a directory of individuals in an office which has four-digit telephone extension numbers. The program example below will read four digits representing a telephone extension and print the name of the individual to whom that extension is assigned. (We ignore the means by which the data would have been placed in the array originally; the purpose of the program is to illustrate n-dimensional indexing.)

The number of subscripts (indices) used in a subscripted name must always be the same as the number of dimensions declared for the name.

```
DIRECTORY:  PROCEDURE OPTIONS (MAIN) ;
            /* EXAMPLE NO. 14
               READ FOUR DIGITS CORRESPONDING TO A
               TELEPHONE EXTENSION AND PRINT THE NAME
               OF THE INDIVIDUAL ON THAT EXTENSION. */

            DECLARE NAME(9,0:9,0:9,0:9) CHARACTER(20),
                    (D1, D2, D3, D4) FIXED ;
            GET LIST(D1, D2, D3, D4) ;
            PUT LIST( NAME(D1,D2,D3,D4) ) ;
            END DIRECTORY ;
```

Array names, without subscripts, may under certain conditions be used to form array expressions. If A is the name of an array, then the expression

2*A means that the value in each element of A is to be doubled. If we want to assign the values obtained to another array, B, we could write

$$B = 2*A ;$$

provided that B has the same number of dimensions and the same subscript bounds as A. If both arrays have three elements, then the above assignment statement is equivalent to

$$B(1) = 2*A(1) ; \quad B(2) = 2*A(2) ; \quad B(3) = 2*A(3) ;$$

Arrays having the same number of dimensions and the same subscript bounds, i.e., arrays which are identical except for their names, can be used in the same way as simple variables. Array operations are performed element by element, so the statement

$$A = A + 1 ;$$

using array A as an operand is identical to the following sequence of statements which use simple variables as operands.

$$A(1) = A(1) + 1 ;$$
$$A(2) = A(2) + 1 ;$$
$$\cdot$$
$$\cdot$$

The following program places the largest number from each corresponding position of two arrays into a third array:

```
MAX:    PROCEDURE OPTIONS (MAIN) ;
            /* EXAMPLE NO. 15
               ILLUSTRATE ARRAY EXPRESSIONS. */

            DECLARE (A(5), B(5), LARGE(5) ) FIXED ;

            GET LIST(A, B) ;
            LARGE = A + (B>A)*(B-A) ;
            PUT LIST( LARGE ) ;
        END MAX ;
```

This table shows how values are computed for the array **LARGE** in Example No. 15, assuming the arrays A and B contain the indicated values:

	A	B	LARGE = A + (B>A)*(B−A)
(1)	1	−1	$1 + (0) * (-2) = 1$
(2)	2	1	$2 + (0) * (-1) = 2$
(3)	3	3	$3 + (0) * (0) = 3$
(4)	4	5	$4 + (1) * (5-4) = 5$
(5)	5	7	$5 + (1) * (7-5) = 7$

Multi-dimensional array operations are performed in "row major" order, which means that the rightmost subscript is varied most rapidly and the leftmost subscript is varied least rapidly. The following examples illustrate row major order in the two contexts where it is most important.

Initialization:

```
DECLARE A(2,3) FIXED INITIAL ( 1, 2, 3, 4, 5, 6 ) ;
```

places the following values in A:

A(1,1) = 1	A(1, 2) = 2	A(1, 3) = 3
A(2, 1) = 4	A(2, 2) = 5	A(2, 3) = 6

Input/Output:

```
DECLARE B(2,3) FIXED INITIAL ( 1, 2, 3, 4, 5, 6 ) ;
PUT LIST( B ) ;
```

causes the following sequence of numbers to be printed:

$$1 \quad 2 \quad 3 \quad 4 \quad 5 \quad 6$$

The principle of row major order applies to arrays of any number of dimensions; two-dimensional arrays were used in the preceding examples only to illustrate the principle. How would initial values be assigned to the array declared in this statement?

```
DECLARE A(2,3,4) FIXED INITIAL ( (12)1, (12)2 ) ;
```

One of the most useful features of arrays is that they simplify the management of large quantities of data. For example, if a program is to add a thousand numbers, these numbers could be placed into an array of a thousand elements, and the required addition could be specified very simply in PL/I:

```
          DECLARE A(1000) FLOAT,
                  I BINARY FIXED INITIAL( 1 ),
                  TOTAL FLOAT INITIAL( 0 ) ;
          .
          .
          .
LOOP:     TOTAL = TOTAL + A(I) ;
          I = I + 1 ;
          IF  I<=1000   THEN GO TO LOOP ;
          .
          .
          .
```

The basic program structure illustrated above is called a loop . Program execution proceeds around the loop, each time adding the contents of the I'th element of the array A to the accumulating sum (TOTAL). Each time through the loop the variable I, used as a subscript, has a different value. After the loop has been executed 1000 times, the variable I will have the value 1001; the condition in the IF statement will be false, and execution will proceed in sequence. The important thing to note is that it is necessary to write only three PL/I statements in order to add 1000 numbers. Of course, 1000 is an arbitrary figure; the limit could have been as large or as small as appropriate; the process would still require only three statements.

The concept of loops is fundamental to data processing, and is practically essential to efficient use of the computer. We have been using loops in almost all of our examples for one purpose or another. Every time we say "GO TO START" we are really implementing a loop.

Chapter 2 showed how the DO statement could be used to group a number of statements together into a logical entity called a DO group. The DO statement can also be used to specify that the statements between the DO and the corresponding END are to be executed repeatedly. This kind of specification is called a DO loop, and here is how a DO loop might be used to add 1000 numbers:

```
DECLARE A (1000) FLOAT,
         I BINARY FIXED,
         TOTAL FLOAT INITIAL ( 0 ) ;
    .
    .
    .
DO I = 1 BY 1 TO 1000 ;
   TOTAL = TOTAL + A(I) ;
END ;
    .
    .
    .
```

The form of the DO statement used in the preceding example specifies that the statements between the DO and the END (a single statement in the example) are to be executed for each value of the variable I from 1 to 1000 in steps of 1. The variable is first set to 1 and the statement is executed. The variable is then "stepped up" by 1 because the DO statement specifies BY 1, and then, assuming the variable is not greater than 1000, the statement is executed again. The process continues until the variable is greater than the limit, at which time execution proceeds to the first statement following the END statement for the loop. A flow chart of the process is included at the end of this chapter.

A recommended practice is to label the DO statement and use that label on the corresponding END statement. This practice, together with indentation, will help to clarify programs and make them easier to read. The program example below illustrates the practice. The program uses the built-in function SIN to compute and print a table of the trigonometric sine function for angles from 0 to 2π radians in steps of 0.1 radian. The limit of 6.28 used in the program is the value of 2π ($\pi = 3.14159$ . . .) to an accuracy within the step size of 0.1.

```
SINE: PROCEDURE OPTIONS (MAIN) ;
         /* EXAMPLE NO. 16
            PRINT TABLE OF SINES. */

         DECLARE X FLOAT ;

LOOP:    DO X = 0 BY 0.1 TO 6.28 ;
            PUT LIST ( X, SIN (X) ) ;
         END LOOP ;
      END SINE ;
```

DO loops have the general form

$$\text{DO } \underline{\text{control variable}} = \underline{\text{specifications}};$$

$$\underline{\text{statement(s)}};$$

$$\text{END};$$

where <u>control variable</u> is a simple or subscripted variable, and <u>specifications</u> specify the various values which the control variable is to assume. The specifications may take several forms:

(a) $\underline{\text{expression}_1}, \ \underline{\text{expression}_2} \ \ldots \ \underline{\text{expression}_n}$
specifies that the statement(s) in the DO loop are to be executed, first with the control variable set to the value of $\underline{\text{expression}_1}$, again with the control variable set to the value of $\underline{\text{expression}_2}$, etc.

(b) $\underline{\text{expression}_1} \text{ BY } \underline{\text{expression}_2} \text{ TO } \underline{\text{expression}_3}$
specifies that the statement(s) in the DO loop are to be executed with the control variable set to the value of $\underline{\text{expression}_1}$ and increased by the value of $\underline{\text{expression}_2}$ at the start of each subsequent pass through the loop, until the value of the control variable exceeds the value of $\underline{\text{expression}_3}$. (If the value of $\underline{\text{expression}_2}$ is negative, the control variable is decremented at the start of each subsequent pass through the loop until its value is less than the value of $\underline{\text{expression}_3}$.) This form of specification may also be written
$\underline{\text{expression}_1} \text{ TO } \underline{\text{expression}_3} \text{ BY } \underline{\text{expression}_2}$

(c) WHILE ($\underline{\text{condition}}$)
specifies that the statement(s) in the DO loop are to be executed repeatedly as long as $\underline{\text{condition}}$ is true. $\underline{\text{Condition}}$ is evaluated prior to each pass through the loop.

In principle, any looping operation can be specified by any of these three forms of DO specifications. The one you should use for a particular purpose is the one which is most convenient for the purpose. Each of the following DO loops sets the first ten elements of the array X to zero:

```
A:      DO I = 1, 2, 3, 4, 5, 6, 7, 8, 9, 10 ;
           X(I) = 0 ;
        END A ;

B:      DO I = 1 BY 1 TO 10 ;
           X(I) = 0 ;
        END B ;

        I = 1 ;
C:      DO WHILE ( I<=10 ) ;
           X(I) = 0 ;
           I = I + 1 ;
        END C ;
```

The labels on the three preceding DO statements correspond to the three forms of DO specifications. For this particular application, form B is the simplest. Form C requires the use of two additional assignment statements.

Forms B and C can be combined into a single specification:

```
BC:     DO I = 1 BY 1 WHILE ( I<=10 ) ;
           X(I) = 0 ;
        END BC ;
```

which simplifies the construction somewhat. Still, for this application, form B is the simplest.°

DO loops have the following characteristics:

1. The specifications may consist of any expressions; they need not contain only decimal integer constants.

2. The expressions in the specifications are evaluated only once, at the time the DO statement is first encountered. Thus, the

---

°The DO loops used for illustration set the first ten elements of array X to zero. If the array contains only ten elements, then of course the simplest way to set all of the elements to zero is the array assignment statement X = 0;

expression values cannot be effectively modified by statements within the loop. However, the control variable can be modified; if such modifications give it a value outside the specified range, the loop will not be repeated after the current pass is completed. In form (a), page 81, each expression is evaluated in turn.

3. A GO TO statement within the scope of a DO loop may transfer control to a point outside the loop, thus terminating the loop prematurely.

4. A GO TO statement outside a DO loop must not transfer to a point within the loop. (A GO TO statement may, however, transfer to a point within a DO group.)

5. The value of the control variable after control has left a DO loop depends on the conditions under which the loop was left. The following two rules are illustrated by Example No. 17, which follows:

If the loop is terminated normally, the control variable has the first value which fails to meet the conditions for execution of the loop.

If the loop is terminated prematurely, e.g., by a GO TO statement which transfers out of the loop, the value of the control variable is the value it had when the GO TO statement was executed.

```
FIND3:    PROCEDURE OPTIONS (MAIN) ;
          /* EXAMPLE NO.  17
             READ 20 NUMBERS INTO AN ARRAY AND PRINT
             THE LOCATION IN THE LIST OF THE FIRST '3'.
             IF NONE OF THE ELEMENTS CONTAINS '3' THE
             ''LOCATION'' PRINTED WILL BE 21. */

          DECLARE (A(20), I) FIXED ;

          GET LIST( A ) ;
L1:       DO I = 1 BY 1 TO 20 WHILE (A(I) ¬= 3) ;
          END L1 ;

          PUT LIST( I ) ;

          END FIND3 ;
```

One very powerful form of the DO loop is a DO WHILE that continuously loops and depends on some other condition to terminate the loop, e.g., a test and a STOP statement. This construction can be used in place of the "backwards" transfers we have been using in our previous examples. Let us rewrite Example 9, page 61.

```
PRINT5:   PROCEDURE OPTIONS (MAIN) ;
            /* EXAMPLE NO.  18
               READ CHARACTER GROUPS AND PRINT ONLY THE
               FIVE-CHARACTER GROUPS. TERMINATE UPON
               READING A ONE-CHARACTER STRING CONSISTING
               OF A ZERO. */

            DECLARE STRING CHARACTER(20) VARYING,
                    CHARS FIXED ;
            /* GROUPS CAN CONTAIN UP TO 20 CHARACTERS. */

          DO WHILE ('1'B) ;
            GET LIST( STRING ) ;
            CHARS = LENGTH( STRING ) ;
            IF (CHARS=1) & (STRING='0')
               THEN STOP ;

            IF CHARS=5 THEN PUT LIST( STRING ) ;

          END ;

          END PRINT5 ;
```

The DO-WHILE construct is particularly useful in very large programs because it may eliminate the need for many (if not all) GO TO statements. The difficulty with GO TO statements is not with those statements themselves, but in determining all of the ways in which control could come to a particular statement label, determination that must often be made in the course of debugging.

Constructing Example No. 10, page 66, to use DO-WHILE instead of GO TO yields a program which is not only easier to understand, but more efficient (fewer statements actually executed):

84

```
SUBLIST: PROCEDURE OPTIONS (MAIN) ;
        /* EXAMPLE NO. 19
           SUBSET MAILING LIST. */

           DECLARE (KEYZIP, ZIP) FIXED(5),
                   (NAME, ADDRESS) CHARACTER(20) VARYING,
                   SWITCH LABEL ;

           GET LIST( KEYZIP ) ; /* READ KEY ZIP CODE. */
           GET LIST( ZIP ) ; /* SUBSCRIBER'S ZIP CODE. */

           DO WHILE (ZIP ¬= 0) ;

              GET LIST (NAME, ADDRESS) ;
              IF ZIP = KEYZIP
                THEN PUT LIST (NAME,ADDRESS, ZIP) ;
              GET LIST (ZIP) ;

           END ;

        END SUBLIST ;
```

DO loops may be nested. That is, any of the statements in a DO loop may themselves be DO statements. In Example No. 20 below, the loop initiated by the DO statement at L2 is an "inner" loop, nested within the loop initiated by the DO statement at L1. What values will be printed by the program?

```
DO_LOOPS:   PROCEDURE OPTIONS (MAIN) ;

            /* EXAMPLE NO. 20
                  ILLUSTRATE NESTED LOOPS */

            DECLARE (I, J, N1, N2) FIXED INITIAL(0) ;

L1:         DO I = 1 BY 1 TO 10 ;
                N1 = N1 + 1 ;
L2:             DO J = 1 BY 1 TO 10 ;
                    N2 = N2 + 1 ;
                END L2 ;
            END L1 ;

            PUT LIST(N1, N2) ;

            END DO_LOOPS ;
```

The answers are, N1 = 10 and N2 = 100. In other words, the assignment statement in the inner loop is executed 100 times; the assignment statement in the outer loop only ten times. Of course, any other statements in the inner loop, had there been any, would also have been executed 100 times, while any other statements in the outer loop would have been executed only ten times. This observation points to a fact which is essential to efficient use of a computer:

> When using nested loops, perform as much computation as possible in the outer loops; perform as little as possible in the innermost loop.

The following two examples illustrate the importance of the rule. Both programs place the integers 1 through 10 in a one-dimensional array and sum the values in a two-dimensional array. Note that the two programs give the same answer.

```
BAD:     PROCEDURE OPTIONS (MAIN) ;
            /* EXAMPLE NO. 21
               INEFFICIENT USE OF DO LOOPS. */

         DECLARE (A(10), B(10,10), I, J, SUM)
                                      FIXED ;

         GET LIST (B) ;

         SUM = 0 ;
L1:      DO I = 1 BY 1 TO 10 ;
L2:         DO J = 1 BY 1 TO 10 ;
S1:            A(I) = I ;
S2:               SUM = SUM + B(I,J) ;
            END L2 ;
         END L1 ;

         PUT LIST (SUM) ;

      END BAD ;
```

```
GOOD:     PROCEDURE OPTIONS (MAIN) ;
          /* EXAMPLE NO. 22
             EFFICIENT USE OF DO LOOPS. */

          DECLARE (A(10), B(10,10), I, J, SUM)
                                   FIXED ;

          GET LIST (B) ;

          SUM = 0 ;
L1:       DO I = 1 BY 1 TO 10 ;
S1:          A(I) = I ;
L2:          DO J = 1 BY 1 TO 10 ;
                SUM = SUM + B(I,J) ;
             END L2 ;
          END L1 ;

          PUT LIST (A, SUM) ;

     END GOOD ;
```

In BAD (Example No. 21) the statements at S1 and S2 will each be executed 100 times, for a total of 200 statement executions. Moving statement S1 into the outer loop (because it doesn't have to be in the inner loop), as in GOOD (Example No. 22), S2 will be executed 100 times, as before, but S1 will be executed only 10 times, for a total of 110 statement executions. Merely by moving a single statement from an inner loop to an outer loop, we have cut the computer time required to solve the problem almost in half!

The END statement corresponding to an inner DO statement must appear prior to the END statement corresponding to the next outer DO statement. The required construction is illustrated schematically on the next page, where each vertical line indicates the scope of a DO statement.

(a) – correct

(b) – incorrect

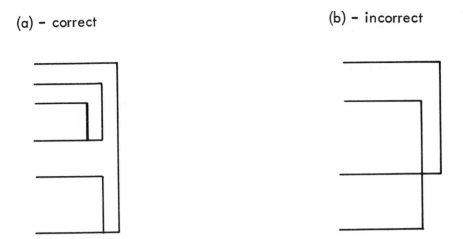

If labels are not used following END statements, the compiler will interpret each END statement as corresponding to the last DO statement for which an END statement has not yet been provided.

If labels are used following END statements, a practice which is highly recommended, then the compiler will interpret each END statement as corresponding to the DO statement having the same label as well as all DO statements within its scope. To illustrate, the following statement will sum the elements of a three-dimensional array:

```
         SUM = 0 ;
L1:      DO I = 1 BY 1 TO 10 ;
             DO J = 1 BY 1 TO 10 ;
                 DO K = 1 BY 1 TO 10 ;
                     SUM = SUM + A(I,J,K) ;
         END L1 ;
```

The END statement terminates all three DO loops because the label, L1, matches the label on the outermost DO statement.

To summarize, this chapter has introduced arrays as collections of data and has shown some of the ways in which arrays can be used to simplify management of data. The DO statement is a very simple but powerful means of specifying iteration, which is one of the things a computer does best. The DO loop has been introduced here predominantly as a device for manipulation of data in arrays, but it is by no means limited to applications of this kind. (See Example No. 16.)

1. The expression A*B where A and B are arrays, does <u>not</u> represent matrix multiplication. Instead, it specifies that corresponding elements of A and B are to be multiplied.

2. PL/I contains several built-in functions which are useful when working with arrays. Two of these are SUM and PROD, which can be used to sum and multiply all the data in an array, respectively. This statement would perform the same function as the loop shown on page 79:

```
TOTAL = SUM( A ) ;
```

3. Another built-in function, MAX, has the value of the largest of its arguments (there must be two or more arguments). This statement could be used to simplify program Example No. 15, page 77:

```
LARGE = MAX( A, B )`;
```

if A and B are arrays, then they, and LARGE also, must have the same bounds.

4. The following example points out a problem that may exist in some implementations. We recommend that you avoid this type of construction.

Array Expressions:

```
DECLARE C (2,2) FIXED INITIAL ( 1, 2, 3, 4 ) ;
C = C + C (2,1) ;
```

places the following values in C:

$$C(1, 1) = 4 \qquad C(1, 2) = 5$$
$$C(2, 1) = 6 \qquad C(2, 2) = 10$$

(Note that the value of C(2, 1) is modified during execution of the array assignment statement.) Instead, use

```
DECLARE C(2,2) FIXED INITIAL ( 1, 2, 3, 4 ) ;
DECLARE TEMP   FIXED ;

TEMP = C(2,1) ;
C = C + TEMP ;
```

5. A DO statement of the form

> DO control variable = expression$_1$ BY expression$_2$
>
> > TO expression$_3$
> >
> > WHILE (condition) ;
>
> statement(s) ;
>
> END ;

can be represented by the flow chart on the following page, assuming that expression$_2$ is positive. If it is not, the loop is terminated when control variable < expression$_3$.

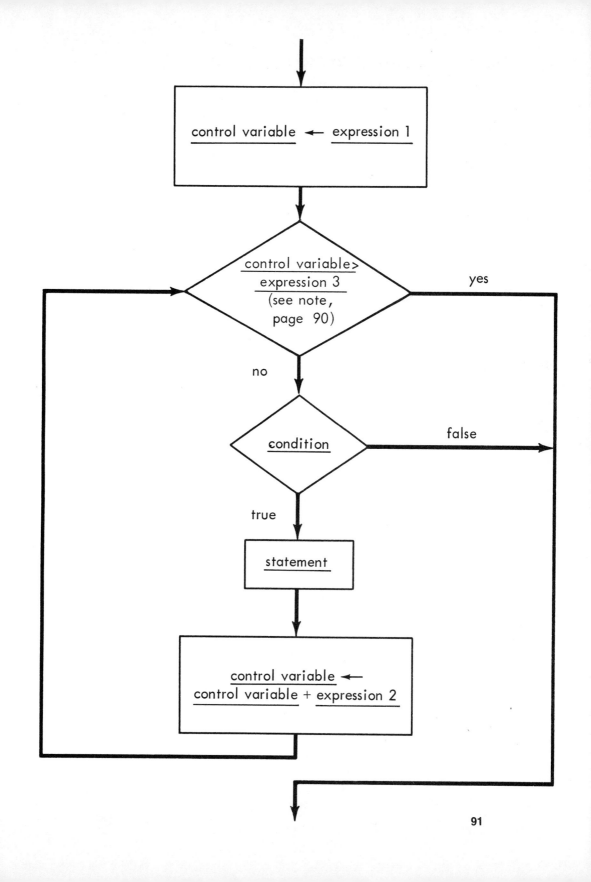

6. BY may be omitted from a DO specification, in which case the step expression (expression₂ in the notation used here) is assumed to be 1. These statements are equivalent:

```
DO V = A BY 1 TO B ;

DO V = A TO B ;
```

7. The DO loop can be further generalized to the form

$$DO \ \underline{\text{control variable}} = \underline{\text{specification}}_1, \ \underline{\text{specification}}_2, \ \cdots$$

where each specification is one of the forms shown on page 81. For example, the PUT statement in the DO loop

```
DO I = 1, 2, 5 BY 1 TO 10, 12 BY 2 WHILE ( I<=16 ), 3, 4 ;
    PUT LIST( I ) ;
END ;
```

will print each value of the variable I, namely,

1, 2, 5, 6, 7, 8, 9, 10, 12, 14, 16, 3, and 4.

8. Chapter 1 stated that, because most computers do not use decimal (base ten) arithmetic, certain common decimal fractions cannot always be represented accurately. The following DO statement causes the decimal fraction 0.01 to be added to itself 100 times; we would expect the final result to be 1.0. The result shown is the result actually obtained when the statement was executed on a computer which uses base sixteen (hexadecimal) arithmetic.

```
DECLARE I FIXED,
        SUM FLOAT INITIAL ( 0 ) ;

DO I = 1 TO 100 ;
    SUM = SUM + 0.01 ;
END ;
PUT LIST( SUM ) ;
```

The result, exactly as produced by the computer, is:

$$9.99999E-01 \quad \text{(i.e., } 0.999999)$$

This example illustrates the characteristic of <u>roundoff error</u>, which is present in some degree in almost every arithmetic operation involving decimal fractions. Uncontrolled, as it is in this example, the error can be compounded and the final results of the computation may be grossly inaccurate.

There is no general remedy for problems due to roundoff, but two simple ways to minimize it are:

1. Increase the precision attribute of the operands. (This may reduce the speed of computation.)

2. Perform operations in a certain sequence in order to maintain accuracy when evaluating expressions. Although this usually requires prior knowledge of the values of the operands, a good general principle is to try to form expressions that do not contain decimal fractions. For example, 10*A will probably give a more accurate result than A/0.1; A/10 may be more accurate than 0.1*A.

It is important to note that the number of digits printed by a particular computer is not necessarily an indication of accuracy, i.e., answers printed to ten decimal places are not necessarily more accurate than answers printed to five decimal places.

EXERCISES

4.1 How many elements are there in the array used in Example No. 14 (page 76)?

4.2 The following program is intended to sum the values in a one-dimensional array and a two-dimensional array. Is the program correct? Is it efficient? What, if anything, should be changed?

```
PROG:      PROCEDURE OPTIONS (MAIN) ;

           DECLARE (A(10), B(10,10), I, J, SUM1, SUM2)
                                     FIXED ;

           GET LIST (A, B) ;

           SUM1, SUM2 = 0 ;
L1:        DO I = 1 BY 1 TO 10 ;
L2:           DO J = 1 BY 1 TO 10 ;
S1:              SUM1 = SUM1 + A(I) ;
S2:              SUM2 = SUM2 + B(I,J) ;
           END L2 ;
        END L1 ;

           PUT LIST (SUM1, SUM2) ;

        END PROG ;
```

4.3 Write a PL/I program which reads 20 fixed-point decimal numbers (precision 5, 2) into an array and then prints the largest value in the array.

4.4 A, B, and C are two-dimensional arrays of 15 elements in each dimension. Write a PL/I program to form the matrix product A×B in C.

Matrix multiplication in the context of this exercise means that each element of C must take on the value

$$C(I, J) = A(I, 1)*B(1, J) + A(I, 2)*B(2, J) + \ldots A(I, 15)*B(15, J)$$

4.5 Write a PL/I program which does the following: reads a string of 15 alphabetic characters into an array (one character per element). Finds each occurrence of the letter Q, and forms a list (using another array) of the positions in which it appears. Use the first element of the list to count the number of appearances of the letter Q.

For example, if the input data were the string

A C G Q X Y P Q R M L A Z Q T

the constructed list would contain

3, 4, 8, 14   (Q appears 3 times, in positions 4, 8, and 14)

4.6 Generalize the program written for Exercise 4.5 so that it will read a single "key" character prior to reading the 15 characters; and forms the list based on the key character.

4.7 Read ten numbers into a one-dimensional array and place them in ascending sequence, i.e., sort them into ascending order. Print the resulting list. Re-sort the numbers into descending sequence, i.e., reverse the array, and print the resulting list. Use only one array.

4.8 Use a DO loop to evaluate the expression

$$\frac{X}{X^2 - 1}$$

for values of X from -3 to $+3$ in steps of 0.5. Allow for the possibility that some values of X in this range may cause division by zero; do not evaluate the expression for these values. Instead, print the message

'CAUSES DIVISION BY ZERO'

For all other values of X, print X and the resulting value of the expression.

4.9 A magazine company wants to send a circular to a particular area of the country which encompasses 10 ZIP codes. Write a program which reads these 10 "key" ZIP codes, then reads the subscription list consisting of—for each subscriber—ZIP code, name, and address. Upon reading a ZIP code of '00000', which marks the end of the list, print each of the ten key ZIP codes followed by all the names and addresses which matched it. Assume a maximum of 20 matches for any particular key ZIP code, but there may be ZIP codes that do not match any of the key ZIP codes.

All ZIP codes, including the key ZIP codes, will be character strings of 5 characters.

Each name and each address will be a character string of not more than 20 characters, but will be of varying length.

4.10 Same as 4.9. Construct the program in such a way that GO TO statements are not used.

4.11 Same as 4.7. Construct the program in such a way that GO TO statements are not used.

Chapter 5

STRUCTURES

Arrays, as shown in Chapter 4, are collections or aggregates of homogeneous data. In many cases you will find it convenient or necessary not only to collect data, but to collect data in some prescribed way; and the data may or may not be homogeneous. For example, in preparing a payroll, there may be several items of information pertaining to each individual employee. These items would include his name (characters), employee number, hours worked, etc. In other words, it would be convenient to group certain items of information under each employee's name: each employee will have his own number, rate of pay, etc. The information pertaining to each employee is non-homogeneous—his name is a character string, but the rest of the information is arithmetic—so the information cannot be organized into an array.

Non-homogeneous and/or logically related data can be organized as a structure in PL/I. The essential difference between a structure and an array is that an array is simply an aggregation of data while a structure is a hierarchical collection of data. Another difference is that an array may contain only homogeneous data, while a structure may or may not contain homogeneous data.

A structure in PL/I can be likened to an outline for a book. The material to be included in the book is divided into parts, and the individual parts may be further subdivided. A typical outline might have the form

I.

    A.

        1.

        2.

    B.

II.

    A.

    B.

where the various levels are denoted by Roman numerals, capital letters, Arabic numerals, etc. Levels which are not further subdivided are called elementary levels.

There are three differences between PL/I structures and outlines:

1. All levels in structures are denoted by numbers.

2. Levels need not be divided into at least two parts, as they must be in an outline.

3. Only the elementary levels in a structure can contain data, while a subdivided level in an outline might correspond to a few general remarks in the text prior to treating the elemental subjects.

In a payroll program, the information pertaining to each employee might be organized as a structure. We could view such a structure as

      1 EMPLOYEE

        2 NAME

        2 NUMBER

        2 HOURS__WORKED

        2 RATE__OF__PAY

        etc.

The number to the left of each identifier is a <u>level number</u>. Within this structure each item with the number 2 is of the same hierarchy; all are subordinate to the item with the number 1.

The preceding structure contains four elementary levels: NAME, NUMBER, HOURS__WORKED, and RATE__OF__PAY. Thus, the structure contains four data items.

It might be convenient to break some of the data down further. For example, it might be desirable to distinguish between straight time and overtime hours worked. We might then visualize the structure as

    1 EMPLOYEE

       2 NAME

       2 NUMBER

       2 HOURS__WORKED

          3 STRAIGHT__TIME

          3 OVERTIME

       2 RATE __OF__PAY

The structure now contains five elementary levels. The name HOURS__WORKED is no longer an elementary level; it is an identifier which refers collectively to the two data items STRAIGHT__TIME and OVERTIME, which are elementary levels.

In principle, we can subdivide a structure into as many levels as we need. In PL/I, a structure must have one and only one level 1. The name given to this level (EMPLOYEE in the preceding representations) is the name of the entire structure.

The structure above would be implemented in PL/I by the statement

```
DECLARE   1 EMPLOYEE,
          2 NAME CHARACTER(20),
          2 NUMBER FIXED,
          2 HOURS_WORKED,
          (3 STRAIGHT_TIME,
           3 OVERTIME) FIXED,
          2 RATE_OF_PAY  FIXED ;
```

The indentation used in the statement on the preceding page is, of course, arbitrary. It is good practice to indent in order to emphasize the data organization being declared.

The DECLARE statement on page 98 is very similar to the structure representation. There are only two differences: attributes have been included in the DECLARE statement, and each level name is separated from the subsequent level number by a comma. Parentheses are used to factor the FIXED attribute, which applies to the elementary items STRAIGHT__TIME and OVERTIME.

Attributes may be applied only to elementary levels, because these are the only levels which contain data.

As a rule, data for any application can be organized into a structure. For example, our program to compute ages involves five data items: four dates and the result. These items could be organized into a structure:

```
DECLARE   1 DATE,
         (2 INPUT_1,
          2 INPUT_2,
          2 INPUT_3,
          2 INPUT_4,
          2 AGE) FLOAT ;
```

This DECLARE statement is rather bulky. It can be simplified considerably by combining the four input items into an array within the structure DATE. This is accomplished simply by giving a dimension attribute to the items:

```
DECLARE   1 DATE,
         (2 INPUT(4),
          2 AGE ) FLOAT ;
```

Now, we have specified the various identifiers to have the following meanings:

DATE is the name of a hierarchical collection of five data items: four input values and one result.

INPUT is the name of an array containing four data items. Individual items are referenced as usual, i.e., INPUT(1),

INPUT(2), INPUT(3) and INPUT(4). The identifier INPUT by itself, of course, refers to all four items.

Suppose we wanted to organize the data for ten people, rather than just one. The data for each of the ten people would consist of five items. The simplest way to declare ten such sets of data is merely to dimension the structure DATE:

```
DECLARE   1 DATE(10),
          (2 INPUT(4),
           2 AGE )  FLOAT ;
```

The above statement allocates space for 50 data items in the computer, 10 sets of 5 items each. The organization of the items can be visualized as

DATE(1)	INPUT(1) element 1 in the computer
	INPUT(2)	2
	INPUT(3)	3
	INPUT(4)	4
	AGE	5
DATE(2)	INPUT(1)	6
	INPUT(2)	7
	INPUT(3)	8
	INPUT(4)	9
	AGE	10
DATE(3)	INPUT(1)	11

.

.

.

.

There is an INPUT(1) in each of the ten elements of DATE. In order to refer to a particular INPUT(1), we must <u>qualify</u> the name by the appropriate element of DATE. That is, we must specify a particular element of DATE in conjunction with INPUT(1) in order to refer to a specific INPUT(1).

Qualification in PL/I is specified by a decimal point. To refer to the data in INPUT(1) within DATE(1) we would write

$$DATE(1).INPUT(1)$$

which qualifies the "minor" name INPUT(1) by the "major" name DATE(1).

How many data items are referenced by each of these names?

DATE(1)	Answer:	5
DATE(1).INPUT(1)		1
INPUT		40

Qualification is in general required in order to make an identifier unique, i.e., to eliminate any ambiguities in referencing it. Another case in which qualification is required occurs when a minor structure has the same name as a minor structure within a different major structure. For example, a program used by a manufacturer might contain three structures:

```
DECLARE   1 PRODUCT_A,
          2 AMOUNT,
          (3 JANUARY,
           3 JULY) FLOAT,

          1 PRODUCT_B,
          2 AMOUNT,
          (3 JANUARY,
           3 JULY) FLOAT,

          1 PRODUCT_C,
          2 AMOUNT,
          (3 JANUARY,
           3 APRIL,
           3 JULY,
           3 OCTOBER) FLOAT ;
```

The identifiers APRIL and OCTOBER are unique; references to them need not be qualified. The identifier JANUARY, however, is not unique, and so references to JANUARY must be qualified by the name of the appropriate structure, e.g., PRODUCT__A.JANUARY. The <u>fully qualified</u> name is

```
PRODUCT_A.AMOUNT.JANUARY
```

which may be used, but which is unnecessary because only partial qualification is needed to refer to a specific JANUARY.

The qualified name AMOUNT.JANUARY would be ambiguous because AMOUNT.JANUARY appears in more than one structure.

Structures which are identical except, perhaps, for the names of various levels, may be used in structure expressions. Two structures are identical when there is a one-to-one correspondence between the elements of the structures.

In a program using the three structures shown on page 101, the statement

```
PRODUCT_A = PRODUCT_B ;
```

would be legal, but the statement

PRODUCT__A = PRODUCT__C ;

would not, because PRODUCT__A and PRODUCT__C are not identical structures: they do not contain the same number of elements. However, by using qualified names, we can move individual data items from PRODUCT__C to PRODUCT__A. For example,

```
PRODUCT_A.JANUARY = PRODUCT_C.APRIL ;
```

is a legal statement.

The following program example might be used by a bank to update 100 checking accounts. The data for each account consist of the individual's name, account number, old balance, service charge, and new balance (which becomes the old balance for purposes of the next update). The name is a character string, the account number is an integer, and the balances are maintained in floating-point form.

```
CHK_ACC: PROCEDURE OPTIONS (MAIN) ;
        /* EXAMPLE NO. 23
            UPDATE 100 CHECKING ACCOUNTS. */
        DECLARE   1 ACCOUNT(100),
                  2 NAME,
                  (3 LAST,
                   3 FIRST)   CHARACTER(12),
                   3 MIDDLE   CHARACTER(2),
                  2 NUMBER    FIXED,
                  (2 OLD_BAL,
                   2 SER_CHG,
                   2 NEW_BAL) FLOAT ;

          /* 'ACCOUNT' CONTAINS DATA FOR EACH OF
             THE 100 ACCOUNTS TO BE UPDATED. */

        DECLARE   1 TOTAL,
                  (2 OLD_BAL,
                   2 NEW_BAL) FLOAT ;

          /* 'TOTAL' WILL CONTAIN THE TOTAL OF THE
             OLD AND NEW BALANCES. */

        DECLARE   1 ED_TOTAL,
                  (2 OLD_BAL,
                   2 NEW_BAL) PICTURE '$999999V.99' ;

          /* 'ED_TOTAL' IS USED TO EDIT THE OUTPUT
             FOR PRINTING. */

        DECLARE   I FIXED,
                    DIFF FLOAT ;

        /* READ DATA FOR 100 ACCOUNTS. */

        GET LIST( ACCOUNT ) ;

        /* INITIALIZE OLD AND NEW TOTALS. */

        TOTAL = 0 ;

        /* SUBTRACT SERVICE CHARGE FROM EACH OLD
           BALANCE, GIVING NEW BALANCE. */
```

```
           ACCOUNT.NEW_BAL = ACCOUNT.OLD_BAL - SER_CHG ;

           /* SUM THE OLD AND NEW BALANCES IN EACH
              ACCOUNT. */

LOOP:      DO I = 1 BY 1 TO 100 ;
              TOTAL.OLD_BAL = TOTAL.OLD_BAL +
                             ACCOUNT(I).OLD_BAL ;
              TOTAL.NEW_BAL = TOTAL.NEW_BAL +
                             ACCOUNT(I).NEW_BAL ;
           END LOOP ;


           /* COMPUTE NET GAIN (OR LOSS). */

           DIFF = TOTAL.NEW_BAL - TOTAL.OLD_BAL ;

           /* CONVERT TOTALS TO FORM FOR PRINTING. */

           ED_TOTAL = TOTAL ;

           /* PRINT TOTAL OLD BALANCE, TOTAL NEW BALANCE,
              AND THE DIFFERENCE. */

           PUT LIST( ED_TOTAL, DIFF ) ;
        END CHK_ACC ;
```

The GET statement reads seven elements for each of the 100 accounts into the structure ACCOUNT.

The assignment statement, TOTAL = 0, sets both elements of the structure TOTAL to zero, element by element. That statement is equivalent to the statements

TOTAL.OLD_BAL = 0 ; TOTAL.NEW_BAL = 0 ;

The DO statement totals the old and new balances in the structure ACCOUNT, keeping the accumulating totals in the appropriate elements of the structure TOTAL.

The net gain or loss is then computed as the difference between the total new balance and the total old balance. The difference is computed after the totals have been obtained, although it could have been computed as the sum of the differences of the old and new balance in each of the 100 accounts. By totaling the 100 old and new balances and then taking the difference, the program eliminates 99 computations of the difference.

The data in the structure TOTAL is then placed into the structure EDIT_TOTAL. The PICTURE specification included in the declaration for EDIT_TOTAL specifies that the data are to be converted into a form suitable for printing at the time it is placed in EDIT_TOTAL. The $ in the specification caused the value printed to be preceded by a dollar sign, and the period caused the decimal point to be printed. By making the assignment to EDIT_TOTAL after the totals have been accumulated, instead of accumulating the totals directly in EDIT_TOTAL, we eliminate 99 conversions.°

Finally, the new information is printed and the update program terminates.

Example No. 23 contains some statements which are perhaps unnecessarily complicated, e.g.,

```
TOTAL.OLD_BAL = TOTAL.OLD_BAL + ACCOUNT(I).OLD_BAL ;
```

Wouldn't the program have been much simpler if OLD_BAL (and NEW_BAL) did not appear in two structures, i.e., if the names had been made unique so that qualification was not required? The answer is yes, but to have made the identifiers different might have introduced some possibility for confusion when reading the program. However, as we shall now see, there is sometimes another advantage to using the same identifiers in different structures.

PL/I provides facilities for structure operations by name. The general form of specifying operations by name is

statement, BY NAME ;

where statement is an assignment statement which contains only structures as operands. The clause BY NAME specifies that only those

---

°In fact, we eliminate many more than 99 conversions. Each time another total is added to EDIT_TOTAL, the existing contents of EDIT_TOTAL must be converted to the form required for the addition, and the sum must then be converted back to the form required by the PICTURE attribute appended to EDIT_TOTAL. Furthermore, every conversion must be performed on each of the two elements of EDIT_TOTAL, further increasing the number of conversions that would be necessary.

names which are common to all structures in the statement are to take part in the specified operations.

If the BY NAME clause had been used in Example No. 23 the two statements in the DO loop could be replaced by the statement

```
TOTAL = TOTAL + ACCOUNT(I), BY NAME ;
```

The only items taking part in the addition and assignment would be those having the names OLD_BAL and NEW_BAL, because these are the only names common to the structures TOTAL and ACCOUNT. (Note that there are 100 items with each name in ACCOUNT.)

The decision to use arrays, structures, or a combination of the two depends upon many things. Sometimes, the particular application of a program will dictate a particular organization; at other times, the way the data are to be referenced will be the deciding factor. In general, you should use whatever means makes a program easiest to write.

Notes on Chapter 5

A structure may be thought of as a list (array), containing sublists which are also arrays. Consider the structure.

```
DECLARE   1 CARS,
          2 DOMESTIC,
          (3 GM(3),
           3 FORD(3) ) CHARACTER(7),
          2 FOREIGN(3) CHARACTER(7) ;
```

which could be visualized as

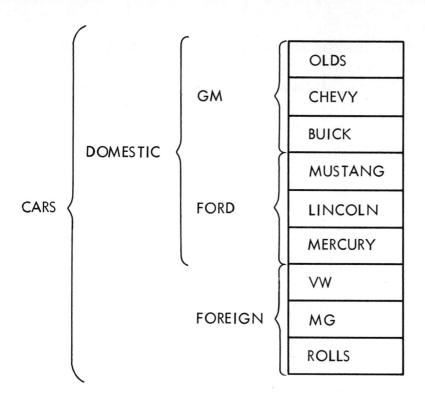

where

CARS is a 9-element list;

DOMESTIC is a 6-element list; and

GM, FORD, and FOREIGN are 3-element lists.

CARS can thus be thought of as a 9-element array containing four other arrays which are proper subsets.° We can refer to any of these subsets, as well as to the entire set (CARS). Suppose we require the domestic automobiles to be printed in a report. We could write:

```
PUT LIST (DOMESTIC) ;
```

Six elements of DOMESTIC would then be printed.

°It is important to remember that CARS is not in fact an array; it is a structure. Thus, it cannot be subscripted as it could if it were an array.

The concept of a structure as containing classes and subclasses of information is very useful in the discipline of information retrieval. The basic purpose of information retrieval is to collect and classify information so that it can be retrieved on request. The organization of CARS, used as an example here, makes it easy to respond to requests like, "give me a list of domestic automobiles" or "give me a list of automobiles made by General Motors."

One of the major applications of information retrieval is in the maintenance of libraries. The books in a library may be classified by subject, author, content, date of publication, etc. Structures can be of great help in classifying such information.

EXERCISES

5.1 The accounting system for a computer installation is to be organized as a structure with the name JOB__ACCOUNT, containing minor elements ACCOUNT__NUMBER, FUNDS, TIME, and RATE (dollars per unit time used on the computer). TIME is to be divided into two categories: COMPILE, and EXECUTE.

> a. Write a DECLARE statement for the structure JOB__ACCOUNT.

> b. Write a PL/I program, using JOB__ACCOUNT, which will update the amount of funds left in an account by means of the formula

$$FUNDS = FUNDS - (RATE *$$
$$EXECUTE +$$
$$0.5 * RATE * COMPILE)$$

5.2 Which elements of the structure A will be modified by the program on the following page?

```
DCL   01  JOB_ACCOUNT,
          03  ACCOUNT-NO      FIXED  (7),
          03  FUNDS           FIXED  (7,2),
          03  TIME,
              05  COMPILE  FIXED  (7,5),
              05  EXECUTE  FIXED  (7,5),
          05  RATE            FIXED  (7,4);
```

```
EX 2:   PROCEDURE OPTIONS (MAIN) ;

              DECLARE  1 A,
                       2 R,
                       2 S,
                       [3 T,]         YES
                       3 U,
                       2 V,
                       3 W ;          NO   A.V = B, BY NAME

              DECLARE  1 B,
                       2 S,
                       3 T,
                       2 W ;

         A = B, BY NAME ;

         END EX2 ;
```

to CHANGE W ⇒ A.V = B, BY NAME;

5.3 A library contains 770 books which are broadly classified as fiction and non-fiction. The fiction class is divided into two classes: novels (275 books) and short stories (200). The non-fiction class is divided into three classes: biography (125), documentary (70), and general reference (100).

a. Declare a structure, BOOKS, which contains the appropriate classifications.

b. Write a PL/I program, using the structure which reads a character string which will be one of the following:

'FICTION'   'BIOGRAPHY'
'NONFICTION'   'DOCUMENTARY'
'NOVELS'   'REFERENCE'
'SHORT STORIES'

and prints a list of those books which fit the indicated classification. Assume that the longest book title is 10 characters.

5.4 Rewrite exercise 4.9 (page 95) so that the names and addresses associated with a matching ZIP code are kept in a structure together with the matching ZIP code.

Chapter 6

INPUT/OUTPUT

There are three basic phases in every computer program:

1. Acquire data

2. Process data

3. Communicate results

Up to this point we have concentrated on phase 2, the processing phase, and have shown some of the facilities in PL/I that can be used during this phase. We have not paid much attention to phases 1 and 3, although they are essential if a program is to be at all useful.

There are two ways in which a program can acquire the data that are to be processed. One way is for the program to generate its own data during execution, and the other is for it to read the data by means of GET statements. Most programs use a combination of these two methods.

There are many ways in which a program can communicate results. For example, results can be printed in order to communicate with a human being; they can be punched into cards which can subsequently be read by another program, etc. The basic statement used to communicate results is the PUT statement, which has been used in the programming examples.

GET and PUT statements perform "input" and "output" functions, respectively. In practice, input and output are frequently considered to be a single function, input/output, (or, simply I/O) because there are many similarities in the way the functions are implemented in most programming languages. For example, the statement

```
GET LIST( A, B, C ) ;
```

causes three data items to be read into the computer from, say, a punched card, and assigned to A, B, and C. The very similar statement

```
PUT LIST( A, B, C ) ;
```

causes the values of A, B, and C to be written out from the computer to, say, the printer.

In short, GET statements cause data to be transmitted to the computer from an external device, and PUT statements cause data to be transmitted from the computer to an external device. Some external devices can be used both for input and output; some can be used only for input; and some can be used only for output. The table below lists some typical external devices and shows how they can be used.

Device	Use
Card reader	Input
Card punch	Output
Printer	Output
Magnetic tape	Input/Output
Typewriter	Input/Output
Graphic display	Input/Output

Collections of data on external devices are called files. GET statements extract data from an input file, and PUT statements place data into an output file. PL/I programs can use several input files and several output files. We will assume for the moment that they use only one of each, called the "standard" files. We will also assume that the output file is a printer.

Three kinds of GET and PUT statements are used in PL/I. Each kind of statement specifies a particular representation of the data in a file. The three kinds of statements and their general forms are

List-directed
  GET LIST(<u>list</u>) ;
  PUT LIST(<u>list</u>) ;

Data-directed
  GET DATA(<u>list</u>) ; or GET DATA ;
  PUT DATA(<u>list</u>) ; or PUT DATA ;

Edit-directed
  GET EDIT(<u>list</u>) (<u>format</u>) ;
  PUT EDIT(<u>list</u>) (<u>format</u>) ;

In every case above, <u>list</u> is a sequence of items separated by commas. The form of each item depends on the kind of statement in use; permissible forms are summarized in the table on page 127. In the case of edit-directed input/output, <u>format</u> specifies the form of the data in a file. Formats are discussed in detail later in this chapter.

For input, the kind of GET statement used depends on how the data are represented in the input file. For output, the kind of PUT statement used depends on how it is desired to represent the data in the output file. In both cases, data representation involves 1) the form of each data item, and 2) the way in which data items are separated from one another, or "delimited." The representations specified by the three kinds of GET and PUT statements are:

DATA REPRESENTATION IN A FILE

	form of each item	items delimited by . . .
List-directed	constant	one or more blanks, or a comma°
Data-directed	variable = constant	one or more blanks, or a comma +
Edit-directed	character, interpreted by format specifications	format specifications

°The comma, if present, may be surrounded by blanks.

+A semicolon must follow the last item when the data are in the input file.

Suppose a PL/I program contains the statements

```
DECLARE   VAR 1     FIXED (2, 1),
          VAR2      FIXED (2),
          ANIMAL    CHARACTER (3)  ;

L:  GET LIST( VAR1, VAR 2, ANIMAL )  ;
```

and the input file contains

```
1.5,   -83,   'CAT',    -3.0, -85,   'DOG'
```

The first time the GET statement is executed, VAR1 will be set to 1.5, VAR2 will be set to -83, and ANIMAL will be set to the character string CAT. If the GET statement is executed a second time, VAR1 will be set to -3.0, VAR2 will be set to -85, and ANIMAL will be set to the character string DOG. Every time the GET statement is executed, three data items are taken from the input file and assigned to the variables in the associated list.

Usually, if the list in a GET statement contains <u>n</u> identifiers, n data items will be extracted from the input file each time the statement is executed. However, a single identifier may cause input of more than one item. For example,

```
DECLARE  A(10) FIXED ;
    .
    .
    .
GET LIST( A ) ;
```

will extract ten items from the input file and assign them to the elements of the array A. The first item will be assigned to A(1) and the tenth will be assigned to A(10).

Once started, list-directed input can be terminated in two ways: satisfaction of the input list, or by an "end of file" condition. The latter is "raised" when there are no more data in the file, and usually causes program execution to terminate.° Unless the condition is raised, the computer will scan the input file as far as necessary to satisfy the input list. There must be one blank space or a comma between data items in the file, but intervening blanks are otherwise ignored.

There are several differences between list-directed input and list-directed output. For input, the list (list in the statement on page 112) may contain identifiers only, although the identifiers may be subscripted if appropriate. For output, the list may contain constants and expressions as well. Constants in an output list are placed in the output file in the same form as they appear in the list, but without the quote marks in the case of string constants. In the case of expressions, the values placed in the output file are those resulting from their evaluation.

During input, data items from the input file are converted to the form required by the attributes of the corresponding variables in the input list. If such an item is subsequently placed in the output file, it will be placed there in its converted form. For example,

---

°Chapter 9 describes a means by which programs can detect the ENDFILE condition and take various courses of action when it is raised.

Input: -1.5

```
DECLARE X FIXED (5, 3) ;
GET LIST( X ) ;
PUT LIST( X ) ;
```

Output: -1.500

List-directed output can be terminated only by exhaustion of the output list. (Note that an input list is said to be "satisfied" but an output list is said to be "exhausted.") The ENDFILE condition cannot be raised during output.

List-directed input/output derives its name from the fact that data to be transmitted are specified in an input or output list in terms of their destination (input) or in terms of their source (output). The input and output files contain only the values of the items.

The second kind of input/output described in this chapter, data-directed input/output, differs from list-directed input/output in that the input and output files contain not only the values of data items, but also the PL/I program names with which the values are associated. Suppose, for example, a PL/I program contains the statements

```
DECLARE  A FIXED,
         B FLOAT,
         C CHARACTER (3)  ;

    L: GET DATA ;
```

and the input file contains

```
    C = 'CAT', A = 4, B = 6.5 ; C = 'DOG' ;
```

The first time the GET statement is executed, the variable A will be set to 4, B will be set to 6.5, and C will be set to the character string CAT. Transmission is terminated by the semicolon in the input file. If the GET statement is executed a second time, the effect will be to change the value of the variable C to the character string DOG. The following semicolon terminates transmission and, since A and B do not appear prior to the

115

semicolon, their values are not altered by the GET statement the second time.

When the list is omitted from a data-directed GET statement, as it is in the illustration on the preceding page, the input file can contain assignments to any of the variables in the program. As shown on page 112, however, a list (exactly like the list used with a list-directed GET statement) may be used with a data-directed GET statement. When a list is used, the input file may specify assignments to any or all of the identifiers in the list, but not necessarily in the same order. The input file must not, however, specify assignment to any identifiers that are not in the list. Thus, a data-directed input list normally specifies those variables whose values could be changed by the particular GET statement.

The variable in an "assignment statement" in the input file must be a simple variable; an array name with all subscripts specified by decimal integer constants, i.e., a single element of an array; or a fully qualified elementary name, i.e., a single element of a structure. The list, if used, may contain simple variables, unsubscripted array names, and major or partially qualified structure names. In the latter cases, the input file may specify assignment to any or all of the elements of the array or structure.

In data-directed output, the names of the sources of the data items are placed into the output file together with the items themselves. A list, specifying the sources, may be used with data-directed PUT statements exactly as with list-directed PUT statements. However, a data-directed output list may contain identifiers only; it may not contain constants or expressions. A semicolon is placed in the output file after the last data item has been transmitted.

Data-directed output provides a simple means of documenting output, because it shows the names of variables as well as their values. The effectiveness is enhanced if the names of variables are descriptive of their meaning, e.g., WIND_VELOCITY. Also, data-directed output can often be useful in debugging, as shown in Chapter 9.

The third kind of input/output described in this chapter, edit-directed input/output, differs from list- and data-directed input/output in that it specifies the format of the input and output files and provides means for editing the transmitted data.

In order to understand edit-directed input/output, it is useful to think of the input and output files as being streams of characters, where every character in the stream—including blanks—is accounted for by a "format specification." During input, characters are accessed from the input stream and interpreted according to the format specifications. During output, characters are placed into the output stream according to the specifications.

The edit-directed input/output statements have the form

$$\text{GET EDIT}\,(\underline{\text{list}}\,)\,(\underline{\text{format}}\,)\,;$$

$$\text{PUT EDIT}\,(\underline{\text{list}}\,)\,(\underline{\text{format}}\,)\,;$$

where list is like the list used with list-directed GET and PUT statements, respectively; and format is a series of editing specifications, called "format phrases," which specify the form of the data in the input file, or the desired form of the data in the output file, i.e., on a printed page.

Suppose a PL/I program contains the statement

```
DECLARE P CHARACTER (5),
        Q FIXED (5)  ;
```

and that it is desired to access a ten-character substream of the input data stream in the following way: place the first five characters into P as a character string, ignore the next two characters, and interpret the next three characters as a decimal integer and assign it to Q. The PL/I statement would be

```
GET EDIT( P, Q )  ( A(5), X(2), F(3) )  ;
```

The "A" format phrase specifies that the input data are to be interpreted as a character string. The "5" specifies the number of characters that are to be so interpreted. Thus, the phrase A(5) specifies that the first data item is to be interpreted as a five-character string. The string is assigned to the variable P because P is the first identifier in the input list and A(5) is the first editing phrase.

The "X" phrase specifies that a certain number of characters—two, in this case—are to be ignored. The X phrase does not cause any transmission; it merely advances the input stream by the specified number of characters.

117

The "F" phrase specifies that the input data are to be interpreted as a fixed-point number. The "3" specifies the number of characters that are to be interpreted to form the number. It does not specify the precision of the number. The number is then assigned to the variable Q because Q is the next identifier in the list. Note: If the three-character number is negative, it can have at most two digits because the minus sign occupies a character position in the input stream. Numbers in the range −99 to 999 can be transmitted by the format phrase F(3).

Some of the more frequently used format phrases are listed below, with their meanings. Additional phrases are given in Appendix E. Note that some of the phrases may have a different form and/or meaning when used for input than they do when used for output.

Phrase		Meaning
A(w)	INPUT:	Interpret the next w characters as a character string.
	OUTPUT:	Place the associated item into the output stream as a character string of length w. If w is omitted, it is assumed to be the current length of the item. If w is greater than the length of the item, the item will be left-justified in a w-character substream, followed by blanks.
E(w,d)	INPUT:	Interpret the next w characters as a floating-point number written in scientific notation (see Chapter 1). If none of the characters is a decimal point, assume the decimal point precedes the rightmost d digits in the field.

Phrase		Meaning

E(<u>w</u>,<u>d</u>) OUTPUT: Place the associated item into the output stream as a floating-point number written in scientific notation rounded to <u>d</u> digits. If the item requires less than <u>w</u> characters, it will be right-justified in a <u>w</u>-character substream, preceded by blanks. The general form of output data edited by the E phrase is

$$n.nnnEnn$$

(one digit to the left of the decimal point, and <u>d</u> digits to the right). Either or both the exponent and the magnitude will be preceded by a minus sign, if appropriate.

F(<u>w</u>)

or

F(<u>w</u>, <u>d</u>) INPUT: Interpret the next <u>w</u> characters as a fixed-point number. If none of the characters is a decimal point, assume the decimal point precedes the rightmost <u>d</u> digits. If d is omitted, it is taken to be 0.

OUTPUT: Place the associated item into the output stream as a fixed-point number rounded to <u>d</u> digits to the right of the decimal point. If the item requires less than <u>w</u> characters, it will be right-justified in a <u>w</u>-character substream,

Phrase		Meaning

		preceded by blanks. Leading zeroes, if any, will be suppressed, i.e., converted to blanks. If _d_ is omitted, no decimal point will appear in the number. If _d_ is 0, no digits will follow the decimal point, but the point will be printed.
X(_w_)	INPUT:	Ignore the next _w_ characters in the input stream.
	OUTPUT:	Insert _w_ blanks into the output stream.

During output, it is not always necessary to use the X phrase to insert blanks into the output stream, because data edited by the E and F phrases may be preceded by blanks. For example, the phrase F(15) is equivalent to (X(5), F(10)), assuming the associated data item as printed will not have more than ten digits.

The field width, _w_, specified for the E and F phrases must account for all of the characters to be printed. The E phrase requires that _w_ be at least _d_+7 to account for

> a leading sign (1 character)
>
> at least one digit
>
> the decimal point (1 character)
>
> the letter "E" (1 character)
>
> the sign of the exponent (1 character)
>
> the exponent (2 characters)

The F phrase must allow for the decimal point, if it is to appear, and a leading sign.

Suppose a PL/I program contains the following statement:

```
DECLARE   A   CHARACTER(3)    INITIAL( 'CAT' ),
          B   FLOAT           INITIAL( 1.25 ),
          C   FLOAT           INITIAL( -6.5 )  ;
```

and the statement

$$PUT \ EDIT(A, B, C)(\ . \ . \ . \ );$$

is executed with (. . .) replaced by each of the formats shown below. The printed results actually produced by a computer are shown to the right of each format specification.

FORMAT	PRINTED RESULTS
(A, F(4,2), F(4,1)) ;	CAT1.25-6.5
(A(10), F(4,2), F(6,1)) ;	CAT 1.25 -6.5
(A, X(5), F(4,2), E(8,1)) ;	CAT 1.25-6.5E+00
(A, F(10,1), E(10,1)) ;	CAT 1.3 -6.5E+00
(A, E(10,1), E(15,6)) ;	CAT␣␣␣1.3E+00 -6.500000E+00

The form of data in a file can also be specified in a way similar to a PICTURE specification, by means of the P format phrase. The general form of the P phrase is

$$P \text{ 'specifications'}$$

where specifications consist of a sequence of characters representing a symbolic "picture" of the data in a file. Some of the more frequently used specification characters are listed below. Additional specification characters are given in Appendix F.

Specification character	Meaning
9	The corresponding character may be any decimal digit, or blank.
A	The corresponding character may be any alphabetic character, or blank.
X	The corresponding character may be any character.
V	A decimal point should be assumed at the corresponding point in the item. V does not specify the appearance of an actual decimal point in an item.

The above characters may be used both for input and output. The following characters may be used for output:

Specification character	Meaning
B	A blank is to be inserted in the output stream.
S	A sign (+ or −) is to be inserted at the corresponding point in the item.

Z	If the associated character is a leading zero (a zero to the left of a non-zero digit) it will be replaced by a blank.
*	Same as Z, above, except that a leading zero will be replaced by an asterisk.
+	If the associated item is greater than or equal to zero, a plus sign is to be inserted at the corresponding point in the output stream. Otherwise, no sign will appear.
−	Same as +, above, except that a sign will appear only if the associated item is less than zero.
.	A decimal point is to be inserted at the corresponding point in the item.
$	A dollar sign is to be inserted at the corresponding point in the item.

The characters S, +, −, and $ can be made to "drift" so that they will appear immediately to the left of the first non-blank character in the output stream. This is important, for instance, when printing checks, to prevent them from being "kited" (raised in value) by the insertion of spurious high order digits between the $ and the original amount of the check. A drifting character is specified by the appearance of the appropriate character in each position through which it may drift. For example, the specification

P'$$$$$9.99'

could be used to print a value from $0.00 to $9999.99 with no spaces between the $ and the first significant digit.

Suppose a PL/I program contains the following statement:

```
DECLARE   A   CHARACTER(3)   INITIAL( 'CAT' ),
          B   FLOAT          INITIAL( 1.25 ),
          C   FLOAT          INITIAL( -6.5 ) ;
```

and the statement

$$PUT \ \ EDIT(A, B, C)(\ . \ . \ . \ );$$

is executed with (. . .) replaced by each of the formats shown below. The printed results actually produced by a computer are shown to the right of each format specification. Note that the P phrase can be used in combination with the other format phrases described previously.

FORMAT	PRINTED RESULTS
(A, P'9V.99', P'S9V.9') ;	CAT1.25-6.5
(A, P'999V.9', P'ZZZV.99') ;	CAT001.2 6.50
(P'AAA', X(3), P'$$$9V.99', P'SSS9V.9') ;	CAT $1.25 -6.5
(A, P'--9V.99', P'+++9V.99') ;	CAT 1.25 6.50
(P'(10)A', 2 P'XXXXXX') ;	CAT 1.250-6.500

A format phrase may be preceded by a replication factor which specifies that the phrase is to be repeated a certain number of times. For example, the phrase

$$(5)F(6, 2)$$

specifies that five consecutive data items are to be edited by the phrase F (6,2).

With the exception of the P phrase, format phrases have the general form

$$(\underline{r})\ \underline{\text{phrase}}\ (\underline{w},\ \underline{d})$$

where

  $\underline{r}$ is a replication factor;

  $\underline{\text{phrase}}$ is one of the letters A, E, F, or X;

  $\underline{w}$ is the total number of characters in the associated item;

  $\underline{d}$, if used, specifies the number of digits to the right of the decimal point in an arithmetic item.

Any of the components, $\underline{r}$, $\underline{w}$, and $\underline{d}$, may be decimal integer constants, or they may be expressions.° The use of expressions can frequently simplify PL/I programs considerably. For example, suppose it is desired to read a character string of length "N" where N is in the input stream as a three-character number preceding the string. The GET statement might be

```
        GET EDIT( N, STRING ) ( F(3), A (N) ) ;
```

A format need not contain as many editing phrases as there are items in the associated list. If the format contains fewer editing phrases than there are items in the list, the format is repeated as necessary to transmit all the

---

°If $\underline{r}$ is a decimal integer constant it need not be parenthesized. If it is not parenthesized, it must be followed by one or more blanks.

data. As in list- and data-directed input/output, transmission stops only when the list is satisfied or exhausted. The statement

```
PUT EDIT ( P, Q, R ) ( F(5,2), X(5), E(10,2), X(3) ) ;
```

will cause the value of P to be edited by the phrase F (5, 2), the value of Q to be edited by the phrase E(10, 2), and the value of R to be edited by the phrase F(5, 2). There will be five blanks between the values of P and Q, and three blanks between the values of Q and R as they are printed.

Format specifications can be very complicated when many data items are to be transmitted. Also, it is not always easy to write a list of items and then write the format specifications for the entire list. In edit-directed input/output, lists and format specifications can be intermixed; the general form of such a GET or PUT statement is

$$\text{EDIT}(\underline{\text{list}}) (\underline{\text{format}}) (\underline{\text{list}}) (\underline{\text{format}}) \ldots ;$$

where each format is associated with the list to its left. Each list-format pair interacts to transmit a certain amount of data. As each list is exhausted, transmission continues using the next list-format pair to the right. Program Example 28 on page 135 illustrates a simple way of putting a large amount of data into a rather complicated printed format.

Edit-directed input/output, together with list- and data-directed input/output, constitute the "stream input/output" facilities of PL/I because the files can be thought of as streams from which data are extracted during input, or into which data are inserted during output. Much of the remainder of this chapter applies to all three forms of stream input/output, so it is useful to review briefly their various characteristics. Each of the three forms specifies a particular representation of data in a file, as shown in the table on page 113. With the possible exception of a data-directed input statement, every input/output statement has a list of data items associated with it. The permissible contents of input/output lists are summarized in the table on the following page.

Unless otherwise stated, the following discussion applies to all three forms of stream input/output statements. Where a particular form, e.g., LIST, is used, the choice is arbitrary; DATA or EDIT could be used just as well.

CONTENTS OF I/O LISTS

	Input	Output
List-directed	identifiers	identifiers, constants, and expressions
Data-directed	identifiers	identifiers
Edit-directed	identifiers	identifiers, constants, and expressions

Data items taken from the input file cannot be assigned to PL/I program variables directly. First, they must be converted to the computer's internal form. Then, possibly, they must be further converted so that they match the attributes declared for the variables that are to receive them. Suppose a PL/I program contains the statements

```
DECLARE ( A, B, C ) FIXED(5,3) ;
GET LIST( A, B, C ) ;
```

and that the input file contains

$$1.5, \quad -1.0625, \quad \text{'XYZ'}$$

The first data item in the file consists of three characters: the digit "1", a period, and the digit "5". These characters are converted to the internal equivalent of the fixed-point decimal quantity 1.5; a quantity having precision (2, 1). The quantity is then further converted to precision (5, 3)—the precision attribute of A, the destination—by the addition of leading and trailing zeroes.°

°If the value of A is subsequently printed by a list-direct PUT statement. leading zeroes will be suppressed. See page 115.

The second data item in the file is converted in the same way, to the internal equivalent of the quantity -1.0625, with precision $(5, 4)$. It is then further converted to precision $(5, 3)$—the precision attribute of B—by truncating the extra digit to the right of the decimal point, and adding a leading zero. The value assigned to B is thus effectively -1.062.

The third data item in the file is first converted to the internal form of the character string XYZ. This string must then be converted to a fixed-decimal number of precision $(5, 3)$, but there is no way in which a character string can be converted to a meaningful numeric quantity (unless the characters happen to be digits). The attempted conversion will raise the "conversion" condition, which will normally terminate program execution. Chapter 9 describes a means by which programs can detect the CONVERSION condition and take various courses of action when it is raised.

When using list- and data-directed input, the internal equivalent of a data item is formed from the appearance of the item in the file, which must be self-describing, e.g., the sequence 'CAT' to represent the 3-character constant CAT. The file used with list- and data-directed input must contain PL/I constants.

When using edit-directed input, the internal equivalent of a data item is formed from the format specifications instead of from the appearance of the item in the file. The internal equivalent may then be further converted before assignment, as described above. In the case of E and F format phrases, the appearance of a decimal point in a data item will override the format interpretation. For example, the format phrase F $(10, 3)$ if the item contains an explicit decimal point, the decimal point need not appear in position 7.

During output, data items are converted to external form as defined by their attributes. That is, an item declared to have precision $(5, 3)$ will be placed in the output file as a five-digit number with three digits following the decimal point. When using edit-directed output, data items are converted to the form specified by the associated format phrases. The end result is that characters are placed in the output file to be printed.

As in the case of input, the CONVERSION condition may be raised in certain cases of output, for instance,

```
DECLARE STR CHARACTER(5) ;
PUT EDIT( STR ) (F(3)) ;
```

Conversion cannot be raised during list- and data-directed output.

It is frequently very useful to print the data read by GET statements, particularly when many data items are involved. Up to this point, we have printed the input data by means of PUT statements, along with the results of the calculation. The COPY option can be used with a GET statement to provide for automatic printout of the input data. The general form of a GET statement with the COPY option is

GET COPY LIST(list) ;

or

GET LIST(list) COPY ;

where LIST is used only for illustration; COPY can be used with data- and edit-directed input as well.

The COPY option does not indicate which values were assigned to which variables, or what conversions, if any, were performed prior to assignment. Thus, it may sometimes be preferable to check the input data by means of a PUT statement immediately following the GET statement.

The SKIP option may be used with a GET statement. When this is done, the next input line° is read immediately. Data are then transmitted as usual for stream input. Note that the next input line is read before any data are transmitted. In some cases this may require the use of a blank line preceding the data.

Three options may be used with PUT statements to provide control over the printer. The general form of a PUT statement with an option is similar to the form of a GET statement with an option; the option may appear after PUT, or before the semicolon. The three PUT options are

———

°The input line may be thought of as a card.

Option	Effect
SKIP or SKIP ($\underline{w}$)	Space the printer to a new print line, and print the data starting at the left margin. If $\underline{w}$ is 0 or negative, printing will start at the left of the current line, overprinting any data previously printed on the line. If $\underline{w}$ is 1, or is omitted, the printer is spaced to the next line, giving single-spaced printing. If $\underline{w}$ is 2, printing will be double-spaced, etc.
LINE ($\underline{w}$)	Space the printer to line $\underline{w}$ on the print page, and print the data starting at the left margin. LINE specifies a skip to a specified line on the page, while SKIP, above, specifies a skip to a new line relative to the current line.
PAGE	Eject the current page. The data will be printed starting at the left margin of the first line (line 1) of the next page.
Note:	LINE ($\underline{w}$) is equivalent to PAGE if $\underline{w}$ is less than the number of the current line, is less than 1, or is greater than the maximum number of lines that can appear on a page.

PUT options always specify an action to be taken by the printer before any data are transmitted. A PUT statement with an option need not cause any transmission at all; the statement

```
PUT PAGE ;
```

merely causes the printer to skip to the top of the next page.

The following two program examples perform the same functions:

summing five numbers and printing them, together with the total. The major difference between the programs is that Example No. 25 uses PUT options, while Example No. 24 does not. The input data are the same in both cases, and both programs use the SUM function, which is a built-in function described in Appendix C.

```
SUM1: PROCEDURE OPTIONS (MAIN) ;

        /* EXAMPLE NO. 24
           SUM FIVE NUMBERS. PRINT RESULTS WITHOUT
           'PUT' OPTIONS. */

        DECLARE (A(5), TOTAL) FIXED DECIMAL (5,2) ;

        GET LIST( A ) ;
        TOTAL = SUM( A ) ;
        PUT LIST( 'OUTPUT FROM EXAMPLE NO. 24' ) ;
        PUT LIST( A, 'TOTAL = ', TOTAL ) SKIP ;
      END SUM1 ;
```

```
OUTPUT FROM EXAMPLE NO. 24
   10.20     5.30     75.00     1.05     2.00     TOTAL =
   93.55
```

```
SUM2: PROCEDURE OPTIONS (MAIN) ;

        /* EXAMPLE NO. 25
           SUM FIVE NUMBERS. PRINT RESULTS USING
           'PUT' OPTIONS. */

        DECLARE (A(5), TOTAL) FIXED DECIMAL (5,2)
                I FIXED ;

        GET LIST( A ) ;
        TOTAL = SUM( A ) ;

        PUT LIST( 'OUTPUT FROM EXAMPLE NO. 25' ) PAGE ;
        PUT SKIP(2) ;

        DO I = 1 TO 5 ;
           PUT LIST( A(I) ) SKIP ;
        END ;

        PUT LIST ( '    _____' ) SKIP(0) ; /* FIVE UNDERBARS */
        PUT LIST( TOTAL ) SKIP ;
      END SUM2 ;
```

```
10.20
 5.30
75.00
 1.05
 2.00
93.55
```

SKIP, LINE, and PAGE may also be used as format phrases in edit-directed PUT statements. In this context, they have the same effects as they do when used as options, except that the specified action occurs when they are encountered in the format. Note that the list may be exhausted before all of the format phrases have been encountered.

Another format phrase that can be used with edit-directed I/O statements is the COLUMN phrase, which has the form

$$\text{COLUMN } (\underline{w})$$

and causes the next data item to be printed beginning at position $\underline{w}$ of the current print line, or taken from the current input line. If $\underline{w}$ exceeds the number of positions available on a line, or is less than the current position on the current print or input line, COLUMN is equivalent to SKIP (1). COLUMN may not be used as an option.

As we have seen, input and output of an entire array can be accomplished simply by placing the array name in an input or output list. In many cases, it is useful to transmit only part of an array, e.g., the first "N" elements. A typical application might be to sum a list of numbers where there are N numbers in the list. Example No. 26 on the following page shows how this might be done for an arbitrary number of lists, when each list is preceded by an integer specifying its length. The numbers in each list are placed into the first "N" elements of an array by means of a repetitive specification, which is described following the example.

```
SUM3: PROCEDURE OPTIONS (MAIN) :

         /* EXAMPLE NO. 26
            SUM LISTS OF NUMBERS. EACH LIST IS PRECEDED
            BY THE NUMBER OF ITEMS IN THE LIST.   TERMINATE
            WHEN THAT NUMBER IS ZERO. */

         DECLARE ( I, N, NUMBER(1000), TOTAL ) FIXED ;

         DO WHILE ('1'B) :

           GET LIST( N, (NUMBER(I) DO I = 1 TO N) ) :
           IF N = 0 THEN DO ;
                         PUT LIST( 'END OF JOB' ) :
                         STOP ;
                         END ;

           TOTAL = NUMBER(1) ; /* INITIALIZE FOR SUM. */
LOOP:      DO I = 2 TO N ;
             TOTAL = TOTAL + NUMBER(I) ;
           END LOOP ;
           PUT LIST( (NUMBER(I) DO I = 1 TO N), TOTAL ) :
         END :

      END SUM3 ;
```

The repetitive specification in the GET and PUT statements in Example No. 26 is the construction

$$(\text{NUMBER(I) DO I} = 1 \text{ TO N})$$

which specifies that the I'th element of the array NUMBER is to be transmitted for each value of I from 1 to N (in steps of 1).

Repetitive specifications are similar to DO loops in many ways; a repetitive specification is essentially a DO loop applied to items in an input or output list. Like DO loops, which can control any number of statements, repetitive specifications can be applied to any number of items in an input or output list. For example, the statement

```
      PUT LIST( (A(I), B(I)   DO I = 1 BY 2 TO 9) ) :
```

will cause data to be transmitted from arrays A and B in the sequence A(1),

B(1), A(3), B(3), . . . A(9), B(9). In general, repetitive specifications have the form

$$(\ \underline{\text{list}}\ \ \text{DO}\ \ \underline{\text{specifications}}\ )$$

where $\underline{\text{list}}$ is a list of items that are permissible in the list in which the repetitive specification appears, and $\underline{\text{specifications}}$ are as defined in Chapter 4.

Items in $\underline{\text{list}}$ can themselves be repetitive specifications; the effect is the same as nesting DO loops. The statement

```
GET LIST( ((A(I,J) DO J = 1 TO 10) DO I = 1 TO 10) ) ;
```

is equivalent to

```
DO I = 1 TO 10 ;
   DO J = 1 TO 10 ;
       GET LIST( A(I,J) ) ;
     END ;
END ;
```

which is equivalent to

```
GET LIST( A ) ;
```

provided that A is declared with the dimension attribute (10, 10).

Finally, like DO loops, repetitive specifications are frequently, but not necessarily, used when working with arrays. The following one-statement program performs the same function as Example No. 16 (page 80), namely, to print a table of sines:

```
SINE: PROCEDURE OPTIONS (MAIN) ;

            /* EXAMPLE NO. 27
            PRINT TABLE OF SINES, PERFORMING ALL COMPU-
            TATIONS IN A 'PUT' STATEMENT. */

        DECLARE X FLOAT ;

        PUT LIST( (X, SIN(X)   DO X = 0 BY 0.1 TO 6.28) ) ;

    END SINE ;
```

The following example program reads data representing a company's monthly sales figures for the years 1974, 1975, and 1976, totals the sales for each year, and prints the results in tabular form. The program uses list-directed input because the data need not appear in any particular format (this convenience would not likely exist in a real-life situation) and list-directed data is the simplest to prepare. The program uses edit-directed input to read three-character abbreviations for the months of the year, because the 36 characters were most convenient to prepare as a 36-character string. All output is edit-directed in order to prepare a neat table.

```
XYZ_4:    PROCEDURE OPTIONS (MAIN) ;

            /* EXAMPLE NO. 28
            XYZ COMPANY, SALES TOTALS FOR 1974-76. */

        DECLARE   SALES( 12,1974:1976) FIXED(5),
                  TOTALS(1974:1976) FIXED(5),
                  MONTH(12) CHARACTER(3),
                  (I, J) FIXED BINARY ;

        /* START OFF WITH NEW PAGE. */
        PUT PAGE ;

        /* HEAD EACH COLUMN WITH YEAR. */
        PUT EDIT( 1974, 1975, 1976 ) ( F(17), 2 F(10) ) ;

        /* INSERT ONE ADDITIONAL SPACE. */
        PUT SKIP ;

        /* BRING IN DATA FOR ARRAY 'MONTH.' */
        GET EDIT( MONTH ) ( 12 A(3) ) ;
```

```
           /* BRING IN SALES DATA. */
           GET LIST( ((SALES(I,J) DO J = 1974 TO 1976)
                               DO I = 1 TO 12) ) ;

           TOTALS = 0 ;

           /* PRINT TABLE AND COMPUTE TOTALS. */

L1:        DO I = 1 TO 12 ;
              PUT EDIT( MONTH(I) ) ( SKIP, A(7) )
                      ( ( SALES(I,J) DO J = 1974 TO 1976) )
                      ( 3 F(10) ) ;
L2:           DO J = 1974, 1975, 1976 ;
                 TOTALS(J) = TOTALS(J) + SALES(I,J) ;
              END L2 ;
           END L1 ;

           /* PRINT TOTALS. */

           PUT EDIT( 'TOTALS', TOTALS )
                   ( SKIP(2), A, F(11), 2 F(10) ) ;

        END XYZ_4 ;
```

Input data to Example No. 28:

```
JANFEBMARAPRMAYJUNJULAUGSEPOCTNOVDEC
120 234 186 199 204 213 208 197 253 244 245 196
179 208 202 196 244 244 256 199 218 223 230 239
226 246 230 247 253 255 229 246 249 253 258 263
```

Output from Example No. 28:

	1974	1975	1976
JAN	120	234	186
FEB	199	204	213
MAR	208	197	253
APR	244	245	196
MAY	179	208	202
JUN	196	244	244
JUL	256	199	218
AUG	223	230	239
SEP	226	246	230
OCT	247	253	255
NOV	229	246	249
DEC	253	258	263
TOTALS	2580	2764	2748

Conceptually, the input and output files are character strings (in which redundant blanks are ignored during list- and data-directed input), and are in many ways similar to PL/I character string variables. Can data be read from and written into character string variables instead of the standard files? Yes, and the facility can be a very useful one.

Data in the input file cannot be read more than once. If it is necessary to read the same data more than once, the items can be taken from the input file and placed in a character string variable by means of an appropriate GET statement. Subsequently, and as often as necessary, the data can then be read from the string by means of other GET statements. A problem might be to interpret the next 50 characters in the input file first as ten 5-digit integers, and again as five 10-digit integers. Here is a solution:

```
DECLARE   A(10)      FIXED (5) ,
          B(5)       FIXED(10) ,
          BUFFER     CHARACTER(50)  ;

/* READ 50 CHARACTERS INTO 'BUFFER' */

GET EDIT( BUFFER ) ( A(50) ) ;

/* INTERPRET CHARACTERS AS 10 FIVE-DIGIT
   INTEGERS; STORE IN ARRAY 'A' */

GET STRING( BUFFER ) EDIT( A ) ( 10 F(5) ) ;

/* INTERPRET CHARACTERS AS 5 TEN-DIGIT
   INTEGERS; STORE IN ARRAY 'B' */

GET STRING( BUFFER ) EDIT( B ) ( 5 F(10) ) ;
```

The first GET statement above is a typical GET statement which places the next 50 characters from the input file into the character string variable BUFFER.

The other two GET statements use the STRING option, which specifies that data are to be taken not from the input file, but from a character string variable in the program. In this case, the variable is BUFFER.

The STRING option may also be used with PUT statements to specify that data are to be transmitted to a character string variable instead of to the output file. The following example program reads five 80-character groups from the input file; each group is preceded by a number from 1 to 5, and then prints the groups in sequence, one group per line. Such a process is not unusual when using a computer to prepare reports.

```
REPORT:  PROCEDURE OPTIONS (MAIN) ;

              /* EXAMPLE NO. 29
                 READ LINES FOR A REPORT, PUT THEM IN
                 SEQUENCE, AND PRINT THE REPORT. */

              DECLARE  ( I, LINE_NO ) FIXED,
                       IMAGE (5)        CHARACTER (80),
                       GROUP            CHARACTER (80) ;

              DO I = 1 TO 5 ;

                  /* BRING IN A GROUP */
                  GET LIST( LINE_NO, GROUP ) ;

                  /* PUT GROUP INTO REPORT IMAGE */
                  PUT STRING( IMAGE (LINE_NO) ) EDIT( GROUP )
                                                        ( A (80) ) ;

              END ;

          /* PRINT THE REPORT */
              PUT EDIT( IMAGE ) ( SKIP, A ) ;

          END REPORT ;
```

The following general rules apply when the STRING option is used:

1. Data are transmitted to or from the string beginning with the first character of the string.

2. Data placed in a string by a list-, data-, or edit-directed PUT statement can be accessed by a list-, data-, or edit-directed GET statement, respectively.

3. When used in a PUT statement, no other options may appear, nor may SKIP, PAGE, LINE, or COLUMN appear as format phrases.

4. The string referenced by a PUT statement must be long enough to hold all of the data. Remember that certain characters, e.g., a decimal point can be inserted during output conversion.

The input/output facilities that have been presented in this chapter are designed primarily for communication between the computer and the people who use it. Although all programs will use some of the facilities described here, PL/I contains many additional input/output facilities that can be used when it is unnecessary to convert data from internal to external form. These facilities are described in Chapter 11.

Notes on Chapter 6

1. Stream files are read and written by GET and PUT statements, respectively. It is a common error to attempt to use READ and WRITE for these purposes, but these words have totally different functions in PL/I. They are described in Chapter 11.

2. It sometimes happens that a certain series of format phrases can be used with many GET and/or PUT statements in a program. Rather than write each such series each time it is to be used, it can be written once and placed in the program remotely from the statements that reference it. The general form of a remotely specified format is

label: FORMAT(specifications);

and the specifications can then be referenced by means of the "R" format phrase in a format associated with a GET or PUT statement. The general form of the R format phrase is

R (label)

where label is the label of a FORMAT statement. The program example below illustrates the use of remote format specifications. The problem is to read ten floating-point numbers into each of two arrays, A and B, and print their contents and the sum of corresponding elements.

```
RFORM:    PROCEDURE OPTIONS (MAIN) ;

          /* EXAMPLE NO. 30
                ILLUSTRATE REMOTE FORMATS. */

          DECLARE (A, B) (10) FIXED (10,3) ;
F1:       FORMAT( 10 F(10,3) ) ;
F2:       FORMAT( A, R(F1) ) ;
F3:       FORMAT( SKIP, X(5), R(F2) ) ;

          GET EDIT( A, B ) ( R(F1) ) ;

          PUT EDIT( 'A = ', A ) ( PAGE, R(F3) ) ;
          PUT EDIT( 'B = ', B ) ( R(F3) ) ;
          PUT EDIT ('TOTAL = ', A+B) (SKIP(2), X(1), R(F2));
          END RFORM ;
```

The example illustrates the fact that remote formats may themselves contain R phrases. However, no format may reference itself with an R phrase, nor may it reference another format that in turn references it. The phrase R (F3), for instance, would be illegal in any of the formats F1, F2, and F3 because it would result in "circular" nesting of formats, regardless of which of the three is referenced by a GET or PUT statement.

3.   Some implementations, such as PL/C, do not include the P format phrase.

EXERCISES

6.1   Name four ways in which a value can be assigned to a character string variable.

6.2   Modify Example No. 5 (page 31) to use data-directed output.

6.3   Why would data-directed input/output be awkward in Example No. 23 (page 103)?

6.4   Would data-directed input/output have any advantage over the list-directed input/output used in Example No. 14 (page 76)?

6.5   Write a PL/I program which reads 51-character groups from the input file. The first character of each group will be the letter A, B, C, D, or E; the next 50 characters will be digits. There will be no blanks between groups, or within a group. The program should perform the following operations, based on the first character:

First Character	Treat the remaining 50 characters as . . .
A	Five 10-digit integers, assigning them to elements 2, 4, 6, 8, and 10 of a fixed-point array named A1.
B	Ten 5-digit integers, assigning them to the first ten elements of A1.
C	Ten floating-point numbers of precision (5, 2), assigning them to the first ten elements of a floating-point array named A2.
D	Ignore; process the next 51-character group.
E	Ignore; terminate the program.

6.6 How many lines, including blank lines, will be printed by the statement (X and Y are scalar arithmetic variables):

DECLARE (X, Y) FLOAT INITIAL (1.0) ;
PUT EDIT (X, Y) (F(3,1), SKIP (2)) ;

6.7 Write a PL/I program which reads two numbers: The first is an integer representing a day of the week (1=Sunday) and the second is the number of days in a month (28, 29, 30, or 31). From these, print a "calendar" for that month. For example, if the inputs are 5 and 30 respectively, your program should print something like:

```
                  1   2   3
   4   5   6   7   8   9  10
  11  12  13  14  15  16  17
  18  19  20  21  22  23  24
  25  26  27  28  29  30
```

6.8 Write a PL/I program which reads one number representing the day of the week corresponding to January 1, (1=Sunday). From this, print a calendar for the entire year. Assume February has 28 days.

6.9 Write a PL/I program which reads one number representing the day of the week corresponding to January 1 (1=Sunday). From this, print the number of Fridays the 13th in the year. Assume February has 28 days.

Chapter 7

PROCEDURES

A procedure in PL/I is a set of statements designed to accomplish some particular objective. Each of the program examples used in this book so far has consisted of a single procedure; the objective of each procedure has been identical to the objective of the whole program. The objective of a program as a whole is called the main objective; it is a result of executing the main program.

In general, some intermediate results must be obtained during the execution of a main program. These intermediate results are then used to obtain other intermediate results and so on, until the main results are obtained. Intermediate results may be obtained directly, by statements in the main program, or they may be obtained by other programs—subordinate to the main program—which are executed as required. Such subprograms, because they consist of PL/I statements designed to accomplish some particular objective, are also procedures.

The general structure of a PL/I program as a whole thus consists of two kinds of procedures: a single main procedure, and any number (including zero) of subprograms, each of which is also a procedure. The main procedure is identified by the option MAIN, as in the program examples.

Every PL/I program must contain at least one procedure with the MAIN option.° This procedure may "call" other procedures—subpro-

---

° If more than one procedure has the MAIN option, the one taken as the main program depends on the particular computer and compiler in use.

grams—in the course of execution, and the subprograms may call other subprograms. Calling a subprogram amounts to transferring control to it, suspending execution of the calling program. When the subprogram has completed its work it "returns" to the calling program, which then resumes execution. Usually, but not necessarily, the subprogram will have performed some operations, the results of which are needed by the calling program when control is returned to it. A subprogram may be called as many times, from as many places, as required; it will normally return to the calling program at the point following the statement which called it.

For an example of a program using a subprogram, we will discuss a program which reads three numbers corresponding to the three dimensions of a rectangular box and computes the length of the diagonal of the box. We can think of the box as having height H, width W, and depth D, as shown in the illustration below. Given values for these dimensions, the program is to calculate the length of the diagonal, E.

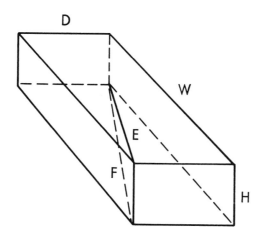

In order to calculate the length of the diagonal, E, we must first calculate the length of the face diagonal, F. The length of F can be determined from the values of W and D by the Pythagorean Theorem:

$$F = \sqrt{W^2 + D^2}$$

The length of E can then be determined, also by the Pythagorean Theorem:

$$E = \sqrt{F^2 + H^2}$$

To solve the problem (in principle) we need only apply the Pythagorean Theorem twice. If we write a subprogram to apply the Pythagorean Theorem, then we need only call the subprogram twice; we do not have to write the necessary PL/I statements each time.

For purposes of writing the subprogram, we will assume that the Pythagorean Theorem means taking the square root of the sum of the squares of two quantities which we will call <u>parameters</u>, which are called SIDE1 and SIDE2. This is the subprogram:

```
HYPOT:    PROCEDURE ( SIDE1, SIDE2 ) RETURNS( FLOAT ) ;

          /* COMPUTE HYPOTENUSE OF RIGHT TRIANGLE
             GIVEN TWO SIDES. */

          DECLARE ( SIDE1, SIDE2 ) FLOAT ;

          RETURN( SQRT( SIDE1**2 + SIDE2**2 ) ) ;

      END HYPOT ;
```

The above sequence of statements declares the identifier HYPOT to be the name of a procedure, the function of which is to compute the square root of the sum of the squares of two quantities and return the result to the calling program. The two quantities, SIDE1 and SIDE2 are the <u>parameters</u> to HYPOT. Parameters to a procedure are enclosed in parentheses to the right of the word PROCEDURE, and are separated by commas.

The attribute FLOAT in the first line specifies that the value returned by HYPOT is to be a floating-point number.

The DECLARE statement serves its usual purpose, to define the attributes of variables used in the program. In this case, the only variables are the parameters.

The RETURN statement specifies the value that HYPOT is to return to the calling program. In this case, it specifies that the value is to be the square root of the sum of the squares of the two parameters.

The complete program to solve the original problem—computing the length of the diagonal of a box—is shown on the following page. The first executable statement in the program is the GET statement. The statements in procedure HYPOT are compiled, but they are not executed until the two statements following the GET statement are executed. In other words, the statement

```
HYPOT:    PROCEDURE( SIDE1, SIDE2 ) RETURNS( FLOAT ) ;
```

tells the compiler three things:

1. Subsequent statements constitute a declaration of a procedure named HYPOT;

2. The procedure has two parameters; and

3. The procedure will return a floating-point value.

   The statement

```
F = HYPOT( W, D ) ;
```

specifies that the subprogram HYPOT is to be executed, using the values of the variables W and D. These identifiers are called arguments; they have a one-for-one correspondence to the parameters, used in the procedure declaration. The above statement is identical to

```
F = SQRT( W**2 + D**2 ) ;
```

```
DIAG: PROCEDURE OPTIONS (MAIN) ;

          /* EXAMPLE NO. 31
             READ THREE SIDES OF A BOX AND COMPUTE THE
             LENGTH OF THE DIAGONAL. */

          DECLARE ( H, W, D, E, F ) FLOAT ;

          HYPOT:    PROCEDURE( SIDE1, SIDE2 ) RETURNS ( FLOAT ) ;

                        /* COMPUTE HYPOTENUSE OF RIGHT
                           TRIANGLE GIVEN TWO SIDES. */

                    DECLARE ( SIDE1, SIDE2 ) FLOAT ;

                    RETURN( SQRT( SIDE1**2 + SIDE2**2 ) ) ;
                  END HYPOT ;

          /* MAIN PROGRAM STARTS HERE. */
          DO WHILE ('1'B) ;
             GET DATA( H, W, D ) ;

             /* COMPUTE DIAGONAL ON FACE. */
             F = HYPOT( W, D ) ;

             /* COMPUTE DIAGONAL. */
             E = HYPOT( F, H ) ;

             /* PRINT DATA AND RESULTS. */
             PUT DATA( H, W, D, E ) ;

          END ;
       END DIAG ;
```

The relationship of arguments and parameters is fundamental to the concept of subprograms. The arguments used when a subprogram is called - are in effect substituted for the parameters. Consequently, it is <u>essential</u> that the attributes of arguments be the same as those of the corresponding parameters.

The names of parameters are unimportant, but they must be identifiers. Parameters have absolutely no relation to any other identifiers in a program, outside of the procedure declaration in which they appear. Consequently, their names can be chosen independently of names chosen for use elsewhere in a program.

Parameters can pass values to procedures, receive values from procedures. The parameters specify how the arguments are to be used when a procedure is called. The following procedure illustrates these two kinds of parameters:

```
QUAD: PROCEDURE ( X, Y, Z, R1, R2, ERROR ) ;

        /* EXAMPLE NO. 32
           SOLVE QUADRATIC EQUATION, GIVEN COEFFICIENTS
           X, Y, AND Z. RESULTS ARE RETURNED IN R1 AND R2.
           SET ERROR FLAG IF X=C OR DISCRIMINATE<0. */

        DECLARE ( X, Y, Z, R1, R2 ) FLOAT,
                ERROR BIT(1),
                ( DISC, DENOM ) FLOAT ;

        IF X=0 THEN  DO ;
                    ERROR = '1'B ;
                    RETURN ;
                    END ;

        DISC = Y**2 - 4*X*Z ;
        IF DISC<0 THEN  DO ;
                    ERROR = '1'B ;
                    RETURN ;
                    END ;

        DISC = SQRT ( DISC ) ;
        DENOM = X + X ;
        R1 = ( -Y + DISC ) / DENOM ;
        R2 = ( -Y - DISC ) / DENOM ;
        RETURN ;
     END QUAD ;
```

When procedure QUAD (Example No. 32) is called, the arguments corresponding to X, Y, and Z will pass values to it. The arguments corresponding to R1, R2 and ERROR will receive values from it.

The parameters X, Y, and Z are sometimes called "value" parameters because their values are important to the procedure. The parameters R1, R2 and ERROR are sometimes called "name" parameters because their names, i.e., their locations in the computer, are important to the procedure.

A fundamental difference between procedure QUAD and procedure HYPOT, which was discussed previously, is that HYPOT itself effectively takes on a value, but QUAD does not. Instead, QUAD merely calculates three values and places them into the arguments corresponding to R1, R2 and ERROR. A procedure like HYPOT, which itself takes on a value, is called a <u>function procedure</u>, or simply, a <u>function</u>. A procedure like QUAD, which does not itself take on a value, is called a <u>subroutine procedure</u>, or simply, a <u>subroutine</u>. Functions are called by using their names in expressions, e.g.,

$$F = HYPOT (W, D) ;$$

Subroutines are called by the <u>CALL statement</u>, which has the general form

$$CALL \ \underline{procedure} \ (\underline{arguments}) ;$$

where

> <u>procedure</u> is the name of the subroutine procedure being called, and

> <u>arguments</u> are the actual variables used.

The following program example uses the subroutine QUAD to solve ten quadratic equations with coefficients in arrays A, B, and C. The roots of each equation are placed in the corresponding elements of two other arrays, ROOT1 and ROOT2. If any set of coefficients results in an error the appropriate elements of ROOT1 and ROOT2 are set to zero and an informative message is printed.

```
SOLVE:    PROCEDURE OPTIONS (MAIN) ;

              /* EXAMPLE NO. 33
                  SOLVE TEN SETS OF QUADRATIC EQUATIONS. */

              DECLARE ( A, B, C, ROOT1, ROOT2 )(10) FLOAT,
                       ERR BIT(1) ,
                       I  FIXED ;

QUAD: PROCEDURE( X, Y, Z, R1, R2, ERROR ) ;

              /* EXAMPLE NO. 32
                  SOLVE QUADRATIC EQUATION, GIVEN COEFFICIENTS
                  X, Y, AND Z. RESULTS ARE RETURNED IN R1 AND R2.
                  TRANSFER TO 'ERROR' IF X=0 OR DISCRIMINANT<0. */

              DECLARE ( X, Y, Z, R1, R2 ) FLOAT, ERROR LABEL,
                       ERROR BIT(1),
                       ( DISC, DENOM ) FLOAT ;
              ERROR = '0'B ;
              IF  X=0 THEN DO ;
                          ERROR = '1'B ;
                          RETURN ;
                          END ;

              DISC = Y**2 - 4*X*Z ;
              IF DISC<0 THEN DO ;
                              ERROR = '1'B ;
                              RETURN ;
                              END ;
              DISC = SQRT( DISC ) ;
              DENOM = X + X ;
              R1 = ( -Y + DISC ) / DENOM ;
              R2 = ( -Y - DISC ) / DENOM ;
              RETURN ;
          END QUAD ;

              /* READ INPUT DATA */
              GET LIST( A, B, C ) ;

      L:     DO I = 1 BY 1 TO 10 ;
                  CALL QUAD( A(I), B(I), C(I), ROOT1(I),
                          ROOT2(I), ERR ) ;
                  IF ERR = '1'B THEN DO ;
                                     ROOT1(I),ROOT2(I) = 0 ;
                                     PUT SKIP LIST ('ERROR, EQUATION',
                                         I, 'COEFFICIENTS = ', A(I),
                                         B(I), C(I)) ;
          END L ;                    END ;

              PUT LIST ( (A(I), B(I), C(I), ROOT1(I), ROOT2(I)
                      DO I = 1 TO 10) ) ;

      END SOLVE ;
```

The form of the RETURN statements in a procedure determines
whether it is a function or a subroutine. If they are of the form

$$RETURN(\underline{expression});$$

the procedure is a function; its value is that of the expression. If the RETURN statements consist of the single word RETURN, the procedure is a subroutine.

Functions must always contain at least one RETURN statement, since by definition they return a value to the calling program. Subroutines return to the calling program either by executing a RETURN statement, or by executing the END statement. (Thus, the RETURN statement in subroutine QUAD is redundant.) There is no restriction on the maximum number of RETURN statements that may appear in a function or in a subroutine.

A single procedure can have the properties of a function and a subroutine at the same time. That is, it can modify the actual parameters and at the same time take on a value itself. For example, subroutine QUAD can be modified to take on a value of 1 or 0 if an equation is or is not solved correctly:

```
QUAD2:    PROCEDURE( X, Y, Z, R1, R2 ) RETURNS( FLOAT ) ;

          /* EXAMPLE NO. 34
             SOLVE QUADRATIC EQUATION, GIVEN COEFFICIENTS
             X, Y, AND Z. RESULTS ARE RETURNED IN R1 AND R2.
             QUAD2 TAKES ON VALUE 0 IF X=0 OR DISCRIMINANT
             <0, ELSE 1. */

          DECLARE ( X, Y, Z, R1, R2 ) FLOAT,
                  ( DISC, DENOM ) FLOAT ;

          IF X=0 THEN RETURN( 0 ) ;

          DISC = Y**2 - 4*X*Z ;
          IF DISC<0 THEN RETURN( 0 ) ;

          DISC = SQRT( DISC ) ;
          DENOM = X + X ;
          R1 = ( -Y + DISC ) / DENOM ;
          R2 = ( -Y - DISC ) / DENOM ;
          RETURN( 1 ) ;
     END QUAD2 ;
```

The essence of Example No. 33 could then be reduced to

```
DO I = 1, BY 1 TO 10 ;
   IF   QUAD2( A(I), B(I), C(I), ROOT1(I), ROOT2(I) )=0
      THEN   ROOT1(I), ROOT2(I) = 0 ;
END ;
```

When a procedure works with the value of an argument rather than its
name, the argument can be an expression. The statements

```
        F = HYPOT( W, D ) ;

        E = HYPOT( F, H ) ;
```

could be combined into a single statement:

```
        E = HYPOT( HYPOT( W, D ), H ) ;
```

That is, the value yielded by HYPOT(W,D) is used as one of the two
arguments (the other is H) in a second call of HYPOT.

Arrays can be passed as arguments to procedures, provided, as usual
that the attributes of the arrays are the same as the attributes of the
corresponding parameters. The following procedure could be used in a
checker-playing program to determine the number of checkers remaining
on the board:

```
CHK_BD:   PROCEDURE( BOARD, REDS, BLACKS ) ;

            /* EXAMPLE NO. 35
               DETERMINE NUMBER OF CHECKERS ON A CHECKERBOARD.
               RED CHECKERS ARE REPRESENTED BY +1, BLACKS BY -1.
               UNOCCUPIED SQUARES CONTAIN 0. */

            DECLARE ( BOARD(8,8), REDS, BLACKS ) FIXED,
                     ( I, J ) FIXED ;

            REDS, BLACKS = 0 ;

            DO I = 1 BY 1 TO 8 ;
               DO J = 1 BY 1 TO 8 ;
                  IF BOARD(I,J)=1 THEN REDS = REDS + 1 ;
                  IF BOARD(I,J)=-1 THEN BLACKS = BLACKS + 1 ;
               END ;
            END ;
          END CHK_BD ;
```

When CHK__BD is called during execution of the checker-playing program, the first argument must be the name of a fixed-point array declared with the dimension attribute (8,8). The second and third arguments must be fixed-point simple variables. All of the arguments must be of default precision, because no precision attribute is specified in the declaration for the parameters.

When structures are passed as arguments to procedures, there are several ways in which they can be treated by the procedures. The program example below calls two procedures, UPDATE and LISTER (declarations for which are not shown).

```
CK_ACC:   PROCEDURE OPTIONS (MAIN) ;

          /* EXAMPLE NO. 36
                  UPDATE CHECKING ACCOUNTS, USING OTHER SUBPRO-
                  GRAMS FOR THE UPDATE AND OUTPUT FUNCTIONS. */

                  DECLARE   1 ACCOUNT,
                            2 NAME,
                            3 LAST       CHARACTER(12),
                            3 FIRST      CHARACTER(12),
                            3 MIDDLE     CHARACTER(3),
                            2 NUMBER     FIXED,
                            2 OLD_BAL    FLOAT,
                            2 SER_CHG    FLOAT,
                            2 NEW_BAL    FLOAT ;

                  GET LIST (ACCOUNT) ;
                  CALL UPDATE( ACCOUNT ) ;
                  CALL LISTER( NAME, NUMBER ) ;
          END CK_ACC ;
```

How would the corresponding parameters be declared in the declarations for UPDATE and LISTER? One way would be to declare parameters in the same way as the arguments, i.e., for UPDATE:

```
UPDATE:    PROCEDURE ( STRUCT ) ;

           DECLARE 1 STRUCT,
                   2 MINOR,
                   (3 ELEM_1     CHARACTER (12),
                    3 ELEM_2     CHARACTER (12),
                    3 ELEM_3     CHARACTER (3),
                   2 ELEM_4      FIXED,
                   2 ELEM_5      FLOAT,
                   2 ELEM_6      FLOAT,
                   2 ELEM_7      FLOAT ;

                   .
                   .
                   .
```

For LISTER:

```
LISTER:    PROCEDURE ( STRUCT, NUM ) ;

           DECLARE 1 STRUCT,
                   2 ELEM_1      CHARACTER (12),
                   2 ELEM_2      CHARACTER (12),
                   2 ELEM_3      CHARACTER (3),

                   NUM FIXED ;

                   .
                   .
                   .
```

All of the elementary items in the DECLARE statement in LISTER are on level 2, but they could have been declared to be on some other level, e.g., 3, without altering the structuring of the parameter STRUCT. The DECLARE statement would still declare STRUCT to be the name of a structure having three elementary items with the indicated attributes. The corresponding arguments must therefore be the name of a structure having three elementary items with the corresponding attributes. In Example No. 36, the argument is NAME, which is a structure having the required characteristics.

A structure parameter must be a level one name, i.e., it cannot be declared as a member of another structure within the called procedure. A parameter structure name may be either non-dimensioned, representing a single structure, or dimensioned, representing an array of structures.

Suppose in Example 36, on page 152, that the structure ACCOUNT were dimensioned as an array of 100 accounts. Then each single ACCOUNT could be passed to the UPDATE procedure on the preceding page as follows:

```
DO  J  =  1  BY  1  TO  100  ;
    CALL  UPDATE( ACCOUNT(J)  )  ;
END  ;
```

On the other hand, the procedure UPDATE could be changed so that the parameter name, STRUCT, is dimensioned 100. Then the entire structure of 100 accounts could be passed and all 100 accounts updated in a single call to UPDATE.

Is there any relationship between identifiers used in a procedure and identifiers used elsewhere in a program? In the case of parameters, there is no relationship, even if the program uses identifiers spelled in exactly the same way outside of the procedure. However, other identifiers used in a procedure may be identical to the same identifiers used outside the procedure. The rule is

> Identifiers appearing as parameters or in a DECLARE statement in a procedure have no relationship to any identifiers used outside of the procedure.

The corollary rule is

> Identifiers, other than parameters, which do not appear in a DECLARE statement in a procedure are identical to the same identifiers used outside of the procedure.

In order to understand the meaning of these rules, consider the following construction:

```
P1:     PROCEDURE OPTIONS (MAIN) ;

            DECLARE   A   FIXED INITIAL( 3 )  ;

            P2:     PROCEDURE ;

                        DECLARE   A   FIXED INITIAL( 10 )  ;

   ③                   P3:     PROCEDURE ;
                                    PUT LIST( A )  ;
                                END P3 ;

   ②                   CALL P3 ;

   ④                   PUT LIST( A )  ;

                   END P2 ;

   ①           CALL P2 ;

   ⑤           PUT LIST( A )  ;

        END P1 ;
```

The numbers to the left of the executable statements in the above construction show the sequence in which they are executed. The first executable statement calls procedure P2, which immediately calls P3.

The PUT statement in procedure P3 prints the value of the variable named A. This "A" is the same "A" that is used in P2, the containing procedure, because the identifier does not appear in a DECLARE statement in P3. The printed value will be 10.

Procedure P3 returns to the PUT statement (④) in P2, the calling program. Since the "A" in P3 is identical to the "A" in P2, the printed value will again be 10.

Procedure P2 returns to the PUT statement (⑤) in P1, the calling program. However, the value printed by that statement will be 3. Because A is declared in P2, it has no relation to the variable of the same name in P1. The "A"s in P1 and P2 are entirely unrelated.

The variable named A declared in P1 is said to be known throughout P1, exclusive of P2. That variable is not known in P2 because another variable of the same name is declared there. This latter variable is known throughout P2, inclusive of P3, because it is not redeclared there. Conversely, the "A" declared in P2 is not known in P1. It is said to be local to P2, and <u>global</u> to P3. In general, the areas in which an identifier is known are called the <u>scope</u> of the identifier.

The appearance of an identifier in a DECLARE statement defines that identifier to be local to the procedure in which it is declared. Consequently, its attributes may be different in different declarations. For example, in the construction

```
P1:     PROCEDURE ;

            DECLARE  XYZ   FIXED ;

            P2:     PROCEDURE ;

                        DECLARE   XYZ   BIT(1) ;

                        P3:     PROCEDURE ;

                                    DECLARE   XYZ   FLOAT ;
                                        •
                                        •
                                    END  P3 ;
                        •
                        •
            END  P2 ;
        •
        •
    END  P1 ;
```

the identifier XYZ is a fixed-point variable in P1, exclusive of P2; a bit string of length 1 in P2, exclusive of P3; and a floating-point variable in P3.

The rules governing the scopes of identifiers can be modified by the <u>EXTERNAL attribute</u> which specifies that identifiers in a procedure are to be identical to the same identifiers in other procedures. In the following illustration the identifier ABC refers to the same variable in procedures P1 and P3. A separate variable having the name ABC is local to P2, and yet another is local to P4.

```
P1:     PROCEDURE ;

            DECLARE  ABC  FIXED EXTERNAL ;

        P2:     PROCEDURE ;

                DECLARE ABC  FLOAT ;

            P3:     PROCEDURE ;

                    DECLARE  ABC  FIXED EXTERNAL ;

                P4:     PROCEDURE ;

                        DECLARE  ABC  FLOAT ;

                        END P4 ;

                END P3 ;

            END P2 ;

        END P1 ;
```

When the EXTERNAL attribute is given to an identifier, any other attributes specified must be identical with other EXTERNAL declarations for the identifier.

Procedures need not be nested in precisely the way they have been in the examples presented up to this point. The rule for nesting procedures is equivalent to the rule for nesting DO loops: if a procedure is begun within another procedure, it must be terminated within the same procedure. Illustration (a) on the following page is a diagram of a properly constructed PL/I program. Illustration (b) shows a construction which is improper because it violates the nesting rule.

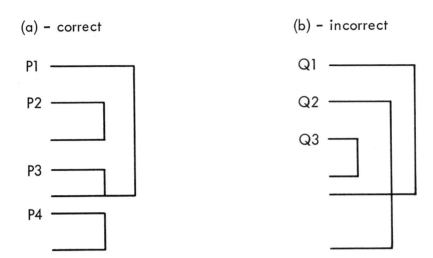

(a) – correct   (b) – incorrect

If illustration (a) is assumed to represent an entire PL/I program, then P1 and P4 are called <u>external</u> procedures. Any identifiers·declared with the EXTERNAL attribute in both P1 and P4 are identical. Thus, the EXTERNAL attribute can be used to establish communication between external procedures as well as between an internal procedure and the outermost procedure of a nest.

Any PL/I program comprises a collection of external procedures. One of these procedures must have the option MAIN which identifies it as the procedure in which execution is to begin. The MAIN option may not be used with an internal procedure.

The name of any external procedure that is to be called by another must be declared in the calling procedure to have the ENTRY attribute. This is done by a statement of the form

DECLARE <u>name</u> ENTRY;

where <u>name</u> is the name of the external procedure that may be called.

The procedures constituting a program may appear in any sequence. Thus, the following is a valid PL/I program:

```
PX:     PROCEDURE ;
            DECLARE PZ ENTRY ;
                .
                .
            CALL PZ ;
                .
                .
        END PX ;

PY:     PROCEDURE OPTIONS (MAIN) ;
            DECLARE (PX,PZ) ENTRY ;
                .
                .
            CALL PZ ;
                .
                .
            CALL PX ;
                .
                .
        END PY ;

PZ:     PROCEDURE ;
                .
                .
        END PZ ;
```

Thus, PY (the main program) can call PZ and PX; PX can call PZ; but PZ can not call PX. In general, any external procedure can call any other external procedure.

The ability to construct PL/I programs by collecting external procedures is a very definite advantage. Any procedure which uses only local identifiers and parameters, if any, can in principle be added to the collection; the only changes required to the main program would be the addition of CALL statements or function references as appropriate.

Procedure QUAD (page 147) could be incorporated into any PL/I program to provide the facility for solving quadratic equations. In order to use the facility, it is necessary to know only

1. the procedure name (QUAD),

2. that the first three arguments are the coefficients,

3. that the next two arguments will be given the values of the roots, and

4. that the last argument is the error indicator.

It is essential that the attributes of arguments be the same as those of the corresponding parameters, but it is not always easy to meet this requirement. In order to get around the difficulty for external procedures we must elaborate the ENTRY attribute to specify the attributes of parameters; the arguments will be converted automatically whenever necessary. The general form of the ENTRY attribute as included in a DECLARE statement is

DECLARE name ENTRY(att, att, . . . , att) ;

where

name is a function or subroutine name, and

att are the attributes of the respective parameters, i.e., the required attributes of the arguments.

If at the time an external procedure is called, the attributes of the arguments do not match the respective attributes stated for them in the ENTRY declaration, they will be converted as necessary before being passed to the procedure. (As usual in all instances of conversion, the CONVERSION condition may be raised during this process.) Arguments to internal procedures will likewise be converted, although internal procedures must not be declared ENTRY within the procedure that contains them.

Conversion, when required, may lead to a variety of errors in the program. Much time and effort can be saved by avoiding the need for conversions. This is done simply by ascertaining that the arguments you use have the same attributes as the parameters used in the respective procedure declarations.

The ENTRY declaration for an external procedure QUAD (page 147) would be

```
DECLARE QUAD ENTRY (FLOAT, FLOAT, FLOAT, FLOAT, FLOAT, BIT(1));
```

and would be included in the procedure which calls QUAD.

When a parameter is an array, the notation in the ENTRY attribute is one or more asterisks (one for each dimension) separated by commas and enclosed in parentheses. The statement

```
DECLARE  PROC  ENTRY( (*,*,*) FIXED, (*) CHARACTER(10) ) ;
```

declares PROC to be an external procedure; the first parameter is a three-dimensional fixed-point array, and the second is a one-dimensional array of character strings of length 10.

When a parameter is a structure, the notation in the ENTRY attribute is a list of level numbers separated by commas. Attributes may be appended to elementary level numbers, but may not be factored. The first level number for each parameter must be 1. The statement

```
DECLARE  P2  ENTRY( 1, 2 FLOAT, 2, 3 FIXED, 3 FIXED, FLOAT ) ;
```

declares P2 to be a procedure; the first parameter is a structure which can be visualized as

> 1 A,
>
>> 2 B FLOAT,
>>
>> 2 C,
>>
>>> 3 D FIXED,
>>>
>>> 3 E FIXED

The statement also specifies that the second parameter to P2 is a floating-point variable of default precision.

It is also essential that the values returned by functions have the attributes expected by the calling program. The RETURNS attribute is used to specify the attributes of values returned by external functions; the values will be converted automatically to the attributes required by the calling program. The general form of the RETURNS attribute as included in a DECLARE statement is

> DECLARE name ENTRY(attributes)
>
>> RETURNS(attributes) ;

The ENTRY declaration for an external procedure HYPOT (page 144) would be

```
DECLARE HYPOT ENTRY( FLOAT, FLOAT ) RETURNS( FLOAT ) ;
```

and would be included in the procedure which invokes HYPOT.

A procedure which is perfectly general can, with no modification whatsoever, be included in any PL/I program. It should use only local identifiers and parameters to be general. Use of such procedures for purposes which are fairly common, yet difficult to program, e.g., solution of a large set of simultaneous equations, can greatly reduce the amount of time and effort required to write programs. Sometimes, such use makes the construction of a program that would otherwise be impossible very simple. For example, linear programming is a very useful technique for finding the optimum solution to problems with many interrelated variables where some of the relationships may be very complicated. An individual with extensive knowledge of linear programming techniques could write a procedure which someone with much less knowledge could then use to solve his problem. Such a procedure could then be written once and stored in a "program library" where it would be available to anyone having need of it.

Notes on Chapter 7

1. In order to minimize the chances for error, the attributes of parameters to a procedure should be specified in two places:

> in an ENTRY declaration contained in the procedure which calls it,

and

> in a DECLARE statement within the procedure itself.

For function procedures, the attributes of the results returned should be specified in a RETURNS attribute appended to an ENTRY declaration, and <u>must</u> be specified in the PROCEDURE statement itself, following the parameter list.

2. In some implementations (excluding PL/C) a procedure may call itself; the process is called <u>recursion</u>. If a procedure is to be recursive, it must have the RECURSIVE attribute, as illustrated below, and there must be some provision for terminating the recursion. The procedure below computes the factorial of its argument. (The factorial of a number is the product of the integers from 1 to the number.)

```
FACT: PROCEDURE( N ) RECURSIVE RETURNS( FIXED ) ;

        /* EXAMPLE NO. 37
           THIS PROCEDURE TAKES ON THE VALUE OF
           N-FACTORIAL. */

        DECLARE N FIXED ;

        IF N<=1 THEN RETURN( 1 ) ;
        ELSE RETURN( N*FACT( N-1 ) ) ;
     END FACT ;
```

3. In some implementations there may be restrictions on ENTRY declarations and arguments.

EXERCISES

7.1 Rewrite Exercise 4.4 as a generalized matrix multiplication subroutine called by the statement

$$\text{CALL MMULT}(\underline{a}, \underline{b}, \underline{c}) ;$$

where $\underline{a}$, $\underline{b}$, and $\underline{c}$ are two-dimensional arrays having bounds (1:15) in each dimension.

7.2 Write a "driver" program that will call MMULT to test it. Include an ENTRY declaration for MMULT.

7.3 Write a non-recursive function to compute factorials. Is your function more, or less, efficient than Example No. 37 above?

7.4 Write a function procedure that evaluates polynomials of the form

$$a_0 + a_1x^2 + a_2x^2 + \ \ . \ . \ . \ a_nx^n$$

and which is called by the expression

$$POLY(A, N, X)$$

where

    A   is a one-dimensional array having a lower subscript bound of zero,

    N   is the degree of the polynomial (N < 20), and

    X   is the value of the variable.

Write a driver program to test your function using several polynomials and several values of the variable for each.

7.5   Write a subroutine which accepts the array of structures ACCOUNT shown in Example No. 23 (pages 103–104) and sorts the contents into ascending order by account number.

7.6   Rewrite Exercise 6.7 as a subroutine which has two parameters to specify the beginning day of the month and number of days in the month.

7.7   Write a driver program which calls the subroutine of Exercise 7.6 in order to produce a 12-month calendar.

7.8   Write a function which has one parameter representing the day of the week corresponding to January 1, (1 = Sunday) and returns as its value the number of Fridays the 13th in that year. Assume February has 28 days.

Chapter 8

BLOCK STRUCTURE

Any PL/I program consists of one or more external procedures, each of which can contain "local" and "global" identifiers. Internal procedures, i.e., procedures contained within other procedures, may also contain local and global identifiers.

A program segment which can contain local identifiers is called a <u>block</u>. Two kinds of blocks are provided for in PL/I: procedure blocks, described in the preceding chapter; and BEGIN blocks, described in this chapter. The term "block" refers to either kind of block and the context indicates which kind is meant.

The general form of a BEGIN block is

BEGIN ;

<u>statement(s)</u> ;

END ;

BEGIN blocks are entered in the normal sequence of execution, as contrasted with procedure blocks which are entered by means of CALL statements or function references. Consequently, a BEGIN block must be contained within another block, which may be either another BEGIN block or a procedure block. The outermost block must, of course, be an external procedure.

The concept of "scope of identifiers" applies to procedure blocks. However, BEGIN blocks cannot have parameters, so the rules become

1. Any identifiers declared within a block are local to the block.

2. Any identifiers not declared within a block are global to the block.

The EXTERNAL attribute can be used to modify the second rule, as described in Chapter 7.

One of the most useful properties of blocks is that they can give a "dynamic" character to programs. That is, they can be used to establish various program characteristics during execution, rather than during compilation. A typical application is the allocation of storage for arrays. For instance, one of the previous program examples using arrays contained the statement

```
DECLARE ( A, B, C ) (10) FLOAT ;
```

to declare three arrays, each having ten elements. The amount of data placed into these arrays may require fewer than ten elements, in which case the DECLARE statement is wasteful of space in storage. The maximum amount of data that can be accommodated is limited to ten items in each array; if more must be accommodated, the DECLARE statement must be rewritten to allocate more storage. In general, it is impossible to write declarations which allocate sufficient space for arrays, yet do not allocate excessive space.

Suppose a program is to read a set of numbers into an array. If the set is preceded by an integer telling how many numbers there are in the set, part of the program might be

```
P1:    PROCEDURE OPTIONS (MAIN) ;

       DECLARE   A(100)    FLOAT,
                 (I, N)    FIXED ;

       GET LIST( N, (A(I) DO I = 1 TO N) ) ;
          .
          .
          .
       END P1 ;
```

166

If the value of N is less than 100, the array declaration is wasteful of storage. If N is greater than 100, an error will occur. Both possibilities can be avoided by reading a value for N and then allocating storage for the array. This can be done easily by using a BEGIN block; the program becomes

```
P2:     PROCEDURE OPTIONS (MAIN) ;

        DECLARE  N  FIXED ;

        GET LIST( N ) ;

        BEGIN ;

            DECLARE  A(N)  FLOAT ;

            GET LIST( A ) ;
                .
                .
                .
        END ;
        .
        .
        .
  END P2 ;
```

Storage for the array A in the above program excerpt is allocated when the BEGIN block is entered. The number of elements allocated is the value of N, a variable which is global to the block. It is important to note that the value of N must have been established prior to entry into the block, i.e., before the array A is declared. It would be useless to place the GET statement ahead of the DECLARE statement for A in the same block because, as stated in Chapter 2, blocks are scanned for DECLARE statements and attributes are established before the executable statements are compiled. In one sense, DECLARE statements are also executable: they allocate storage and assign attributes. In this sense, they are always the first statements to be executed when a block is entered, regardless of their physical placement within a block.

The following example illustrates the use of a BEGIN block in a complete PL/I program:

```
SUMLIST: PROCEDURE OPTIONS (MAIN) ;

        /* EXAMPLE NO. 38
           READ LISTS OF NUMBERS INTO AN ARRAY, ADD THEM, AND
           PRINT THE TOTAL OF THE ITEMS IN EACH LIST. LISTS
           MAY BE OF VARYING LENGTH; ALLOCATE JUST ENOUGH
           STORAGE TO ACCOMMODATE THE PARTICULAR LIST IN
           PROCESS. */

        DECLARE ( I, N ) FIXED ;

   DO WHILE( 1 ) ;

     GET LIST ( N ) ; /* NUMBER OF ITEMS IN NEXT LIST. */

        BEGIN ;
           DECLARE A(N) FLOAT,
                   TOTAL FLOAT INITIAL(0) ;

           GET LIST( (A(I) DO I = 1 TO N) ) ;
           DO I = 1 TO N ;
              TOTAL = TOTAL + A(I) ;
           END ;

           PUT LIST( N, TOTAL ) ;
        END ;

   END ;

   END SUMLIST ;
```

The DECLARE statement in the BEGIN block causes the array A and the variable TOTAL to be defined anew each time the block is entered. TOTAL is initialized to zero each time storage is allocated for it.

BEGIN blocks may be entered only in the normal course of program execution, and procedure blocks may be entered only as a result of CALL statements and function references.

Blocks may be exited by executing the END statement for the block, by transfers (GO TO statements), and, in the case of procedure blocks, by the RETURN statement.

It is an error to attempt to transfer to the interior of a block from a point outside the block. The arrows in the diagram on the next page represent permissible transfers; transfers in the opposite direction are not permissible.

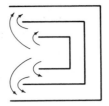

The arrows in the diagram also apply to procedure calls: a procedure may not be called from a point outside the block in which it is contained. External procedures, of course, may be called from any point in a program because they are not contained in any block.

When an identifier is used in a block, the block is checked to determine if the identifier is declared in that block. If not, the next outer block is checked, and so on, until the identifier is found to be defined or until the outermost block (an external procedure) is checked. If the identifier is not defined it is given the default attributes if it is a data item, or is in error if it is a label. The abbreviated program below shows how identifiers are interpreted:

```
P:   PROCEDURE OPTIONS (MAIN) ;

   A:   BEGIN ;
        DECLARE  X FIXED INITIAL (3) ;
           .

        B:   BEGIN ;
             DECLARE  X FLOAT INITIAL (5) ;
                .

             C:   BEGIN ;
                     .
                  PUT LIST (X) ;
                  END C ;
             END B ;

        PUT LIST (X) ;
        END A ;

   END P ;
```

The DECLARE statement in Block A establishes X as an identifier with the value 3. The DECLARE statement in Block B establishes a different X with a value of 5. When execution enters Block C, X is referenced. Because X does not appear in a DECLARE statement in Block C, the containing block is searched for a declare for X. The X declared in Block B is used and the value 5 is printed. The PUT statement in Block A prints the value 3.

The scope of identifiers, i.e., where the identifier is known, is important in determining the results of the execution of the program. BEGIN blocks may alter the scope of identifiers in the same way as PROCEDURE blocks may alter the scope.

The principal advantage of blocks is that they permit programs to make the most efficient use of storage. Storage is allocated upon entry to a block, and freed upon exit; the space that is used in one block may be used for some other purpose in another block. For instance, a program might need to use an array with the dimension attribute (50, 50) during the earlier phases, and an array with the dimension attribute (2500) during some later phases. Both arrays have 2500 elements, but it is not necessary to allocate 5000 elements if both arrays need not be available at the same time. The program would be organized like this:

```
P:  PROCEDURE OPTIONS (MAIN) ;

        BEGIN ;

            DECLARE  A(50,50) ;
            .
            .
            .
        END ;

        BEGIN ;

            DECLARE  B(2500) ;
            .
            .
            .
        END ;

    END P ;
```

Any storage areas that are required in both blocks would be declared in a DECLARE statement preceding the first block.

A certain amount of time is required to perform allocation, initialization, and other functions upon block entry. Therefore, it is preferable to declare as much storage as possible in outer blocks, and as little as possible in inner blocks.

EXERCISE

8.1   Write a subroutine that multiplies two square matrices and is called by the statement

CALL MMULT(A, B, C, N) ;

where A and B are the matrices to be multiplied, C is the resulting matrix, and N is the size of each of of the three matrices.

Chapter 9

TESTING AND DEBUGGING

Once a program has been compiled without any error messages, it still may not execute correctly because of mistakes in the logic, "bugs". Finding and correcting these—"debugging"—is often the most time-consuming phase of programming. Anything that can reduce the time and effort required for debugging is worthwhile.

Generally, the most difficult part of debugging is finding the error—making the actual correction is relatively simple. Much of this effort can be saved by approaching the writing of programs in the correct way at the outset. The objective must be to write a program that is easy to understand and, since most programs are changed during their lives, easy to modify. It has been found that such programs are easier to write if approached in a certain way, from the "top down".

"Top-down" programming means starting with a very few details, just the outline of the program and gradually filling in the details, in much the same way that an artist fills in the details into an outline of a picture. In practice, the program is first written in skeleton form and expanded in a series of steps to make the complete program. The important thing is that, at each stage, the programmer can assure himself of the correctness of the program.

For an example of the way that top-down development of a program works, let us construct the solution of Example 26 (page 133).

The first step is to understand the specification of the problem:

The program sums lists of numbers. Each list is preceded by the number of items in the list. The end of input is marked by this number being zero.

Omitting all details, the solution to this problem is the program:

```
SUM3:   PROCEDURE OPTIONS(MAIN) ;

        /* Solve example no. 26 */

        END SUM3 ;
```

If PL/I had such a statement as "Solve example no. 26," our task would be complete! Since there is no such statement, we must split this statement into substeps. As with all problems, before the computation can be done, some initialization must be done first. Thus, we can rewrite our program as:

```
SUM3:   PROCEDURE OPTIONS(MAIN) ;

        /* Initialize  */
        /* Perform computation   */

        END SUM3 ;
```

Again, we have a complete program. We can easily see that it is correct, obviously the initialization must be done <u>before</u> the computation. In order to elaborate the program further, we must use some of the important details given in the comment. It is an iterative process and at each iteration, the sum of a list of numbers is computed and printed. Using this information, our program becomes:

```
SUM3:   PROCEDURE OPTIONS(MAIN) ;

        /* Initialize  */
        /*  Loop while not end of input */
            /* compute and print sum of list */
            /* reinitialize */
        /* terminate looping  */

        END SUM3 ;
```

At each stage, as the program becomes PL/I, we write it in upper case; those parts yet to be expanded are left in lower case. Since the problem statement tells us that the end of input is marked by the length of the list being zero, we can use this fact in our next expansion. Note that, as we introduce variables into the program, their declaration is added.

```
SUM3:   PROCEDURE OPTIONS (MAIN) ;

        DECLARE N FIXED ;
        GET LIST (N) ;
        DO WHILE (N ¬= 0) ;
           /* Read and sum next N numbers */
           /* Print result */
           GET LIST (N) ;
        END ;
     END SUM3 ;
```

In the next step we will establish the array of numbers and read them.

```
SUM3:   PROCEDURE OPTIONS (MAIN) ;

        DECLARE N FIXED,
                I FIXED,
                NUMBER(1000) FIXED ;
        GET LIST (N) ;
        DO WHILE (N ¬= 0) ;
           GET LIST ((NUMBER(I) DO I = 1 TO N)) ;
           /* Calculate sum of numbers */
          /* Print result */
           GET LIST (N) ;
        END ;
     END SUM3 ;
```

Finally, the whole problem can be written in PL/I, giving:

```
SUM3:   PROCEDURE OPTIONS (MAIN) ;

        DECLARE N FIXED,
                I FIXED,
                NUMBER (1000) FIXED,
                TOTAL FIXED ;
        GET LIST (N) ;
        DO WHILE (N ¬= 0) ;
           GET LIST ((NUMBER(I) DO I = 1 TO N)) ;
           TOTAL = NUMBER (1) ;        /* INITIALIZE FOR SUM */
           DO I = 2 TO N ;
              TOTAL = TOTAL + NUMBER(I) ;
           END ;
           PUT LIST ((NUMBER(I) DO I = 1 TO N), TOTAL) ;
           GET LIST (N) ;
        END ;
     END SUM3 ;
```

By developing a program in this way, top-down, it is straightforward and readable at each level. We have a PL/I program at each stage. We take the comments and break them down into simpler steps and then into PL/I executable statements. The PL/I compiler does this type of thing when it takes PL/I statements and translates them into machine instructions.

At any stage, the elaboration of one of our "programming language" statements can be a subprocedure call as shown in Chapter 7. If a procedure extends over one page it becomes harder to read; therefore, it is often convenient and clearer to group some detailed processing into another procedure.

This type of approach also has the advantage that it is easy to change the program by changing only the routine involved and perhaps the routines that depend on it but not the entire program. After the change is made and verified, the rest of the program does not need to be verified.

A great deal has been written on "correct programming" using this approach and we refer you to several other books to learn more about the techniques involved.°

°Mills, H. D., "Top Down Programming in Large Systems," Debugging Techniques in Large Systems, Courant Computer Science Symposium No. 1, ed. Randall Rustin, New York University, pp. 41–55. Prentice-Hall, Inc., Englewood Cliffs, N. J., 1971.
References are continued on the next page.

Often, a bug or a data error will give rise to a condition which can be detected by the program. Some of the more common conditions (which may or may not indicate errors) are listed below. Other conditions are given in Appendix D.

Condition	Meaning
OVERFLOW	A floating-point quantity has become too large to be represented in the computer.
UNDERFLOW	A floating-point number has become too small (in magnitude) to be represented in the computer.
FIXEDOVERFLOW	A fixed-point number has become too large to be represented in the computer.
ZERODIVIDE	The expression used as the denominator has the value zero, leading to an undefined operation.
SUBSCRIPTRANGE	The value of an expression used as a subscript has a value outside of the bounds declared for an array.
ENDFILE	There are no more data in the standard input file.

When a condition is raised, it causes the PL/I program to be interrupted while control is transferred to a special program called the operating system.[†] The operating system analyzes the cause of the interrupt and then performs a "standard system action" which depends on the specific condition.

[†]Also known as the monitor, supervisor, or control program.

Wirth, Niklaus, Systematic Programming: An Introduction. Prentice-Hall, Inc., Englewood Cliffs, N. J., 1973.

Dahl, O. L., E. W. Dijkstra, and C. A. R. Hoare, Structured Programming. Academic Press, New York, 1972.

It is frequently very useful to specify, by means of PL/I statements, actions to be taken in lieu of the standard system action for various conditions. The specification is accomplished by means of the ON statement, which has the general form

ON <u>condition</u> <u>on-unit</u> ;

where

<u>condition</u> is the name of a condition, e.g., ENDFILE, and

<u>on-unit</u> is a PL/I statement (other than a DO statement), or a BEGIN block.

The unit associated with an ON statement is not executed at the time ON statement is executed; it is executed when and if the specified condition subsequently arises.

The program example below uses an ON statement for the FIXEDOVERFLOW condition in order to accomplish its purpose: to determine the largest binary integer that can be stored in the particular computer on which the program is executed.

```
LARGEST: PROCEDURE OPTIONS (MAIN) ;

          /* EXAMPLE NO. 39
             DETERMINE THE LARGEST INTEGER THAT CAN BE
             CONTAINED IN THE COMPUTER, ASSUMING THAT
             INTEGER IS OF THE FORM 2**N-1 (A VALID
             ASSUMPTION FOR MOST COMPUTERS). */

          DECLARE NUMBER BINARY FIXED INITIAL( 1 ) ;

          ON FIXEDOVERFLOW BEGIN ;
                    NUMBER = NUMBER +
                             (NUMBER - 1) ;
                    PUT LIST ( NUMBER ) ;
                    STOP ;
                    END ;

          DO WHILE( '1'B ) ;
          NUMBER = NUMBER + NUMBER ;
          END ;

     END LARGEST ;
```

177

In Example No. 39, the value of NUMBER is added to itself repeatedly. At some point the expression

$$NUMBER + NUMBER$$

will give a result that is greater than the largest number that can be contained in the computer, and the attempted addition will raise the FIXEDOVERFLOW condition. The condition will be raised before the assignment operation is performed and control will be transferred immediately to the appropriate on-unit. The unit is a BEGIN block which completes the process and prints the result.

The assignment statement in the BEGIN block produces a number of the form 2^n-1, consistent with the assumption mentioned in the comment. You can verify this by assuming that the largest number is 7, for example, and working through the calculations just as the computer would.

What would happen if the ON statement were removed from Example No. 39? The fixed-point overflow condition would still be raised, but the action taken would be the standard system action. The standard action differs for various conditions, but two things usually happen: a message is printed to inform you that the condition arose, and then either execution is terminated or it resumes – perhaps with data which became invalid as a result of the condition.

In some cases, it may be desirable to specify an action to be taken when, for example, the FIXEDOVERFLOW condition is raised in one part of a program, and a different action if it is raised in another part of the program. This is easily done by writing another ON statement:

```
        .
        .
        .
ON  FIXEDOVERFLOW  GO  TO  BIGA  ;
        .
        .
        .
ON  FIXEDOVERFLOW  GO  TO  BIGB  ;
        .
        .
        .
```

The second ON statement completely overrides the first. Any fixed-point overflow occurring in statements between the two ON statements will cause the program to transfer to the statement labeled BIGA. Any fixed-point overflow occurring after the second ON statement has been executed will cause a transfer to the statement labeled BIGB.

When ON statements appear in nested blocks, they do not necessarily override ON statements that were executed previously. For example, in this construction

```
A: BEGIN ;
       •
       •
   ON FIXEDOVERFLOW GO TO BIGA ;
       •
       •
   B: BEGIN ;
          •
          •
      ON FIXEDOVERFLOW GO TO BIGB ;
          •
          •
      BIGB:
          •
          •
       END B ;
       •
       •
   BIGA:
       •
       •
 END A ;
```

any fixed-point overflow condition arising prior to execution of the first ON statement will result in standard system action. The first ON statement, when it is executed, establishes the statement GO TO BIGA as the on-unit for the FIXEDOVERFLOW condition. This unit remains in effect as execution proceeds into block B until the ON unit in that block is executed. At that time, the effective on-unit for the FIXEDOVERFLOW condition becomes the statement GO TO BIGB.

What happens when control passes out of block B? The statement GO TO BIGA is re-established as the on-unit for the FIXEDOVERFLOW condition. In other words, when the ON statement in block B is executed, the on-unit GO TO BIGA is temporarily suspended; the unit GO TO BIGB is "stacked" on it. When control leaves block B, the unit GO TO BIGA is restored. On-units can thus be redefined in much the same way that identifiers can be redefined by DECLARE statements in nested blocks.

An on-unit may specify that no action is to be taken if a condition is raised, i.e., that the condition is to be ignored. This is accomplished simply by using a null statement as the on-unit.

Once an on-unit has been established for a condition, it may be canceled in two ways. One way is to execute an ON statement with the word SYSTEM as the on-unit. SYSTEM specifies that the standard system action is to be taken if the associated condition is subsequently raised. (At the start of execution the operating system establishes SYSTEM as the on-unit for every possible condition.)

The second way to cancel an on-unit is to execute a REVERT statement, which has the general form

REVERT condition ;

Execution of a REVERT statement within a block causes execution to proceed as though no ON statement for the specified condition had been executed in the same block. If the statement

```
REVERT FIXEDOVERFLOW ;
```

had been executed in block B in the illustration on page 179 after the ON statement in that block had been executed, the effect would have been to restore the on-unit GO TO BIGA.

In order to investigate conditions more closely, recall that programs are executed under the control of the operating system. The diagram on the following page illustrates the general way in which conditions are processed. The diagram is not a flow chart in the usual sense, because it does not represent a program; instead, it represents a sequential process.

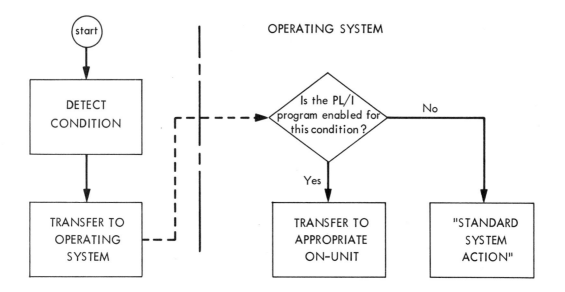

The first two steps in processing a condition are first, to detect its existence; and second, to transfer control to the operating system. There are two distinct ways in which these steps can be accomplished. One way is for the computer circuits to detect the existence of a condition and automatically signal the operating system. Conditions that can be detected in this way are called initially enabled conditions. The other way is for the PL/I program to detect the existence of a condition by means of programmed tests and transfer to the operating system if appropriate. Conditions that must be detected in this way are called initially disabled conditions. Thus, on any computer there are two classes of conditions: those that are initially enabled, and those that are initially disabled. The specific conditions in each class may differ among various computers.

In order to enable conditions that are initially disabled, the compiler must generate the appropriate instructions when it is compiling the program. Inclusion of these instructions is specified by means of prefixes associated with particular statements or blocks. The general form of a prefix is

$$(\text{condition}_1, \text{condition}_2, \ldots) : \text{unit} ;$$

where each condition is the name of a condition to be enabled, and unit is a statement, a procedure, or a BEGIN block. Each condition is enabled for the duration of execution of the associated unit.

Assuming that SUBSCRIPTRANGE is initially disabled, the on-unit in the illustration below will not be executed, despite the fact that the subscript obviously takes on values outside the permissible range. The instructions necessary to detect the condition will not be generated by the compiler, so the condition will not be detected during execution.

```
ANOMALY: PROCEDURE OPTIONS (MAIN) ;

         DECLARE  A(-3:3)  FLOAT,
                  I  FIXED ;

         ON SUBSCRIPTRANGE PUT LIST( I ) ;

LOOP:    DO I = -5 BY 1 TO 5 ;
            A(I) = 0 ;
         END LOOP ;
         .
         .
   END ANOMALY ;
```

In order to detect the error (by raising the SUBSCRIPTRANGE condition), the first line in the above illustration must be changed to read

```
(SUBSCRIPTRANGE): ANOMALY:   PROCEDURE OPTIONS (MAIN) ;
```

It is not necessary to use an ON statement for conditions that are enabled by prefixes. As long as a condition is enabled, whether it is initially enabled, or is enabled by its appearance in a prefix, there is an associated standard system action. An ON statement would be used only if the standard action is not satisfactory. The standard actions for various conditions are given in Appendix D.

Just as disabled conditions can be enabled by prefixes, enabled conditions can be disabled by prefixes. To disable a condition, the condition is written in a prefix preceded by NO. Assuming that FIXEDOVERFLOW is enabled, the on-unit in the illustration below can be executed as a result of statements L1 and L3, but not as a result of L2.

```
INHIBIT: PROCEDURE OPTIONS (MAIN) ;

            DECLARE  ( A, B, C )  FIXED ;

            ON FIXEDOVERFLOW GO TO ERROR ;
            .
            .
            .
    L1:     A = B + C ;
            .
            .
            .
   (NOFIXEDOVERFLOW): L2:
            B = A + C ;
            .
            .
            .
    L3:     C = A + B ;
            .
            .
            .
         END INHIBIT ;
```

Sometimes, during program checkout, it is useful to "simulate" various conditions that may arise in order to verify that the program reacts to them in the proper way. Conditions are raised by the SIGNAL statement, which has the general form

$$\text{SIGNAL} \; \underline{\text{condition}};$$

where condition is the name of the condition to be raised. The effect of the statement

```
    L:   SIGNAL FIXEDOVERFLOW ;
```

is precisely the effect that would occur had a fixed-point overflow occurred in the statement labeled L. If the statement were used in a program to simulate an overflow condition, then it would be replaced by the actual statement required at L after the program had been checked out.

Although conditions such as OVERFLOW can be processed to recover from contingencies during execution, they are not usually very helpful when you are trying to find logical errors. Logical errors can usually be located by inspecting the PL/I source program and the results, but sometimes it may be necessary to monitor the sequence in which the program is executed.

A very effective way to monitor the sequence of execution is to place PUT statements in strategic points in the program. PUT DATA is especially useful, as it prints both the name and the value of the variables specified. The sequence in which the PUT statements are executed is significant in discovering actual execution sequences, but equally significant may be the sequence in which the statements are not executed.

The ON and SIGNAL statements can be used in conjunction with each other to monitor program execution. An ON statement can specify a "programmer-defined" conditions, and a SIGNAL statement can be used to raise the condition. Programmer-defined conditions are arbitrary identifiers, and have no relation to the conditions described previously. The general forms of corresponding ON and SIGNAL statements for a programmer-defined condition are

ON CONDITION (identifier) on-unit ;

and

SIGNAL CONDITION (identifier) ;

The ON, REVERT, and SIGNAL statements are very useful for tracking down elusive program bugs. As you gain experience in programming you will also gain experience in debugging, and will find that you will be able to use these statements to great advantage in getting good results back from the computer. Remember that by

- approaching the problem from top down,

- avoiding most if not all GO TOs in order to determine the logical flow,

- keeping each procedure a readable size and,

- establishing ON conditions to take care of errors in data the logical "bugs" will be few.

ON statements have many uses aside from debugging. A complete list of conditions is given in Appendix D; many of them can be used to simplify and generalize your programs. For instance, the ENDFILE condition makes it relatively easy to write a program which will read and process data from a file of unknown length. You retain control when the end of data has been read; therefore, no special information needs to be placed at the end to signal the last data item. As a practical matter, you may not have control over the data you are to process, and it is impossible to impose what the last data will be.

The name of the standard input file is SYSIN which is assumed for GET statements but which must be specified in ON statements.° The appropriate ON statement is

ON ENDFILE(SYSIN) <u>on-unit</u>;

Files are discussed at length in Chapter 11.

The following two abbreviated programs show two different ways that the use of the ON ENDFILE condition can be helpful in structuring a program that establishes the values of all variables and then computes.

```
SOLVE1:  PROCEDURE OPTIONS  (MAIN)  ;

         DECLARE   EOF BIT (1) INITIAL('0'B)  ;
         ON ENDFILE(SYSIN)   EOF = '1'B ;

         DO WHILE (EOF = '0'B)  ;
            /* ESTABLISH VALUES */
            .
            .
         END ;

         /* COMPUTE */

         END SOLVE1 ;
```

°The standard output file is SYSPRINT and is assumed by default with PUT statements.

```
SOLVE2:   PROCEDURE OPTIONS (MAIN) ;

            ON ENDFILE(SYSIN)
               BEGIN ;
                 /* COMPUTE */
                     .
                     .
               END ;

            DO WHILE (1) ;
               /* ESTABLISH VALUES */
                   .
                   .
            END ;

          END SOLVE2 ;
```

Note on Chapter 9

One feature which is not in all implementations is the CHECK condition which provides a simple way of monitoring execution: it can be used to indicate each change in the value of a variable, each execution of a labeled statement, and each procedure call.

The CHECK condition is initially disabled, and must, therefore, be enabled by means of a prefix. Further, the particular identifiers to be checked must be specified so that the compiler can generate the appropriate instructions to check each one. The general form of the prefix enabling the CHECK condition is

(CHECK(identifier list)) :

where identifier list is a list of variables, unsubscripted array names, structure names, procedure names, and/or labels. Parameters may not be used.

The standard system action for the CHECK condition depends on the kind of identifier for which the condition is raised. For variables, the standard action is to print the name of the variable followed by the value; for labels, the standard action is to print the label and a count of the number of times the associated statement has been executed. Similar information is printed for the other kinds of identifiers for which the condition can be raised. In the following example, an informative message will be printed each time the variable I and the array A (any element) take on new values; and each time the statement labeled L is executed.

```
CHECKIT: PROCEDURE OPTIONS (MAIN) ;

           /* EXAMPLE NO. 40
              MONITOR EXECUTION. */

           DECLARE ( A(10), I ) FIXED ;
           A = 0 ;

(CHECK( A, I, L )): B:
              BEGIN ;
       LAB:       DO I = 1 BY 1 TO 10 ;
       L:            A(I) = 3*I ;
                  END LAB ;
              END B ;
           END CHECKIT ;
```

The CHECK condition should be enabled as infrequently as possible, and for as few identifiers as are absolutely necessary. The condition can easily result in a great deal of output, which may be more confusing than helpful. Usually, a great deal of information can be obtained by enabling the CHECK condition until it has been raised a certain number of times for a particular identifier, and then disabling it by means of a REVERT statement. Another way is to enable the CHECK condition and then specify a non-standard action which does not cause printing until the condition has been raised a certain number of times. The following program illustrates the principle: no CHECK-output is printed for the variable I until its value has been changed three times; no CHECK-output is printed for the label L until the associated statement has been executed three times.

```
LIM_CK:   PROCEDURE OPTIONS (MAIN) ;

              /* EXAMPLE NO. 41
                 HYPOTHETICAL PROGRAM TO ILLUSTRATE LIMITED
                 CHECKING. */

              DECLARE ( I, ICOUNT, LCOUNT ) FIXED INITIAL( 0 ) ;

(CHECK( I, L )): B:
              BEGIN ;
                 ON CHECK( I ) ICOUNT = ICOUNT + 1 ;
                 ON CHECK( L ) LCOUNT = LCOUNT + 1 ;

      LA:        DO I = 1 BY 1 TO 10 ;
      L:            PUT LIST ( I ) ;
                    IF ICOUNT=3 THEN REVERT CHECK (I) ;
                    IF LCOUNT=3 THEN REVERT CHECK (L) ;
                 END LA ;
              END B ;
         END LIM_CK ;
```

EXERCISES

9.1 What is the effective on-unit for OVERFLOW in each of these programs at the time the statement labeled X is executed?

```
P1:        PROCEDURE OPTIONS (MAIN) ;
              ON OVERFLOW GO TO Y ;
Y:            .
              .
              .
           ON OVERFLOW GO TO Z ;
           BEGIN ;
              ON OVERFLOW ;
              .
              REVERT OVERFLOW ;
              .
              REVERT OVERFLOW ;
              .
           END ;
X:            .
              .
              .
Z:         END P1 ;
P2:        PROCEDURE OPTIONS (MAIN) ;
              ON OVERFLOW GO TO Y ;
Y:            .
              .
           BEGIN ;
              ON OVERFLOW SYSTEM ;
              .
              .
              .
           END ;
X:            .
              .
              .
           END P2 ;
```

9.2 Rewrite exercise 4.10 using the ENDFILE condition to check for the last data item.

Chapter 10

CHARACTER MANIPULATION

All of, the uses of computers discussed so far in this book have been concerned with the processing of arithmetic data. That is, in most cases, we have read numbers into the computer and used these numbers to calculate other numbers; the final results have been numbers. In some cases, we have carried alphabetic (character string) data along with the computations, but we have not performed any operations on them.

PL/I contains a number of facilities for processing string data, i.e., non-numeric data. In this chapter, we will be concerned exclusively with character strings, but the same principles apply to bit strings.

One of the characteristics of any string is its length, i.e., how many characters it contains. The character string 'COMPUTER' has a length of 8, and we can think of it as appearing in the computer as

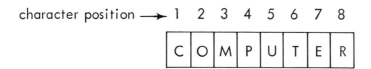

Each character in the string has a unique position, noted by a number. Position number 1 is the leftmost character.

String data can be assigned to string variables by means of the familiar assignment statement. The program example on the following page illustrates a few string assignment statements.

```
ASSIGN:   PROCEDURE OPTIONS (MAIN) ;

          /* EXAMPLE NO. 42
             STRING ASSIGNMENT */

          DECLARE   STRING_1  CHARACTER(8),
                    STRING_2  CHARACTER(10),
                    STRING_3  CHARACTER(5) ;

          STRING_1 = 'COMPUTER' ;
          STRING_2 = STRING_1 ;
          STRING_3 = STRING_2 ;

          PUT EDIT( STRING_1, STRING_2, STRING_3 )
                  ( SKIP, A ) ;

      END ASSIGN ;
```

The DECLARE statement established three character string variables. We can visualize these strings as in the following illustration. Initially, the content of each character position is undefined.

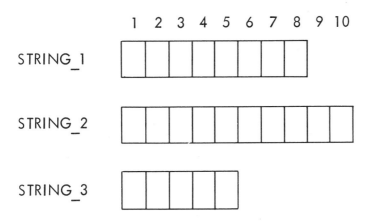

The first assignment statement in Example No. 42 places the string COMPUTER into STRING__1. The contents of each character position in STRING__1 is now defined, namely:

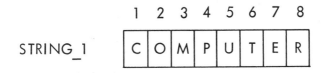

The second assignment statement transfers the contents of STRING__1 to STRING__2, which can then be thought of as containing

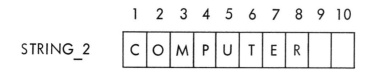

What are the contents of positions 9 and 10 of STRING__2 after the assignment statement is executed? The answer is, blanks. STRING__2 is longer (10 positions) than STRING__1 (8 positions). The rule is

> When a shorter string is assigned to a variable which is the name of a longer string, the string is filled out to the right with blanks.°

> Note: The character "b" will be used in this chapter to represent a blank.

We can now visualize the assignment statement

$$STRING\_2 = STRING\_1 ;$$

by the illustration

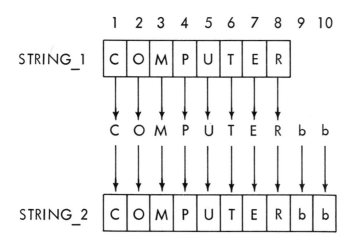

°The process of adding characters to make a data item assume a specified length is called padding. In PL/I, the padding character for character strings is the blank.

The contents of STRING_2 would have been the same if the assignment statement had been

$$\texttt{STRING\_2 = 'COMPUTER' ;}$$

The third assignment statement in Example No. 42 transfers the contents of STRING_2 to STRING_3. However, the length of STRING_3 is only 5 characters. The rule in this case is

> When a longer string is assigned to a variable which is the name of a shorter string the string is truncated on the right.

We can now visualize the assignment statement

$$\texttt{STRING\_3 = STRING\_2 ;}$$

by the illustration

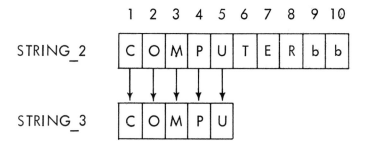

In general, a string assignment statement has the form

$$\text{destination string} = \text{source string};$$

which means, simply, that characters are transferred from the source string to the destination string. The number of characters transferred depends entirely on the length of the destination string:

> If the lengths of the destination and source strings are equal, the strings will be identical after the assignment.

> If the length of the destination string exceeds that of the source string, blanks are added to the right of the source characters.

193

If the length of the destination string is less than that of the source string, the excessive characters on the right are ignored.

Suppose, now, that we want to perform the following operation:

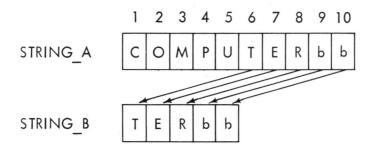

That is, STRING__A is the source string and STRING__B is the destination string, but instead of beginning the transfer with the first character of STRING__A we want to begin with the sixth character. In other words, we want to replace STRING__B with a <u>substring</u> of STRING__A.

Substrings are specified in PL/I by the built-in function SUBSTR, which has two general forms. One of them is

$$\text{SUBSTR(string, position) ;}$$

where

        <u>string</u> is a character string, and

        <u>position</u> is an arithmetic expression.

The PL/I statement to perform the operation above would be

```
STRING_B = SUBSTR ( STRING_A, 6 ) ;
```

which states, "beginning with character 6 of STRING__A, transfer characters to STRING__B." As usual, blanks will be added if STRING__B is longer than the substring of STRING__A; the substring will be truncated if STRING.__B is shorter.

The second form of SUBSTR allows us to specify the number of characters to be transferred, in addition to specifying the starting character position. This form is

$$SUBSTR(\underline{string},\ \underline{position},\ \underline{nchars})\ ;$$

where nchars is an arithmetic expression specifying the number of characters to be transferred.

If the string specified by SUBSTR does not lie completely within the source string then anomalous characters will be placed into the destination string. The STRINGRANGE condition, if enabled, returns a null string for that portion which lies outside the source string.

The following example illustrates some of the things that can be done with SUBSTR.

```
PLAY: PROCEDURE OPTIONS (MAIN) ;

        /* EXAMPLE NO. 43
           ILLUSTRATE THE SUBSTR FUNCTION */

        DECLARE WORD CHARACTER(8) INITIAL( 'COMPUTER' ),
                LETTER(8) CHARACTER(1),
                LETTERV(8) CHARACTER(8) ,
                Q FIXED ;

L:      DO Q = 1 BY 1 TO 8 ;
           LETTER(Q)  = SUBSTR( WORD, Q, 1 ) ;
           LETTERV(Q) = SUBSTR( WORD, 1, Q ) ;
        END L ;

        PUT EDIT( (LETTER(Q),LETTERV(Q) DO Q = 1 TO 8) )
               ( SKIP, 2 A(10) ) ;
        END PLAY ;
```

Initially, the character string variable WORD has the following contents:

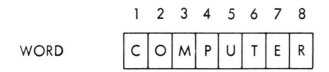

At the time the PUT statement is executed the two arrays have the contents illustrated below. That is, the Qth element of LETTER contains the Qth character of WORD. The Qth element of LETTERV contains the first Q characters of WORD.

	LETTER		LETTERV
(1)	C		C ƀ ƀ ƀƀ ƀƀƀ
(2)	O		CO ƀ ƀƀ ƀƀƀ
(3)	M		COM ƀ ƀƀƀƀ
(4)	P		COMP ƀ ƀƀƀ
(5)	U		COMPU ƀƀƀ
(6)	T		COMPUT ƀƀ
(7)	E		COMPUTE ƀ
(8)	R		COMPUTER

The SUBSTR function can also be used to specify a substring of the destination string, i.e., it may be used to the left of the = in an assignment statement.° Example No. 44 on the following page places a character string into an array in the same way Example No. 43 placed a string into the array LETTER (page 195), and then reconstructs the string in another character string variable.

_____

°When so used, SUBSTR is called a <u>pseudo-variable</u> because it specifies the destination in an assignment operation, but SUBSTR itself – the function – is not the destination.

```
PLAY_1:    PROCEDURE OPTIONS (MAIN) ;
           /* EXAMPLE NO. 44
              BREAK A STRING INTO INDIVIDUAL CHARACTERS,
              PLACING ONE CHARACTER INTO EACH ELEMENT OF
              AN ARRAY. THEN RECONSTRUCT THE WORD. */

           DECLARE ( OLD_WORD, NEW_WORD ) CHARACTER (8),
                    LETTER (8)   CHARACTER(1),
                    Q  FIXED ;

           OLD_WORD = 'COMPUTER' ;

           /* DECOMPOSE THE WORD. */
     L:    DO Q = 1 BY 1 TO 8 ;
              LETTER(Q) = SUBSTR( OLD_WORD, Q, 1 ) ;
           END L ;

           /* RECONSTRUCT THE WORD IN NEW_WORD. */
     L2:   DO Q = 1 BY 1 TO 8 ;
              SUBSTR( NEW_WORD, Q, 1 ) = LETTER(Q) ;
           END L2 ;

           PUT LIST( OLD_WORD, NEW_WORD ) ;
        END PLAY_1 ;
```

The SUBSTR function, as we have seen, can be used to break strings apart in various ways, and can also be used to put them together. Another way to build a string is to add characters to the end of it by the process of concatenation. The concatenation operation, ‖, read "concatenated with," operates in the following way:

$$'A' \, \| \, 'B' \quad \text{yields} \quad 'AB'$$

$$'T' \, \| \, 'H' \, \| \, 'E' \, \text{yields} \quad 'THE'$$

The example on the following page uses concatenation to form the plurals of words by adding the character "S"

```
PLURAL:    PROCEDURE OPTIONS (MAIN) ;

              /* EXAMPLE NO. 45
                 READ A WORD, ADD THE CHARACTER 'S', AND
                 PRINT THE RESULT. */

              DECLARE  WORD  CHARACTER(20) VARYING ;

           DO WHILE ('1'B) ;
             GET LIST( WORD ) ;
             WORD = WORD || 'S' ;
             PUT LIST( WORD ) SKIP ;
           END ;

           END PLURAL ;
```

The identifier WORD in the above example has the VARYING attribute. One reason for this is that the words read in may be of differing lengths. The primary reason, however, is that concatenation itself – by definition – changes the length of a string. The strings being concatenated may be of fixed lengths, but as a general rule, the destination string should be of varying length.

Suppose we have a string of characters and it is desired to know where a certain substring, e.g., 'ABC', appears in the string. We could examine the string using the SUBSTR function and several IF statements, but that would make for a rather complicated program. Problems of this nature arise frequently, especially in the discipline of information retrieval, and so PL/I contains a built-in function, INDEX, to simplify the process of finding the desired substring.

The INDEX function has the general form

$$INDEX(\ \underline{string},\ \underline{argument}\ ) ;$$

where

>   <u>string</u> is the string to be examined, and

>   <u>argument</u> is the desired substring. In the vocabulary of information retrieval, this argument is called the <u>search argument</u>.

The value of the INDEX function is the character position in the string of the leftmost character of the substring represented by the search argument. If the argument does not occur in the string, the value of INDEX is zero. If it occurs more than once, the value of INDEX is the position of its first occurrence.

To illustrate the use of INDEX, assume we have a string named ALPHABET of length 26, containing the alphabet in the usual sequence. Then the following statements will have the indicated results:

```
P = INDEX ( ALPHABET, 'XYZ' ) ;        P is set to 24

P = INDEX ( ALPHABET, 'E' ) ;               "      5

P = INDEX ( ALPHABET, 'EF' ) ;              "      5

P = INDEX ( ALPHABET, 'AZ' ) ;              "      0
```

The SUBSTR function can be combined with the INDEX function to give added character-handling facilities to PL/I programs. Example No. 46 on the following page reads a sentence and counts the frequency of appearance of each letter.

The variable named SEARCH is used in Example No. 46 for two reasons. First, it is used to reduce the amount of computation required in the inner loop. Second, it simplifies the statements which reference INDEX.

The facilities for manipulating characters permit use of the computer in many non-numeric applications. Typical applications include text-editing and justification, language translation, and composition of music. Some of the following exercises indicate typical applications of non-numeric uses of computers.

```
FREQ:    PROCEDURE OPTIONS (MAIN) ;

         /*   EXAMPLE NO. 46
              READ A SENTENCE AND PREPARE A FREQUENCY
              TABLE OF LETTERS IT CONTAINS.              */

         DECLARE   ALPHABET   CHARACTER(26) INITIAL
                              ('ABCDEFGHIJKLMNOPQRSTUVWXYZ'),
                   SENTENCE   CHARACTER(100) VARYING,
                   SEARCH     CHARACTER(1),
                   FREQUENCY  FIXED,
                   P          FIXED,
                   P1         FIXED,
                   Q          FIXED ;

         ON ENDFILE (SYSIN)   STOP ;

         DO WHILE ('1'B) ;
           GET LIST (SENTENCE) COPY ;

           DO Q = 1 BY 1 TO 26 ;   /* LOOP THRU ALPHABET */
             SEARCH = SUBSTR (ALPHABET, Q, 1) ;
                               /* FIND FIRST OCCURANCE */
             P1, P = INDEX (SENTENCE, SEARCH) ;

             DO FREQUENCY = 0 BY 1 WHILE (P¬= 0) ;
                               /* THIS LOOP IS VACUOUS
                                  IF ARGUMENT DOES NOT
                                  OCCUR AT ALL.      */
               P = INDEX (SUBSTR (SENTENCE, P1+1), SEARCH) ;
               P1 = P1 + P ;
             END ;

             PUT SKIP LIST  (SEARCH, '=', FREQUENCY) ;
           END ;
         END ;
     END FREQ ;
```

EXERCISES

10.1 Read a character string of arbitrary length (not more than 20 characters) and reverse the order of the characters. (Use the LENGTH function to determine the length of the string.) For example, if the input string is ABC, the output string should be CBA.

10.2 Read a character string of arbitrary length (not more than 100 characters) and print the first non-blank character. Assume the string includes at least one non-blank character.

10.3 Read a character string of arbitrary length (not more than 200 characters). Delete all blanks and print the resulting condensed string.

10.4 Read a character string of arbitrary length (not more than 200 characters), representing text. Print out those words which begin with "A".

10.5 Read a character string of arbitrary length (not more than 200 characters), representing text. Print

      1.   The number of sentences in the text.
      2.   The average number of words in a sentence.
      3.   The average number of letters per word.

10.6 Read a character string of arbitrary length (not more than 200 characters), representing a sentence. Convert each word to Pig Latin by the following rule:

      Move all the characters preceding the first vowel to the end of the word and append "AY".

    Print the resulting sentence, including the terminal period.

Chapter 11

ADDITIONAL INPUT/OUTPUT FACILITIES

Computers, as we have discussed them so far, have for the most part operated on internal data, with input/output operations being almost incidental to the total operation. In many applications, the opposite relationship is the case: input/output operations predominate, while the internal processing plays a relatively minor part. There is no fundamental difference in the language used, but some additional considerations become important when input/output is a primary concern.

When input/output is a relatively minor concern the "standard" files can usually be used for input and output; all that is needed is one input file, and one output file. When input/output is the primary concern, however, the reason is usually that there are large quantities of data to be processed. The input data may exist in several input files, and it may be desirable to route output data to several output files.

Whenever it is inappropriate to use the standard files, we can use files to which we have given specific names. A name is declared to be a file by means of the FILE attribute in a DECLARE statement:

DECLARE name FILE ;

The effect of the FILE attribute is to associate name (which must of course be an identifier) with an external device, such as a magnetic tape unit, a typewriter, or a printer. The particular external device with which a name is associated must also be specified outside the PL/I program, but the way in which this is done varies among computer installations. The important thing is that a file name refers to a single external device, and when we specify the name in a GET or PUT statement, as shown below, we are stating that data are to be read from or written on a particular file, i.e., a specific input/output device.

When the standard input file is used, a typical GET statement might be

```
GET LIST ( A, B, C ) ;
```

When a non-standard file is to be used, the statement must be written

GET FILE (name) LIST (A, B, C) ;

where name has been declared with the FILE attribute. A non-standard file is specified in a PUT statement in the same way as for a GET statement, e.g.,

PUT FILE (name) EDIT (list) (format) ;

As you know, the standard output file is equivalent to a printer, but a non-standard output file is not necessarily equivalent to a printer. To make a name refer to a printer, it must have the PRINT attribute as well as the FILE attribute:

DECLARE name FILE PRINT ;

(where the attributes FILE and PRINT need not appear in that order). If the file name used in a PUT statement does not have the PRINT attribute, the options LINE, PAGE, and COLUMN are meaningless.

Depending on the device with which it is associated, a file may be an input file, an output file, or an input/output file. (See the table on page 111.) If a file name is associated with an output device, it may appear only in a PUT statement; if it is associated with an input/output device, it may appear in GET and/or PUT statements.

We can specify in a file declaration how the file is to be used, namely, as an input file, an output file, or an input/output file. A file function is specified by the INPUT or OUTPUT attribute in a DECLARE statement, e.g.,

DECLARE <u>name</u> FILE INPUT ;

(where the attributes FILE and INPUT need not appear in the order shown). The PRINT attribute mentioned on the preceding page applies only to output files, and may not be used in combination with the INPUT attribute. It may be used in combination with the OUTPUT attribute, in which case OUTPUT is redundant.

The association of a particular file name to a particular device will (depending on the computer installation) be made outside the PL/I program, independently of any attributes specified for the name in a DECLARE statement in the program. Since the attributes might be specified independently of the actual association with a physical device, it is very important to make sure that the device actually associated with a file name is consistent with the attributes specified for it.

The term "file" in the present context is in many ways similar to a file such as you might find in an office. In an office, before information can be filed or extracted, the file must first be opened. In PL/I, files can be opened by the first input/output statement that references them. Files opened in this way are said to be opened <u>implicitly</u>. The operating system performs the opening operation before the input/output statement is executed.

In an office, once a file has been used, it may be closed or may be left open. The PL/I files we have used so far have been opened implicitly by the first input/output statement that referenced them, and have been left open for the remainder of program execution. They have been closed (implicitly) at the end of execution.

PL/I files can be opened and closed <u>explicitly</u> by means of the OPEN and CLOSE statements, respectively. These statements have the general form

OPEN FILE (<u>name</u>) ;

and

CLOSE FILE (<u>name</u>) ;

If the purpose of a file is not predetermined by the INPUT or OUTPUT attribute in its declaration, we can specify the purpose when we open it. In this case, after using it for the specified purpose, we can close the file, and then open it again for some other purpose. The following example takes three numbers from the standard input file, writes them in another file, and then reads them back from that file into different variables.

```
INOUT:     PROCEDURE OPTIONS (MAIN) ;

           /* EXAMPLE NO. 47
              READ THREE NUMBERS FROM STANDARD INPUT FILE,
              WRITE THEM ON TEMPORARY FILE, READ THEM BACK
              FROM THE TEMPORARY FILE INTO DIFFERENT
              VARIABLES. */

           DECLARE ( X, Y, Z, A, B, C ) FLOAT,
                   TEMP  FILE ;

           GET LIST( X, Y, Z ) ;

           OPEN FILE( TEMP ) OUTPUT ;
           PUT FILE( TEMP ) LIST( X, Y, Z ) ;
           CLOSE FILE( TEMP .) ;

           OPEN FILE( TEMP ) INPUT ;
           GET FILE( TEMP ) LIST( A, B, C ) ;

           PUT LIST( A, B, C ) SKIP ;

        END INOUT ;
```

The most important things to note about Example No. 47 are:

- The physical device associated with TEMP must be an input/output device.

- No attributes (other than the FILE attribute) are included in the declaration for TEMP, because it is used both as an input and as an output file.

- TEMP can be referenced only in PUT statements during the time it is open as an output file and only by GET statements during the time it is open as an input file.

- No input/output statements may refer to TEMP during the time it is closed, i.e., between the CLOSE statement and the subsequent OPEN statement.

- The CLOSE statement has the effect of repositioning TEMP so that the first data item to be read after TEMP has been reopened is the first data item in the file.

One final thing to note about files is that if an output file associated with an input/output device is closed and then opened again as an output file, any data subsequently written in that file will destroy the data previously placed there. In other words, when a file associated with an input/output device is closed, it is repositioned to the beginning; any subsequent input/output operations (after the file is reopened) will either re-read or re-write the first data item(s). In the latter case, the data previously in the file will be destroyed.

It is sometimes useful to have the same file name associated with different external devices at different times. This may be done by means of the TITLE option in the OPEN statement. The TITLE option thus allows a number of external devices to be associated with a file name in the course of program execution. The general form of the OPEN statement with the TITLE option is

OPEN FILE (name) TITLE (string) ;

where

> string is a character string variable or character string constant. Permissible values for string may depend upon the particular computer in use. INPUT and OUTPUT attributes may also be specified.

The following program might be used to collect data from three files prior to processing:

```
FILL:    PROCEDURE  OPTIONS(MAIN) ;
         /*FILL AN ARRAY FROM THREE FILES */
         DECLARE X(100)     CHARACTER(80),
                 FF         FILE,
                 TI         CHARACTER(6),
                 EOFSW      BIT(1),
                 (N,I)      FIXED ;

         N = 1 ;
         DO I = 1 TO 3 ;
            GET LIST (TI) ;
            OPEN FILE (FF) INPUT TITLE (TI) ;
            EOFSW = '0'B ;
            ON ENDFILE (FF) EOFSW = '1'B ;
            DO WHILE (N<100  & EOFSW='0'B) ;
               GET FILE(FF) EDIT (X(N))  (A(80)) ;
               N = N+1 ;
            END ;
            CLOSE FILE (FF) ;
         END ;
         /* BEGIN PROCESSING  */
                         .
                         .
                         .
     END FILL ;
```

By this time, you should have a pretty good idea of what files are, and how they can be used. Let us now look more closely at what happens when we read information into the computer from a file and write information into a file from the computer.

If we execute the statement:

$$\text{GET FILE (\underline{name}) LIST (A) ;}$$

the data item (singular, assuming A is a simple variable) is not transmitted directly from the file into the computer memory location corresponding to A. Instead, it is brought from the file into another area of computer memory, called a <u>buffer</u>, and is then transferred from the buffer to the location corresponding to A. Any data conversion necessary is performed during the transfer from the buffer to A; not during transmission from the file to the buffer. Data input is thus a two-step operation: from the file to a buffer, and from the buffer to the destination. Only the file and the destination are specified in a GET statement; the operating system establishes and controls the buffer automatically. Data output is similarly a two-step operation.

There is one buffer for each open file; there is no buffer associated with a closed file. (This is why input/output statements cannot be used with closed files.)

When a buffer is first established, that is, when the associated file is opened, the buffer is empty. The first GET statement to be executed (which may be the same statement that opened the file) causes data to be brought into the buffer from the associated physical device. However, the amount of data brought in is determined by the size of the buffer, and not by the GET statement. The data are brought into the buffer without conversion, meaning, in the case of list-directed input for example, that all blanks between data items are brought in along with the data items themselves. Transmission stops when the buffer is full, or an end-of-file is sensed. In the latter event, a special character might be set into the buffer to mark the position of the end-of-file, or the position of the last data item in the buffer might be noted by the operating system.

After the buffer has been filled, it is scanned for data. The scan commences at the first location in the buffer. For list- and data-directed input, if the first location contains a blank, the scan proceeds to the next location, continuing until a data item is found. The scan then continues to the end of the item, which occurs, say, at point p in the buffer. The item is then converted as necessary (based on the attributes of the current variable needed by the GET statement) and transferred to the location in memory corresponding to that variable. The same process applies to edit-directed input, except that blanks are treated as any other characters.

If there are more data to be transmitted, i.e., the input list is not yet satisfied, the scan then resumes from point p, and subsequent items are converted and transferred to their appropriate locations in memory. The process continues until one of two things happen;

- The scan reaches the end of the buffer. In this case, the buffer is re-filled from the file and the scan starts over from the first location in the buffer.

- The input list is satisfied. In this case, the operating system saves the location of point p and returns control to the PL/I program. When a subsequent GET statement refers to the same file, the scan will resume from that point.

For output, the process is reversed. The data in each of the items in the output list is converted and placed into the buffer associated with the output file. When the buffer is full, its contents are written on the associated external device and the process begins again. If the output list is exhausted before the buffer is full, the location in the buffer into which the next data item is to be placed is saved; the first data item from the subsequent PUT statement will be placed into the buffer starting at that point. When an output file is closed, either implicitly by the end of the program, or explicitly by a CLOSE statement, an end-of-file character is added to the associated buffer and the contents of the buffer are written into the file. The buffer is then "freed," meaning that that area of memory can be used for some other purpose.

Buffer contents are written on external devices as "physical records." To understand the meaning of this term, suppose we want to write the contents of a buffer on magnetic tape. In order to record the data so that it can later be read, the tape must be brought up to a defined constant speed. After the data are written, the tape must come to a stop, but it cannot stop instantly. The result is that there will be some blank tape on each end of the data record that was written. There are thus distinct "data" and "non-data" areas on the tape. The "data areas" are physical records, and the "non-data" areas are called inter-record gaps. (See the illustration on following page.) We can think of a physical record as being equivalent to one "bufferful" of information.

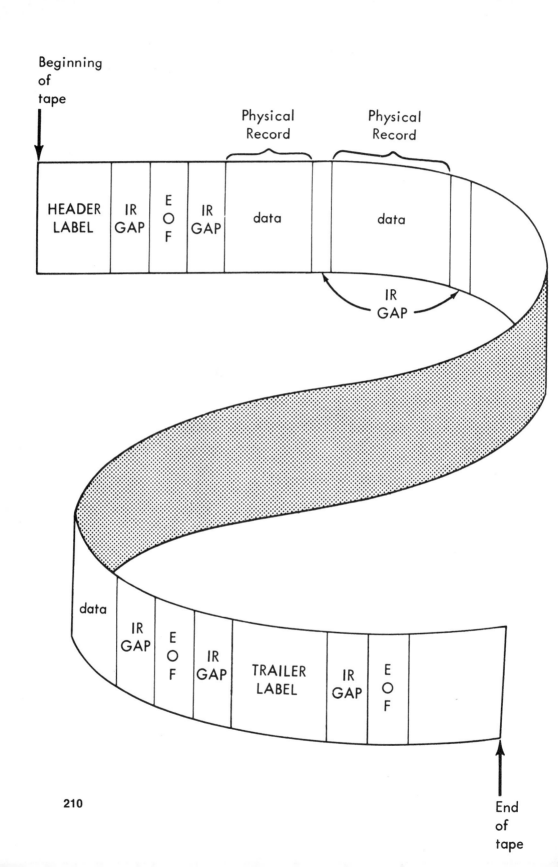

Once the tape has come up to the proper speed we can write as large a physical record as we like by having a buffer as large as we like. The input buffer required for reading a record back in must be at least as large as the buffer used for writing it because a physical record must be read in all at once just as it must be written out all at once. There is no problem if the input buffer is larger than the physical record to be read; the buffer will merely be incompletely filled.

Because the contents of stream files are always characters, i.e., the external form of data, data must be converted during input into the computer's internal form before being stored. During output, data must be converted into characters before being written.

It is frequently useful to organize files so that each physical record contains a certain amount of data, and it happens that in such cases it is unnecessary or undesirable to convert data from internal form to external form. For instance, we might want to write the contents of a structure into a file to be read later. Since the data will be read only by the program, it is wasteful of time to convert the items to external form when writing and then to convert them back into internal form when subsequently reading. Furthermore, if we write the contents of the structure as one physical record, we need a buffer that is just large enough to contain the structure contents. And, since it is unnecessary to convert the contents, why not use the structure itself as the buffer?

The kind of file needed to perform the desired operation is called a RECORD file. The main difference between RECORD and STREAM files is that information in RECORD files is maintained in the computer's internal form on the external device, while information in STREAM files consists of characters. (One consequence of this difference is that PRINT cannot be used as an attribute of a RECORD file.) Because no conversion is performed during record input/output, large quantities of data can be read and written in a relatively short time. From a practical standpoint, this is the major advantage of record input/output.

The input/output statements for RECORD files are READ and WRITE, corresponding to GET and PUT which are used with STREAM files. The general forms of READ and WRITE statements are:

READ FILE (name) INTO (variable) ;

and

$$\text{WRITE FILE (}\underline{\text{name}}\text{) FROM (}\underline{\text{variable}}\text{)};$$

where <u>variable</u> is

> a simple variable,
> an array name, or
> a structure name associated with a major or minor structure

Only one variable may be read or written by a single READ or WRITE statement. However, the name that is used might cause a great deal of data to be transmitted, e.g., it could be the name of a major structure. There is in fact a great advantage in organizing data so that a great deal can be transmitted by a single READ or WRITE statement. Each record input/output statement causes a single record to be transmitted. If the associated file happens to be magnetic tape, for example, and the transmitted records are very short, a very small portion of the tape would be used for data; most of the tape would be inter-record gaps. Thus, we might find it useful to organize a number of simple variables into a structure simply to improve the efficiency of input/output operations. The following two examples show how this might be done:

```
SLOW: PROCEDURE OPTIONS (MAIN) ;

    /* EXAMPLE NO. 48
       INEFFICIENT I/O. */

    DECLARE   FF   RECORD OUTPUT,
              A   FIXED,
              B   FLOAT,
              C CHARACTER(10) ;

    WRITE FILE( FF ) FROM( A ) ;
    WRITE FILE( FF ) FROM( B ) ;
    WRITE FILE( FF ) FROM( C ) ;

END SLOW ;
```

```
FAST: PROCEDURE OPTIONS (MAIN) ;

        /* EXAMPLE NO. 49
           EFFICIENT I/O. */

        DECLARE  FF  RECORD OUTPUT,

                 1 COLLECT,
                 2 A   FIXED,
                 2 B   FLOAT,
                 2 C   CHARACTER(10) ;

        WRITE FILE( FF ) FROM( COLLECT ) ;

   END FAST ;
```

A bank might wish to read data for each of its customers and build a file containing data on those customers whose balances are less than $500. The bank's program might be:

```
LOW_BAL: PROCEDURE OPTIONS (MAIN) ;

        /* EXAMPLE NO. 50
           ESTABLISH FILE OF CUSTOMERS WITH BALANCES
           BELOW $500. */

        DECLARE   CUST_IN   RECORD INPUT,
                  LT500     RECORD OUTPUT,
                  EOFSW  BIT( 1 ) INITIAL( '0'B ),

                  1 PROFILE,
                  2 NAME,
                   3 LAST        CHARACTER(15),
                   3 FIRST       CHARACTER(10),
                  2 ACCOUNTNO  FIXED,
                  2 BALANCE    FLOAT ;

        ON ENDFILE (CUST_IN)  EOFSW = '1'B ;

        READ FILE( CUST_IN ) INTO( PROFILE ) ;

        DO WHILE( EOFSW = '0'B ) ;
        IF BALANCE<500 THEN
           WRITE FILE( LT500 ) FROM( PROFILE ) ;

        READ FILE( CUST_IN ) INTO( PROFILE ) ;
        END ;

        CLOSE FILE( LT500 ) ;
   END LOW_BAL ;
```

213

The data for every customer is checked, and those with balances below $500 are recorded in file LT500, which is organized exactly like CUST__IN, except that there are fewer (presumably) records in LT500. There is very little calculation performed in Example No. 50, but a great deal of input/output is performed. Thus, it is extremely valuable not to have to convert the data during each input/output operation.

Suppose the bank wanted to print the data for each customer whose balance was below $500. That could be done very simply, by replacing the statement WRITE with a PUT statement, possibly a very simple PUT statement referencing the standard output file. If some other file were to be used, it must have been declared with the attributes STREAM and PRINT. Still, only a fraction of the total data to be processed will be converted, since the WRITE statement is not executed for every customer.

The rate of data transmission between an external device and a buffer is very slow compared to the internal speed of the computer, because external devices are mechanical in nature. For this reason, it is sometimes very desirable to 1) transfer data to a device less frequently, by transferring more of it each time, and 2) avoid having to wait for a buffer to be filled or emptied.

If, in Example No. 50, the buffer had been large enough to hold five replications of the structure PROFILE, the data would have to go to external devices only one-fifth as often as when the buffer is large enough to hold only one copy of PROFILE. Such a buffer could be used, and, in fact might have been set up by the operating system automatically. If such a buffer exists, then each physical record contains a number of replications of PROFILE. Each replication is called a logical record.

In general, the number of logical records in a physical record is called the blocking factor. Usually, the blocking factor will be an integer, greater than or equal to 1, but this is the case only because logical records in a physical record are usually of the same length. There is no requirement that this be the case; we could combine a very short structure and a very long structure together in one physical record. Also, a structure might be longer than the maximum length of a physical record permitted by the operating system; in this case there will be less than one logical record in a physical record. The most important thing to remember about logical records is that they are not distinguishable from one another in the same way that physical records are (except when the blocking factor is 1: in that case, each logical record corresponds to a physical record, and records are distinguishable by inter-record gaps).

Up to this point we have brought data into the buffer and then transferred it to some other area, say, a structure in the program, in order to work on it. The transfer takes time, and also means that we have used twice as much of the computer's memory in some cases; i.e., we have had to have a buffer (for which the operating system allocated space) and a structure which we declared. The similar situation existed for output.

The operating system keeps track of logical records in buffers by means of a "pointer" which always indicates the beginning of a logical record. We can overlay a structure on the buffer, starting at the current pointer position. (When this is done, the structure is said to be based on the pointer.) We can then use the structure in whatever way we wish, but we are really operating on the contents of the buffer. In a sense, we are using the structure to format the data in the buffer.

For an example, we will modify Example No. 50 so that it works on the data in PROFILE not by moving the data in the buffer to the structure, but by moving the structure to the data in the buffer.

It is very important to recognize that none of the computer memory is set aside for the structure PROFILE1 in Example No. 51 (following page), as it was for PROFILE in Example No. 50. Rather, the structure declaration in Example No. 51 serves merely to define a pattern which can be overlaid on data in a buffer. The variable BASE1 is an arbitrary identifier, which because of the context in Example No. 51 is called a pointer variable. The same variable is used in the READ statement, and the effect is to overlay the pattern associated with BASE1, i.e., PROFILE1, on the data in the buffer. Then, when we refer to PROFILE1.BALANCE in the next statement, we are really referring to the data in the buffer that lies under that part of the pattern.

```
LOW_BAL: PROCEDURE OPTIONS (MAIN) ;
              /* EXAMPLE NO. 51
                 ESTABLISH FILE OF CUSTOMERS WITH BALANCES
                 BELOW $500. DO NOT MOVE DATA FROM BUFFERS,
                 BUT TRANSFER DATA DIRECTLY FROM INPUT TO
                 OUTPUT BUFFER WHEN NECESSARY TO WRITE. */

           DECLARE   CUST_IN   SEQUENTIAL RECORD INPUT,
                     LT500     SEQUENTIAL RECORD OUTPUT,

                     1 PROFILE1   BASED (BASE1),
                      2 NAME,
                       3 LAST          CHARACTER(15),
                       3 FIRST         CHARACTER(10),
                      2 ACCOUNT_NO  FIXED,
                      2 BALANCE       FLOAT ;

           DECLARE   1 PROFILE2  BASED (BASE2),
                      2 NAME,
                       3 LAST          CHARACTER(15),
                       3 FIRST         CHARACTER(10),
                      2 ACCOUNT_NO  FIXED,
                      2 BALANCE       FLOAT ;

           ON ENDFILE( CUST_IN ) BEGIN ;
                                 CLOSE FILE( LT500 ) ;
                                 STOP ;
                                 END ;

           DO WHILE ('1'B) ;

           READ FILE( CUST_IN ) SET( BASE1 ) ;
           IF PROFILE1.BALANCE < 500 THEN
               DO;
     LOW:      LOCATE PROFILE2 SET( BASE2 ) FILE( LT500 ) ;
               PROFILE2 = PROFILE1 ;
               END;

           END ;

        END LOW_BAL ;
```

It is useful to compare the kind of READ statement used here with the
kind of READ statement we have used before.

> READ FILE (name) INTO (variable);

causes data to be read from the file named name into a buffer,
and thence to the computer memory location corresponding

to variable. Variable may be a simple variable, an array, or a major or minor structure.

READ FILE (name) SET (pointer);

causes data to be read from the file named name into a buffer, and then the pattern controlled by pointer is associated with the record. The pattern name (which does not appear explicitly in the READ statement) is called a based variable. The file name must have the attributes RECORD, SEQUENTIAL, and INPUT. These attributes may be specified in any sequence.° The pattern which is used to access the data must be the same as the pattern that was used to write it.

The LOCATE statement at LOW in Example No. 51 is used to establish an output buffer. The assignment statement then transfers the data from the input buffer (more precisely, from that part of the input buffer that lies under the pattern PROFILE1) into the output buffer (more precisely, to that part of the output buffer that lies under the pattern PROFILE2). The general form of the LOCATE statement is:

LOCATE pattern SET (pointer) FILE (name);

where pattern is a based variable and pointer is the pointer variable associated with it. Pattern must be the name of a major structure.

Data placed into a LOCATEd buffer remains there until another LOCATE or a WRITE statement is executed. At that time, the buffer may be emptied to an external device, or the buffer pointer may be repositioned to point to the next logical record to be placed in the buffer.

It frequently happens that the records in a file do not all have the same form. In this case, we will have in our program a number of variables, typically structures, one for each possible record form. We base all of these variables on the same pointer. As has been pointed out, each of these

---

°Further, some may be specified in the file declaration, and the rest in an OPEN statement. If the file is opened implicitly, then all must appear in the declaration.

variables defines a pattern for the data in the buffer. Only one of these patterns is appropriate for the particular record that was read. We determine which pattern applies by testing an item that is common to all.

For example

```
LEDGER: PROCEDURE OPTIONS(MAIN) ;

                /* EXAMPLE NO. 52
                   PROCESS A FILE WITH A MIXTURE OF DATA TYPES */

                DECLARE 1 CASH BASED (P),
                        2 TRANSACTION   CHARACTER(8),
                        2 AMOUNT        FLOAT,

                        1 CREDIT BASED  (P),
                        2 TRANSACTION   CHARACTER(8),
                        2 CUSTOMER,
                        3 NAME          CHARACTER(30),
                        3 STREET        CHARACTER(30),
                        3 CITY          CHARACTER(25),
                        3 STATE         CHARACTER(15),
                        2 AMOUNT        FLOAT,

                        1 INV  BASED (I),
                        2 TRANSACTION   CHARACTER(8),
                        2 CUSTOMER,
                        3 NAME          CHARACTER(30),
                        3 STREET        CHARACTER(30),
                        3 CITY          CHARACTER(25),
                        3 STATE         CHARACTER(15),
                        2 AMOUNT        FLOAT,

                        (PURCH,
                         INVOICE) FILE SEQUENTIAL RECORD,
                        (CREDITAMT, CASHAMT)   FLOAT INITIAL (0) ;

                ON ENDFILE (PURCH) GO TO OUT ;

START:          READ FILE (PURCH) SET (P) ;
                IF CASH. TRANSACTION = 'CASH' THEN GO TO CASHPROC ;

CREDITPROC:     CREDITAMT = CREDITAMT + CREDIT.AMOUNT ;
                LOCATE INV SET (I) FILE (INVOICE) ;
                INV = CREDIT ;
                GO TO START ;

CASHPROC:       CASHAMT = CASHAMT + CASH.AMOUNT ;
                GO TO START ;

OUT:            PUT DATA (CREDITAMT, CASHAMT) SKIP ;
                END LEDGER ;
```

The structures CASH and CREDIT are both based on P. Since CREDIT.TRANSACTION and CASH.TRANSACTION are both identical data type and the structures are identical to this point, either could be tested. The correct process is then determined.°

The file name associated with a LOCATE and a READ with SET option statements must have the attributes RECORD and SEQUENTIAL. These attributes may be specified in any sequence.

What is a sequential file? As the name implies, a sequential file is one in which the records are organized sequentially; to access a particular record it is necessary to go through the file, beginning with the first record, until the particular record is found. All files can be sequential.

A direct access file, in contrast to a sequential file, is one from which records can be extracted (or written) in any sequence. The concept of the "next record" does not apply to direct access files.

Whether an external device can be associated with a direct access file depends on its physical characteristics. Card readers, printers, and magnetic tape units cannot be associated with direct access files; they are sequential devices. Other devices, such as magnetic disk units, can be associated with direct access or sequential files.

In order to access a particular record in a direct access file, we must have some way of identifying the record. Records are identified by "keys" which determine their positions in the file. Every direct access file operation must reference a key, and the length of the key must be specified outside the PL/I program.

A direct access file is declared by a statement of the form:

DECLARE name RECORD DIRECT;

where the indicated attributes must appear, but not necessarily in that order. The INPUT or OUTPUT attribute and the KEYED attribute, implied by DIRECT, may also appear.

A typical use of a direct access file might be to maintain personnel records as part of a management information system. To access the record pertaining to a particular employee, we do not want to search through all of the records until we find the one we want.

°In order for this to work properly, attention must be given to the way in which variables are represented internally to the computer.

Each record must have a unique key. Assuming that the key for a given record is the associated employee's social security number, we can write a program which will accept social security numbers and print the appropriate employee's personnel records.

```
EMPL2:    PROCEDURE OPTIONS (MAIN) ;

          /* EXAMPLE NO. 53
          READ SOCIAL SECURITY NUMBERS AND PRINT
          EMPLOYEE RECORD ACCESSED FROM DIRECT
          ACCESS FILE.
          NOTE:
          THE DECLARE STATEMENT FOR 'FILENAME' IS
          NOT ADEQUATE FOR ALL IMPLEMENTATIONS OF
          PL/I.   ADDITIONAL INFORMATION MAY BE
          REQUIRED BY THE OPERATING SYSTEM.   */

          DECLARE   1 EMPLOYEE,
                    2 NAME,
                    3 LAST        CHARACTER(15) ,
                    3 FIRST       CHARACTER(10) ,
                    2 SOCIAL_SECURITY  FIXED DECIMAL(9),
                    /* USED AS RECORD KEY */
                    2 DEPARTMENT  FIXED DECIMAL(3) ,
                    2 RATE_OF_PAY,
                    3 REGULAR     FLOAT,
                    3 OVERTIME    FLOAT,
                    2 DATE_OF_LAST_REVIEW CHARACTER(6) ;

          DECLARE   EMPLFIL   RECORD DIRECT KEYED INPUT ;

NEXT:     GET LIST( SOCIAL_SECURITY ) ;

          /* ACCESS EMPLOYEE'S RECORD FROM DIRECT ACCESS
             FILE. */
          READ FILE( EMPLFIL ) INTO( EMPLOYEE )
                               KEY( SOCIAL_SECURITY ) ;

          /* PRINT RECORD */
          PUT LIST( EMPLOYEE ) SKIP ;

          GO TO NEXT ;

          END EMPL2 ;
```

The key specified in the READ statement in Example No. 53 is used by the computer to find the desired record, but we need not concern ourselves with how a social security number is transformed into a record location on a direct access device.

The general form of the READ statement referencing a direct access file is:

READ FILE (name) INTO (variable) KEY (expression);

The WRITE statement for a direct access file is similar, except that KEY becomes KEYFROM:

WRITE FILE (name) FROM (variable) KEYFROM (expression);

In the case of WRITE, the KEYFROM expression is converted to a character string. This string is the key for the record to be written. It is placed into the buffer ahead of the information in variable. The KEYFROM expression also determines the position of the record in the file.

In the case of READ, the KEY expression is converted to a character string which determines the position of the record in the file. This record is then read into variable.

Now we can write a PL/I program that could be used to create the file that is accessed by Example No. 53.

```
EMPL1:    PROCEDURE OPTIONS (MAIN) ;

                    /* EXAMPLE NO. 54
                    CREATE DIRECT ACCESS FILE FOR USE BY
                    EXAMPLE NO. 51
                    NOTE:
                    THE DECLARE STATEMENT FOR 'FILENAME' IS
                    NOT ADEQUATE FOR ALL IMPLEMENTATIONS OF
                    PL/I.  ADDITIONAL INFORMATION MAY BE
                    REQUIRED BY THE OPERATING SYSTEM.  */

                    DECLARE  1 EMPLOYEE,
                               2 NAME,
                                 3 LAST        CHARACTER(15),
                                 3 FIRST       CHARACTER(10),
                               2 SOCIAL_SECURITY FIXED DECIMAL(9),
                                 /* USED AS RECORD KEY */
                               2 DEPARTMENT  FIXED DECIMAL(3),
                               2 RATE_OF_PAY,
                                 3 REGULAR    FLOAT,
                                 3 OVERTIME   FLOAT,
                               2 DATE_OF_LAST_REVIEW CHARACTER(6) ;

                    DECLARE  EMPLFIL  RECORD DIRECT KEYED OUTPUT ;

         NEXT:      /* READ EMPLOYEE'S RECORD FROM STANDARD INPUT
                       FILE. */
                    GET LIST( EMPLOYEE ) ;

                    /* PLACE RECORD IN DIRECT ACCESS FILE. */
                    WRITE FILE( EMPLFIL ) FROM( EMPLOYEE )
                                        KEYFROM( SOCIAL_SECURITY ) ;

                    GO TO NEXT ;

            END EMPL1 ;
```

Direct access files are most advantageous when there are many records in a file, but it is necessary to process only a few of them. They are also superior to sequential files (in terms of time required) when it is necessary to process records in random order.

Sequential files, on the other hand, are more useful when a large proportion of the records in a file are to be processed, since it usually takes less time to access the "next" record in a sequential file than it does to access a random record in a direct access file.

The records in a direct access file can be organized sequentially, i.e., records can be placed in the file in ascending order, by key; an organization of this kind combines the best features of both organizations. For example, this is the best organization for processing a number of sequential records, the first of which is somewhere near the middle of the file. A typical example is a company which sends out invoices at certain times of the month to all customers whose names begin with a certain letter; the customers' records are placed in the file alphabetically, so the first customer whose name begins with a certain letter can be found quickly through direct access. The rest of the names would appear in sequence in subsequent records.

As we have seen the same file may be used for both input and output as long as the physical device permits it. However, you cannot write on a file which is open for input or read a file which is open for output. The UPDATE attribute allows the same file to be open for input and output at the same time. An UPDATE file allows you to change items in a file without creating a new, separate file. The general form of the DECLARE statement for UPDATE files is:

DECLARE name FILE UPDATE ;

The RECORD attribute is assumed. UPDATE is not allowed for stream files. INPUT, OUTPUT, and UPDATE are mutually exclusive.

UPDATE files are read with READ statements. Changes may be made to the information last read or new information may be written in place of it. The REWRITE statement is used to insert the changed data or new data into the file in place of the original information.

For SEQUENTIAL files, the general form of the REWRITE statement is

REWRITE FILE (name) FROM (variable) ;

which writes the current contents of the variable into the same place the previous READ statement read the data from the file name.

If the record was read by the statement:

$$\text{READ FILE (\underline{name}) SET (\underline{pointer}) ;}$$

and the data is corrected in the buffer, then the record may be rewritten directly from the input buffer by the statement

$$\text{REWRITE FILE (\underline{name}) ;}$$

If a new variable is to be written in place of the variable in the buffer the FROM clause is required. Both variables must be of the same size.

A store might use an UPDATE file to record payments to credit accounts as shown in Example 55:

```
PAYMENT:   PROCEDURE OPTIONS (MAIN) ;

           /* EXAMPLE 55
               UPDATE A FILE
               FROM PAYMENTS RECEIVED.*/

           DECLARE 1 ACCOUNT BASED (P),
                      2 NAME,
                        3 LAST      CHARACTER (20),
                        3 FIRST     CHARACTER (12),
                      2 BALANCE   FLOAT,

                      1 PAYER,
                      2 NAME,
                        3 LAST      CHARACTER (20),
                        3 FIRST     CHARACTER (12),
                      2 AMOUNT    FLOAT,

                      FF   FILE RECORD BUFFERED SEQUENTIAL
                                                  UPDATE ;

           ON ENDFILE (SYSIN) GO TO OUT ;
           ON ENDFILE (FF) GO TO OUT ;

TOP:       GET LIST (PAYER) ;
SEARCH:    READ FILE (FF) SET (P) ;
           IF ACCOUNT.LAST ¬= PAYER.LAST THEN GO TO SEARCH ;

           BALANCE = BALANCE - AMOUNT ;
           REWRITE FILE (FF) ;
           GO TO TOP ;
OUT:
           CLOSE FILE (FF) ;
           END PAYMENT ;
```

For files that have the DIRECT attribute we can read, write, and rewrite when the file has been opened as UPDATE. The general form of the REWRITE statement then becomes

REWRITE FILE (name) FROM (variable) KEY (expression) ;

The FROM and KEY clauses are required.

For an example of UPDATE on a DIRECT file, we can use a report stored in a file. Each line of the report is one record, and we find that in the sixth line the word "write" should be "wrote". We could then write:

```
CORRECT:   PROCEDURE OPTIONS(MAIN) ;

           /* EXAMPLE 56
           CORRECT A REPORT
           NOTE:
           THE DECLARE STATEMENT FOR 'FILENAME' IS
           NOT ADEQUATE FOR ALL IMPLEMENTATIONS OF
           PL/I.  ADDITIONAL INFORMATION MAY BE
           REQUIRED BY THE OPERATING SYSTEM. */

           DECLARE LINE     CHARACTER(80),
                   NO       FIXED INITIAL (6),
                   REPORT FILE UPDATE RECORD DIRECT ;

           READ FILE (REPORT) INTO (LINE) KEY (NO) ;
           I = INDEX(LINE, 'WRITE') ;
           SUBSTR(LINE, I, 5) = 'WROTE' ;

           REWRITE FILE (REPORT) FROM (LINE) KEY (NO) ;
       END CORRECT ;
```

Note

Some implementations, e.g., PL/C do not include direct access files. The LOCATE and REWRITE statements are thus excluded, as is the SET option on the READ statement.

11.1   A bank has decided to open a new branch and wants to notify its customers. Each customer having a savings account or a checking account should be notified, but a customer having both types of accounts should receive only one notification. The names in each file are in alphabetical order. The records in both files have the form

        1 SAVING or CHECKING

        (2 NAME

        2 ADDRESS) CHARACTER(20)

        2 ACCT_NO FIXED

        2 BALANCE FLOAT

Write a program to read two files, SAVE and CHECK, and print the mailing list.

11.2   A direct file has been created which contains a 100 line document; each line is a separate logical record. The key for each record is its position in the document.

Write a PL/I program which reads a key, a string of existent text, and a string of new text which is to replace the old text in the appropriate record.

11.3   Rewrite Example No. 52, page 218, without GO TO statements.

11.4   Rewrite Example No. 53, page 220, without GO TO statements.

11.5   Rewrite Example No. 54, page 222, without GO TO statements.

Chapter 12

STORAGE MANAGEMENT

Chapter 8 has shown how storage can be allocated when needed and how that same storage can be used for several purposes. Allocation of storage for variables was done when a PROCEDURE block or BEGIN block was entered; and the storage was freed or released upon exit from the block. This happens automatically. Variables which are allocated and freed in this manner are of the AUTOMATIC storage class.

If, on the other hand, a certain variable must be allocated at all times you may declare it to be of the STATIC storage class. The general form of the DECLARE statement is

DECLARE name attributes STATIC;

This allocates space for name when execution begins and does not free it until execution terminates.

The reason for using STATIC is to cause the value of the variable to remain set for the next invocation of the procedure. For example

```
SUBA: PROCEDURE ;
         DECLARE I FIXED STATIC INITIAL (0) ;
         .
         .
         .
         IF I=0
            THEN DO ;    /* INITIAL CASE */
                 I = I + 1 ;
                 .
                 .
                 .
                 RETURN ;
                 END ;
         /* ALL OTHER CASES */
         .
         .
         .
     END SUBA ;
```

The first time SUBA is entered the path taken is the DO group. For all other invocations the DO group is skipped.

PL/I also provides a facility for the programmer to control when space for a variable is allocated and when it is freed. Variables which are allocated and freed explicitly are of the CONTROLLED storage class and are declared by statements of the general form:

DECLARE name attributes CONTROLLED;

Because the attribute CONTROLLED is specified, no storage is allocated for name until the statement:

ALLOCATE name;

is executed. When you need the variable, you allocate space for it; and when you no longer need the variable, you write:

FREE name;

The combination gives you complete control over when a variable is allocated.

The attributes of the variable may be explicitly stated in the

DECLARE statement; when the ALLOCATE statement is executed, these attributes apply. The bounds of an array or the number of characters in a string are specified as arithmetic variables in the DECLARE statement. At the time the ALLOCATE statement is executed the bounds of the array or the number of characters in the string is determined by the current value of those arithmetic variables. For example:

1)
```
DECLARE ( X (L:M) FLOAT,
          Y CHARACTER (J) )
          CONTROLLED ;
```
X is declared as a single dimensioned array and Y is a character string.

2)
```
L = 1 ;
M = 120 ;
J = 200 ;
ALLOCATE X, Y ;
```
X is allocated with 120 elements; Y is allocated as a string of 200 characters.

3)
```
FREE X ;
```
X is freed.

4)
```
L = -50 ;
M = 50 ;
   ALLOCATE X ;
```
X is again allocated but this time as an array of 101 elements.

5)
```
FREE X ;
```

6)
```
DECLARE Z (J+5) FLOAT
          CONTROLLED ;
J = 30 ;
ALLOCATE Z ;
```
Expressions, as well as variables may be used. Z is allocated with 35 elements.

Let us see how we can allocate storage for an array of "N" elements where "N" is an input data item, first using AUTOMATIC variables, and then using CONTROLLED variables.

Automatic
```
GET LIST( N) ;
BEGIN ;
    DECLARE A(N) FLOAT ;
    .
    .
    .
END ;
```

Note: AUTOMATIC is the default storage class attribute but may be explicitly stated if desired.

Controlled
```
DECLARE A(N) FLOAT CONTROLLED ;
GET LIST( N ) ;
ALLOCATE A ;
.
.
.
```

The amount of storage available for any particular user is limited. The ability to allocate and free is valuable because you can specify the exact amount of storage needed and you can use the same storage for different purposes.

The three ways to allocate storage that we have been discussing are:

AUTOMATIC–   Storage is allocated upon entry to a block and freed upon exit. This is the default storage class.

STATIC –   Storage is allocated once and remains allocated.

CONTROLLED – Storage is allocated and freed by execution of ALLOCATE and FREE statements, respectively.

Sometimes the amount of storage required changes during execution. For example, an airline reservation system requires more storage each time an additional passenger makes a reservation. This storage will be used for pertinent information relating to the additional passenger. A structure (for instance) is established describing a typical passenger and defining the amount of storage required. Each time an additional passenger requests a reservation more storage of this format is allocated.

We accomplish this by allocating a variable which has been declared with the BASED attribute. BASED is the fourth storage class attribute. As

we have seen in Chapter 11, the general form of the DECLARE statement
for BASED variables is

DECLARE name BASED (pointer) ;

No storage is allocated for name until a statement of the form

ALLOCATE name;

is executed.

When the ALLOCATE statement is executed storage is allocated for
name, and pointer is set to the location of name in storage. When we need
another allocation, we again ALLOCATE and the associated pointer is set
to the new allocation. The previous value of the pointer must be saved so
that we can still refer to the previous allocation.

For an example of how storage might be managed using based
variables, consider a technique that might be used by an airline for
handling passenger reservations for certain flights. The objective is to
write a program which requires only the amount of storage needed to build
a list of the passengers for a particular flight. As passengers request
reservations they will be added to the list.

The following structure used in Example 57 has the general format for
each person requesting a reservation. To add a passenger to the list, we
merely allocate a new generation of PASSENGER and assign the
appropriate specific information.

```
DECLARE 1 PASSENGER BASED (P),
         2 NAME CHARACTER(20),
         2 SEAT CHARACTER(3),
         2 MENU CHARACTER(40),
         2 LINK POINTER,

         FLIGHT POINTER ;
```

Variables used as pointers are of "locator" data type and may be
explicitly declared by means of the POINTER attribute. The general form
of the DECLARE statement is

DECLARE name POINTER;

As we have seen in Chapter 11, pointer variables may also be declared contextually in the declarations for BASED variables.

In the structure PASSENGER we have a variable named LINK which is a pointer variable. The program also uses a pointer variable named FLIGHT which locates the first passenger allocation.

How do we add the first passenger? First we allocate PASSENGER with the statement

```
ALLOCATE PASSENGER ;
```

Our storage could then be visualized as

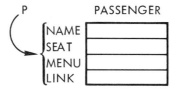

Then we assign the value of P (which was set at allocation) to FLIGHT. This is done by a conventional assignment statement, i.e.,

```
FLIGHT = P ;
```

How do we add the second passenger? First we allocate a second instance of PASSENGER with an ALLOCATE statement. Our storage could then be visualized as

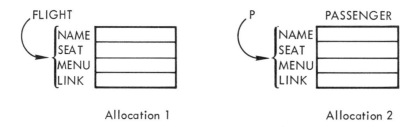

Allocation 1   Allocation 2

Then we assign the value of P (which has been set to the second allocation) to the LINK of the first passenger. As more passengers are added, the location of the "next" passenger is kept in the LINK of the preceding passenger.°

There is a LINK in each allocation of PASSENGER. In order to refer to a particular LINK we must qualify the name by the appropriate pointer. This is done by means of the "locator qualifier" symbol made by a "minus" and "greater than" symbol. In the case of the second passenger, we are interested in the LINK that is pointed to by FLIGHT. The appropriate assignment statement is thus

$$\text{FLIGHT->LINK = P ;}$$

and our storage could now be visualized as

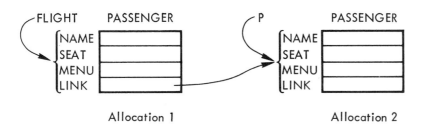

Allocation 1   Allocation 2

Finally, the LINK of the second allocation of PASSENGER must be set to NULL to signify the last passenger in the list. This is done by the statement

$$\text{P->LINK = NULL ;}$$

NULL is a built-in function which returns the locator value "nothing", which has meaning for pointers only. A pointer with the value NULL references nothing.

The pointer associated with PASSENGER is P because of its

°This kind of data organization is called a linked list, or chained list.

appearance in the DECLARE statement. When the locator qualifier is omitted, P is assumed.

It is useful to keep track of the last passenger in the list and this is done with the pointer LAST.

```
AIRRES:   PROCEDURE OPTIONS( MAIN ) ;
              /* EXAMPLE NO 57
              ADD NAMES TO A RESERVATION LIST */

          DECLARE 1 PASSENGER BASED( P ),
                    2 NAME CHARACTER (20),
                    2 SEAT CHARACTER (3) ,
                    2 MENU CHARACTER (40),
                    2 LINK POINTER,

              (FLIGHT, LAST) POINTER ;

          DECLARE NULL BUILTIN ;
          ON ENDFILE(SYSIN) STOP ;

          FLIGHT = NULL ;

          DO WHILE ('1'B) ;
          ALLOCATE PASSENGER ;
          GET LIST( NAME, SEAT, MENU ) ;

          IF FLIGHT=NULL THEN FLIGHT = P ;
          ELSE LAST->LINK = P ;

          P->LINK = NULL ;
          LAST = P ;
          END ;

      END AIRRES ;
```

Two kinds of operations are permitted with locator data: assignment and comparison. The only permissible comparisons are "equal" and "not equal."

Now we will change the program to both add and cancel names for the flight. Passengers are added in the same manner as in Example 57, but to delete a passenger we must search the list for the name to be canceled. This list is scanned until a match is found. When the correct name is found, we make the LINK of the preceeding passenger point to the following passenger and then free the storage taken by the person to be canceled. We may visualize cancellation of passenger #2 in the following way.

Passenger list before cancellation

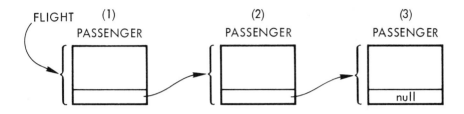

Update LINK of previous passenger

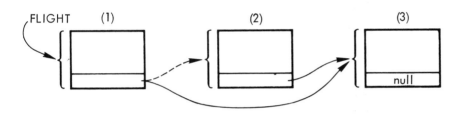

Free storage for canceled passenger

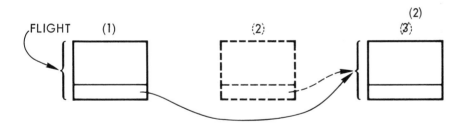

The statement

```
FREE TEST->PASSENGER ;
```

releases the storage. The locator qualifier is required in order to specify which allocation of PASSENGER is to be freed.

```
AIRRES:   PROCEDURE OPTIONS( MAIN ) ;

   /* EXAMPLE NO. 58
      ADD AND DELETE PASSENGERS   */

   DECLARE NULL BUILTIN ;

   DECLARE P POINTER ;

   DECLARE 1 PASSENGER BASED (P),
             2 NAME CHARACTER (20),
             2 SEAT CHARACTER (3) ,
             2 MENU CHARACTER (40),
             2 LINK OFFSET (DAY);

   DECLARE (FLIGHT, LAST, TEST, PREV) POINTER ;
   DECLARE PERSON CHARACTER(20),   FUNCTION CHARACTER(6) ;
   DECLARE FOUND_FLAG  BIT(1) ;

   ON ENDFILE (SYSIN)
     BEGIN;
       TEST = FLIGHT;
       DO WHILE (TEST ¬= NULL) ;
         PUT LIST (TEST->NAME) SKIP;
         TEST = TEST->LINK;
         END;
       STOP;
       END;

   FLIGHT = NULL;

   /* MAIN LOOP FOR PASSENGER PROCEESING */

   DO WHILE ('1'B) ;

     GET EDIT (FUNCTION) (SKIP,A(6)) ;

     IF FUNCTION = 'ADD'
       THEN DO; /* ADD A NEW PASSENGER */
            ALLOCATE PASSENGER ;
            GET EDIT (NAME, SEAT, MENU)
                     (SKIP,A(20),A(3),A(40)) ;
            IF FLIGHT = NULL
               THEN FLIGHT = P ;
               ELSE LAST->LINK = P ;
            P->LINK = NULL ;
            LAST = P ;
            END ;
```

```
      ELSE IF FUNCTION = 'CANCEL'
          THEN DO;  /* CANCEL A PASSENGER */
            GET EDIT (PERSON) (SKIP,A(20));
            /* NAME TO BE CANCELLED */
            PREV = NULL;
            TEST = FLIGHT;
            FOUND_FLAG = '0'B;

            /* GO THROUGH LIST TO FIND PERSON */
            DO WHILE (TEST ¬= NULL);
              IF TEST->NAME = PERSON
                THEN DO;  /* PERSON FOUND */
                      FOUND_FLAG = '1'B ;
                      IF PREV = NULL
                         THEN FLIGHT = TEST->LINK ;
                         ELSE PREV->LINK = TEST->LINK ;
                      IF TEST = LAST
                         THEN LAST = PREV ;
                      FREE TEST->PASSENGER ;
                      TEST = NULL ;
                      END ;
                  ELSE DO ;   /* SET POINTERS TO TEST */
                                  /* NEXT PASSENGER */
                      PREV = TEST ;
                      TEST = TEST->LINK ;
                      END ;
            END ;
            IF ¬ FOUND_FLAG
              THEN PUT EDIT ('NOT ON FLIGHT: ',PERSON)
                  (A) SKIP;
            END;
        ELSE PUT EDIT ('ILLEGAL FUNCTION: ',FUNCTION)
            (A) SKIP;
END ;

END AIRRES ;
```

The input data for Example 58 appears on page 238.

```
**********SAMPLE DATA FOR EXAMPLE 58   **********
ADD
LARRY BROWN              4C STANDARD
ADD
PATRICIA FOX             17ASTANDARD
ADD
JAMES MCDONALD           12FNO SALT
ADD
ROY ANDERSON             9D STANDARD
ADD
JOAN ANDERSON            9F LO-CAL SPECIAL
CANCEL
JAMES MCDONALD
ADD
PHILIP COCHRAN           15ASTANDARD
CANCEL
PATRICIA FOX
```

Example 58 is limited to one specific flight. To make it operate for
many flights we can make FLIGHT an array of pointers. There will be an
element of FLIGHT corresponding to each flight number; each element is
a pointer to the appropriate list of passengers. LAST is also made an array
of pointers. We can visualize this as:

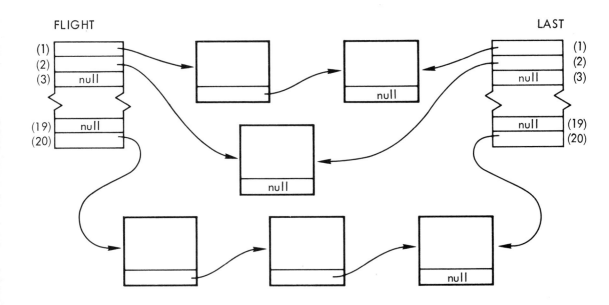

The arrays FLIGHT and FLIGHTNO in Example 59 are organized so
that, for example, FLIGHT(5) points to the list of passengers for the flight
number contained in FLIGHTNO(5).

238

```
AIRRES: PROCEDURE OPTIONS (MAIN) ;

  /* EXAMPLE NO. 59
     MAINTAIN PASSENGER LISTS FOR SEVERAL FLIGHTS */

  DECLARE NULL BUILTIN ;

  DECLARE P PCINTER ;

  DECLARE 1 PASSENGER BASED (P),
            2 NAME CHARACTER (20),
            2 SEAT CHARACTER (3),
            2 MENU CHARACTER (40),
            2 LINK OFFSET (DAY);

  DECLARE ( FLIGHT(20), LAST(20), TEST, PREV) POINTER ;
  DECLARE ( FLIGHTNO(20), NO, NUM, I) FIXED ;
  DECLARE PERSON  CHARACTER(20),  FUNCTION  CHARACTER(6) ;
  DECLARE  FOUND_FLAG  BIT(1) ;

  ON ENDFILE (SYSIN)
     BEGIN;
       DO I = 1 TO NO;
         PUT SKIP LIST (FLIGHTNO(I));
         TEST = FLIGHT(I) ;
         DO WHILE (TEST ¬= NULL);
           PUT LIST (TEST->NAME) SKIP;
           TEST = TEST->LINK;
           END;
         END;
       STOP;
       END;

  GET LIST (NO) ;
    IF NO<0 | NO>20
      THEN DO;
        PUT LIST ('INVALID NUMBER OF FLIGHTS ',NO);
        NO = C;
        END;
      ELSE DO;
        FLIGHT = NULL;
        GET LIST ((FLIGHTNO(I)  DO I = 1 TO NO));

        /* MAIN LOOP FOR PASSENGER PROCESSING */

        DO WHILE ('1'B);

          GET EDIT (NUM,FUNCTICN) (SKIP,F(3),A(6));
```

```
        /* FIND THIS FLIGHT IN THE LIST */
        DO I = 1 TO NO;
          IF FLIGHTNO(I) = NUM
            THEN DO;     /* FLIGHT FOUND */

              IF FUNCTION = 'ADD'
                THEN CALL ADD ;

                ELSE IF FUNCTION = 'CANCEL'
                  THEN CALL CANCEL ;
                  ELSE PUT SKIP EDIT('ILLEGAL FUNCTION: '
                      ,FUNCTION) (A);
              I = 9999;   /* FORCE END OF DO-LOOP */
              END;
          END;
        IF I < 9999
          THEN DO;
            PUT SKIP EDIT('INVALID FLIGHT NUMBER: ',NUM)
                (A,F(5));
            GET SKIP;
            END;
        END;
      END;


ADD: PROCEDURE ;
    /* ADD PASSENGER TO LIST FOR FLIGHT */
    ALLOCATE PASSENGER ;
    GET EDIT (NAME, SEAT, MENU)
            (SKIP,A(20),A(3),A(40)) ;
    IF FLIGHT(I) = NULL
        THEN FLIGHT(I) = P ;
        ELSE LAST(I)->LINK = P ;
    P->LINK = NULL ;
    LAST(I) = P ;
END ADD ;


CANCEL: PROCEDURE ;
    /* DELETE PASSENGER FROM LIST */
    GET EDIT (PERSON) (SKIP,A(20));
    FOUND_FLAG = '0'B;
    PREV = NULL;
    TEST = FLIGHT(I);
    DO WHILE (TEST ¬= NULL);
```

```
                IF TEST->NAME = PERSON
                  THEN DO;
                    FOUND_FLAG = '1'B;
                    IF PREV = NULL
                      THEN FLIGHT(I) = TEST->LINK;
                      ELSE PREV->LINK = TEST->LINK;
                    IF TEST = LAST(I)
                      THEN LAST(I) = PREV;
                    FREE TEST->PASSENGER ;
                    TEST = NULL;
                    END;
                  ELSE DO;
                    PREV = TEST;
                    TEST = TEST->LINK;
                    END;
              END;
            IF ¬FOUND_FLAG
              THEN PUT SKIP EDIT
                  ('NOT ON FLIGHT: ',PERSON) (A);
        END CANCEL ;
END AIRRES ;
```

Input Data for Example 59

```
    10        3 12 321 689 37 322 1 703 29 266
     12ADD
    LARRY BROWN            4C STANDARD
     37ADD
    PATRICIA FOX           17ASTANDARD
    322ADD
    JAMES MCDONALD         12FNO SALT
     3ADD
    ROY ANDERSON           9D STANDARD
    322CANCEL
    JAMES MCDONALD
     37ADD
    JOAN ANDERSON          9F LO-CAL SPECIAL
    123ADD
    PHILIP COCHRAN         15ASTANDARD
     37CANCEL
    PATRICIA FOX
```

Two potential difficulties related to input-output arise when using based variables for applications such as the airline reservation example. One of these is that if we were to write the information for each individual in the list we would write many small records. As shown in Chapter 11 this can be very inefficient. It would be better to collect all the allocations of PASSENGER into one area of storage and write the area as one long record. PL/I provides for this by means of AREA variables. An allocation of based variable may then be specified to occur within the appropriate AREA. For example,

DECLARE name1 AREA (size) ;

DECLARE name2 BASED (pointer) ;

.

.

.

ALLOCATE name2 IN (name1) ;

Name1 identifies the area and size specifies how much space is reserved for it. If size is not included a default size is given the area.* An area may be of any storage class, i.e., AUTOMATIC, CONTROLLED, STATIC or BASED.

The other difficulty is that a program and its data will not usually occupy the same storage locations from run to run.† At the time a based variable is allocated, the associated pointer is set to the absolute location of the variable in storage. For this reason, pointer values written by one program become meaningless when read by another. In fact, they may be meaningless even if they are read by the same program.

This difficulty is likewise overcome by means of area variables. When a based variable is allocated in an area it is of necessity allocated at some position relative to the beginning of the area. This relative position, which does not change when the area is written or read by the same or any other program, is called the "offset." Names with the OFFSET attribute are declared by statements of the general form:

---

*The units and value of the default size depend on the computer used.

†Normally, this is of no concern to the programmer because data locations are referred to by their names and not by their absolute locations in memory.

DECLARE name OFFSET (area) ;

The identifier used for <u>area</u> is contextually declared to be an AREA name. It may be explicitly declared as shown on page 242.

Pointers and offsets are known as "locator" data. Pointers reference absolute locations in memory; offsets reference locations relative to the beginning of an area.

Example 60 (starting below) shows how Example 58 could be rewritten to process the reservation list in an area DAY. We assume the reservation list exists in file FUTURE. Each record in FUTURE contains the passenger list for one day's flight, and the offsets of the first and last passengers. The offsets must be retained in the record so that we know how to find the first (and last) allocation when the area is read. Once the first passenger is located, the second passenger can be located by referring to the LINK of the first, etc. This is possible because LINK is an offset, and not a pointer. The allocations occupy the same relative positions within the area, so the offsets remain valid even though the area itself will probably not occupy the same location from which it was written.

Because no size is specified for DAY in Example 60 the default size is assumed. In practice, we would specify the size of DAY large enough to accommodate the maximum number of passengers for each flight.

```
AIRRES: PROCEDURE OPTIONS (MAIN);

   /* EXAMPLE NO. 60
      KEEP PASSENGER LIST IN AN AREA  */

   DECLARE NULL BUILTIN ;
   DECLARE (P, RES) POINTER ;

   DECLARE 1 PASSENGER BASED (P),
             2 NAME CHARACTER (20),
             2 SEAT CHARACTER (3),
             2 MENU CHARACTER (40),
             2 LINK OFFSET (DAY);

   DECLARE 1 RESERVATION BASED (RES),
             2 FLIGHT OFFSET (DAY),
             2 LAST OFFSET (DAY),
             2 DAY AREA;
```

```
DCL TEST OFFSET (DAY);
DECLARE PO POINTER ;
DECLARE PERSON CHARACTER(20),  FUNCTION CHARACTER(6) ;
DECLARE FUTURE FILE RECORD SEQUENTIAL UPDATE ;   /* THIS
          DECLARE MAY NOT BE SUFFICIENT FOR SOME COMPILERS */
DECLARE READ_FLAG  BIT(1) ;

ON ENDFILE (FUTURE)
  SIGNAL ENDFILE (SYSIN);

ON ENDFILE (SYSIN)
  BEGIN;
    CLOSE FILE (FUTURE);

    ON ENDFILE (FUTURE)
      BEGIN;
        CLOSE FILE (FUTURE);
        STOP;
        END;

    DO WHILE ('1'B);
      READ FILE (FUTURE) SET (RES);
      PUT EDIT ('--- FLIGHT LIST ---') (A) SKIP (2);
      TEST = FLIGHT;
      DO WHILE (TEST ¬= NULL);
        PUT EDIT (TEST->NAME) (A) SKIP;
        TEST = TEST->LINK;
        END;
      END;
    END;

DO WHILE ('1'B);
  READ FILE (FUTURE) SET (RES);
  READ_FLAG = '1'B;
  DO WHILE (READ_FLAG);
    GET EDIT (FUNCTION) (SKIP,A(6)) ;

    IF FUNCTION = 'ADD'
      THEN CALL ADD ;
      ELSE IF FUNCTION = 'NEXT'
        THEN DO;
          /* UPDATE LIST FOR THIS DAY'S FLIGHTS */
          REWRITE FILE (FUTURE);
          READ_FLAG = '0'B;
          END;

        ELSE PUT EDIT ('UNKNOWN FUNCTION: ',FUNCTION)
            (A) SKIP;
    END;
```

```
            END;


ADD: PROCEDURE ;
        /* ADD A PASSENGER TO THE LIST */
        ALLOCATE PASSENGER IN (DAY);
        P->LINK = NULL;
        GET EDIT (NAME,SEAT,MENU)
           (SKIP,A(20),A(3),A(40));
        IF FLIGHT = NULL
          THEN FLIGHT = P;
          ELSE LAST->LINK = P;
        LAST = P;
END ADD ;


CANCEL: PROCEDURE ;
        /* DELETE A PASSENGER FROM THE LIST */
        GET EDIT (PERSON) (SKIP,A(20));
        IF FLIGHT ¬= NULL
          THEN DO;
            PO = NULL;
            TEST = FLIGHT;
            DO WHILE (TEST ¬= NULL);
              IF TEST->NAME = PERSON
                THEN DO;   /* DELETE */
                    IF TEST = FLIGHT
                       THEN FLIGHT = FLIGHT->LINK;
                       ELSE PO->LINK = TEST->LINK;
                    IF TEST = LAST
                       THEN LAST = PO;
                    FREE TEST->PASSENGER IN (DAY);
                    TEST, PO = NULL;
                    END;
                ELSE DO;   /* CHAIN */
                    PO = TEST;
                    TEST = TEST->LINK;
                    END;
              END;
            IF PO ¬= NULL
              THEN PUT SKIP EDIT ('NOT ON FLIGHT: ',
                  PERSON) (A);
            END;
          ELSE PUT SKIP EDIT ('FLIGHT EMPTY') (A);
END CANCEL ;

END AIRRES ;
```

Areas may be assigned to other areas. The portion of the source area used for allocated variables directly maps into the destination area. If the destination area is not large enough to accomodate the source then the AREA condition is raised. The AREA condition is also raised by the ALLOCATE statement if there is insufficient space remaining in the area.

Notes on Chapter 12

1. An ALLOCATE statement may specify a pointer to be set. The general form is

$$\text{ALLOCATE } \underline{\text{name}} \text{ SET } (\underline{\text{ptr}}) ;$$

If $\underline{ptr}$ is the same as the pointer used in the declaration for $\underline{name}$ the SET option is redundant.
If $\underline{ptr}$ is a different pointer variable from the pointer used in the declaration for $\underline{name}$ then it alone is set.

2. If a CONTROLLED variable is allocated a second time without freeing the first allocation, the second allocation is "stacked." That is, the first variable allocated cannot be referenced again until the second is freed. For example:

```
DECLARE A(N) FIXED CONTROLLED ;

N = 10 ;
ALLOCATE A ;
A = 1 ;
N = 5 ;
AILCCATE A ;
A = 2 ;
PUT LIST (A) ;
FREE A ;
PUT LIST (A) ;
FREE A ;
```

2	2	2	2	2
1	1	1	1	1
1	1	1	1	1

3. Some implementations, e.g. PL/C, do not include the storage management capabilities described in this chapter.

EXERCISES

12.1 Modify Example No. 58 (page 236) to print any special meal required and the number of "regular" meals after the list of passengers is completed.

12.2 What is the advantage, if any, of the variable LAST in Example No. 58 (page 236)? How could the program be written without using this variable?

12.3 Modify Example No. 60 (page 243) so that the file FUTURE is a direct file keyed on day number. A day number should be read along with each instruction to add or cancel a passenger. The record for that day should then be updated and rewritten.

12.4 Write a PL/I program which reads a file of names and addresses, establishes a linked list. Sort the names alphabetically by rearranging the pointers only; do not move the actual records. Then print the sorted list. The records in the file have the form:

           1   Person,
           2   Name CHARACTER (20),
           2   Address CHARACTER (20);

Appendix A

CHARACTER SETS AND OPERATORS

I.   60-CHARACTER SET

Graphic	Description
A thru Z	Alphabetic
$, @, #	Alphabetic
0 thru 9	Numeric
	Blank
=	Equal or Replacement
+	Plus
—	Minus
*	Asterisk
/	Slash
(	Left parenthesis
)	Right parenthesis
,	Comma
.	Radix point or Structure name qualification
'	Quote
%	Percent
;	Semicolon
:	Colon
—	Break character

Graphic	Description
¬	Not
&	And
|	Or
<	Less Than
>	Greater Than
?	Question mark

II.   48-CHARACTER SET°

Graphic	Description
A thru Z	Alphabetic
$	Alphabetic
0 thru 9	Numeric
	Blank
=	Equal or Replacement
+	Plus
—	Minus
*	Asterisk
/	Slash
(	Left parenthesis
)	Right parenthesis
,	Comma
.	Radix point or Structure name qualification
'	Quote

Some language elements require two graphics for their representation in the 48-character set. These are:

Element	48-Character Representation
Semicolon	, .
Colon	. .
Percent	/ /

°Some implementations, e.g. PL/C, do not allow the 48-character set.

No blanks may appear between the two graphics constituting a single element. To avoid confusion, it is a good idea to use at least one blank on each side of a two-graphic element.

Operation	Operator 60-Char.	48-Char.°
Assignment	=	=
Exponentiation	**	**
Multiplication	*	*
Division	/	/
Addition	+	+
Subtraction	−	−
Negation (arithmetic)	−	−
Negation (logical)	¬	NOT
And	&	AND
Or	|	OR
Less Than	<	LT
Less Than or Equal	<=	LE
Equal	=	=
Greater Than or Equal	>=	GE
Not Equal	¬=	NE
Not Less Than	¬<	NL
Not Greater Than	¬>	NG
Concatenation	||	CAT

°Operators composed of alphabetic characters must be delimited by one or more blanks on both sides. Alphabetic operators may not be used as identifiers; they are "reserved" words. Some implementations, e.g. PL/C, do not allow the 48-character set.

	Operator	
Operation	60-Char.	48-Char.
Qualification (structures)	.	.
Qualification (locator)	->	PT
Begin comment	/'*	/*
End comment	*/	*/

ABBREVIATIONS FOR KEYWORDS

ALLOCATE	ALLOC
BINARY	BIN
CHARACTER	CHAR
COLUMN	COL
CONTROLLED	CTL
CONVERSION	CONV
DECIMAL	DEC
DECLARE	DCL
EXTERNAL	EXT
FIXEDOVERFLOW	FOFL
INITIAL	INIT
OVERFLOW	OFL
PICTURE	PIC
POINTER	PTR
PROCEDURE	PROC
SEQUENTIAL	SEQL
STRINGRANGE	STRG
STRINGSIZE	STRZ

SUBSCRIPTRANGE	SUBRG
UNDERFLOW	UFL
VARYING	VAR
ZERODIVIDE	ZDIV

Appendix C

BUILT-IN FUNCTIONS

Function values have the same base, scale, and precision as the arguments. Arguments to trigonometric functions are assumed to be expressed in radians.

Function	Value
ABS(arg)	The absolute value of arg.
ATAN(arg)	ABS(arctan (arg)) modulo $\pi/2$.
ATAN(arg_1, arg_2)	arctan(arg_1/arg_2). The result is positioned in the correct quadrant. Error if $arg_1 = 0$ and $arg_2 = 0$.
CEIL(arg)	The smallest integer greater than or equal to arg.
	Example: X = −1.23 ;
	Y = CEIL(X) ;
	then Y contains −1.
COMPLEX(arg_1, arg_2)	Arg_1 becomes the real part and arg_2 becomes the imaginary part of the complex function value.
CONJ(arg)	The complex conjugate of arg.
COS(arg)	cos(arg)

254

Function	Value
COSH(arg)	cosh(arg)
EXP(arg)	e^{arg}
FLOOR(arg)	The largest integer less than or equal to arg.

FLOOR example:

    Example: X = 1.23;

                 Y = FLOOR(X);

                 then Y contains 1.

Function	Value
IMAG(arg)	The imaginary part of arg.
LOG(arg)	ln(arg). Error if arg<=0.
LOG2(arg)	$\log_2$(arg). Error if arg<=0.
LOG10(arg)	$\log_{10}$(arg). Error if arg<=0.
MAX(arg1, arg2, . . .)	The maximum value of an arbitrary number of arguments.

    Example: A = 1 ;

                 B = 2 ;

                 C = 3 ;

                 D = −2 ;

                 Z = MAX(A,B,C,D) ;

                 then Z contains 3

Function	Value
MIN(arg1, arg2, . . .)	The minimum value of an arbitrary number of arguments.

    Example: A = 1 ; B = 2 ;

                 C = 3; D = −2;

                 Z = MIN(A,B,C,D) ;

                 then Z contains −2.

Function	Value
MOD(arg1, arg2)	The remainder of (arg 1/arg2).

    Example: A = 16 ;

                 B = 3;

                 Z = MOD(A,B) ;

                 then Z contains 1.

Function	Value
REAL(arg)	The real part of arg.
SIGN(arg)	1 if arg >0
	0 if arg = 0
	−1 if arg <0

Function	Value
SIN(arg)	sin(arg)
SINH(arg)	sinh(arg)
SQRT(arg)	Positive square root of arg. Error if arg<0.
TAN(arg)	tan(arg)
TANH(arg)	tanh(arg)
TRUNC(arg)	Arg truncated to an integer.

Examples: A = 1.875 ;

B = −3.625 ;

Y = TRUNC(A) ;

Y contains 1.

Z = TRUNC(B) ;

Z contains −3.

II. STRING FUNCTIONS

Function	Value
INDEX(arg1,arg2)	The position in the string arg1 where arg2 first appears. If arg2 does not appear, the value returned is zero. Example:

DECLARE A CHAR(8), Z FIXED;

A = 'COMPUTER' ;

Z = INDEX(A, 'MP') ;

Z contains 3.

Z = INDEX(A, 'Y') ;

Z contains 0.

Function	Value
LENGTH(arg)	The length of the string, arg: the number of bits if arg is a bit string; the number of characters if arg is a character string.
SUBSTR(arg, s, n)	A substring of arg. The substring starts at position s of arg and is n characters (or bits) long. If n is omitted the substring starts at position s in arg and continues to the end of

Function	Value

arg. If the specified substring does not lie wholly within arg anomalous results will occur. See STRINGRANGE, Appendix D. Example:

DECLARE (A,Z) CHAR(8) VARYING ;
A = 'COMPUTER' ;
Z = SUBSTR(A, 4, 3) ;
Z contains 'PUT'.
Z = SUBSTR(A, 7, 4) ;
Z contains 'ER??' where ? means "undefined".

TRANSLATE(arg, r, t)

A character string of the same length as arg. Each character in arg is examined. If it occurs in t the corresponding character in r replaces the character in the result. If the character in arg does not occur in t it is placed unchanged in the result.

DECLARE A CHAR(25) VARYING ;
DECLARE (LOWER, UPPER) CHAR(5) ;
LOWER = 'aeiou' ;
UPPER = 'AEIOU' ;
A = 'DOGCAT' :
DECLARE Z CHARACTER(25) VARYING;
Z = TRANSLATE(A, UPPER, LOWER) ;
Z contains 'DoGCaT'

UNSPEC (arg)

The bit string which is the internal representation of arg.

VERIFY(arg, t)

The position in arg of the first character which does not occur in t. If all characters in arg occur in t, the value is zero.

DECLARE   A CHAR(5),
               B CHAR(9),
               Z FIXED;

Function	Value

A = 'DOGCAT' ;
B = 'CATDOGCOW' ;
Z = VERIFY (B, A) ;
Z contains 9, the location of 'W' which does not occur in A.

III. ARRAY FUNCTIONS

The arguments noted as <u>arg</u> to the following functions must be unsubscripted array names. The arguments noted as <u>n</u> must be integer expressions.

Function	Value
ALL(<u>arg</u>)	A bit string equal in length to the length of the greatest element of <u>arg</u>. If there is a 1 in the same bit position of every element, the corresponding bit position in the result contains 1. Otherwise, the corresponding bit position in the result contains 0. Example: A(1) = 5 ; A(2) = 3 ; Y = ALL(A) ; A(1) contains '101'B A(2) contains '011'B Y contains '001'B
ANY(<u>arg</u>)	A bit string equal in length to the length of the greatest element of <u>arg</u>. If there is a 1 in any bit position of any element, the corresponding bit position in the result contains 1. Otherwise, the corresponding bit position in the result contains 0. Example: A(1) = 5 ; A(2) = 3 ; Y = ANY(A) ; A(1) contains '101'B A(2) contains '011'B Y contains '111'B

Function	Value
DIM(arg, n)	The extent of the nth dimension of arg. Example: DECLARE A(5, 10, 20); Y = DIM(A, 2) ; Y contains 10.
EVERY(arg)	See ALL
HBOUND(arg, n)	The upper bound of the nth dimension of arg.
LBOUND(arg, n)	The lower bound of the nth dimension of arg. Example: DECLARE A(−1:10) ; DO I = LBOUNDA(A, 1) TO HBOUND(A, 1) ; means DO I = −1 TO 10;
PROD(arg)	The product of all the elements of arg. Example: DECLARE A(3) ; A(1) = 1 ; A(2)=5 ; A(3)=10 ; Y = PROD(A) ; Y contains 50.
SOME(arg)	See ANY
SUM(arg)	The sum of all the elements of arg. Example: DECLARE A(3) ; A(1)=1 ; A(2)=5 ; A(3)=10 ; Y = SUM(A) ; Y contains 16.

IV.   BASED STORAGE FUNCTIONS (not available in PL/C)

In the following descriptions:

arg   is any variable
ptr   is any pointer variable
off   is any offset variable
area   is the name of an area.

Function	Value
ADDR(arg)	The location in storage of arg. If arg has not been allocated, the value of ADDR is NULL (see below). Example: DECLARE X FLOAT; P POINTER; P = ADDR(X); P contains the location of X.
EMPTY	An area containing no allocations. The initial value of an allocated area is EMPTY. Example: area = EMPTY; IF area = EMPTY THEN . . .
NULL	The locator value signifying "nothing." Example: ptr = NULL;
OFFSET(ptr, area)	The offset value in area corresponding to ptr. Example: ALLOCATE X IN (A) SET (P); OFF = OFFSET(P,A);
POINTER(off, area)	The pointer value corresponding to off in area. Example: P = POINTER(O,A)−> LINK; means convert the offset O in area A to a pointer to the variable LINK. ALLOCATE X IN (A) SET (O); P = POINTER(O, A);

Function	Value
ALLOCATION(arg)	The number of generations of arg currently allocated. The value is zero if arg is not allocated. ALLOCATION is not included in some implementations, e.g. PL/C.

Example:
```
DECLARE X CONTROLLED ;
ALLOCATE X ;
IF ALLOCATION (X) THEN FREE X ;
```

Function	Value
DATE	Character string of the form YYMMDD:

YY = Year
MM = Month
DD = Day

Function	Value
ROUND(arg, p)	Arg rounded to the pth digit after the decimal point.
TIME	Character string of form HHMMSSTTT:

HH = Hours
MM = Minutes
SS = Seconds
TTT = Milliseconds

CONDITIONS

The classification of conditions into "initially enabled" and "initially disabled" classes holds for the IBM System/360–370 computers. Some conditions may fall into the other class when other computers are used.

A more complete and detailed list of conditions is given in PL/I Language Specifications, IBM Form Y33-6003.

I. INITIALLY ENABLED CONDITIONS

The following conditions are enabled initially. Some of them may be disabled by means of prefixes (see Chapter 9).

Condition	Description
AREA	Raises by the ALLOCATE statement if there is insufficient storage in an area to allocate a variable. Raised by assignment when the destination area is smaller than the source area. Standard action: raise the ERROR condition.
CONDITION(name)	Raised by a SIGNAL statement. Name is a programmer-defined condition. Standard action: comment and continue.

Condition	Description
CONVERSION	Raised when a character conversion is illegal or arithmetic value exceeds the width of the field. Raised internally or during I/O. Result is undefined. Standard action: raise the ERROR condition.
ENDFILE(filename)	Raised during a GET or READ statement when an attempt is made to read past an end of file. Standard action: raise the ERROR condition.
ENDPAGE(filename)	Raised when an attempt is made to write on the line beyond the maximum for the page. Standard action: start a new page.
ERROR	Raised by a SIGNAL statement, or as standard action for other conditions. Standard action: terminate the program.
FIXEDOVERFLOW	Raised when a fixed-point number exceeds the field width allowed for it. Result is undefined. Standard action: comment and continue.
KEY(filename)	Raised when a key is not found when reading a keyed record. Raised when trying to WRITE or LOCATE a key that already exists. Standard action: raise the ERROR condition.
NAME(filename)	Raised during a data-directed GET statement if an unrecognizable identifier is found. Standard action: comment and continue.
OVERFLOW	Raised when the exponent of a floating point number exceeds maximum. Result is undefined. Standard action: raise the ERROR condition.

Condition	Description
UNDERFLOW	Raised when the exponent of a floating point number is smaller than permitted minimum. Resulting value is zero. Standard action: comment and continue.
ZERODIVIDE	Raised when an attempt is made to divide by zero. Result is undefined. Standard action: raise the ERROR condition.

II. INITIALLY DISABLED CONDITIONS

The following conditions must be enabled by prefixes (see Chapter 9) before they will be raised.

Condition	Description
CHECK(list)	Raised when the value of a variable named in the list is changed, when a statement named in the list is executed, and when a procedure named in the list is called. Standard action: comment and continue.
SIZE	Raised during a conversion between different scales or bases or precision if high-order bits will be lost. Result is undefined. Standard action: raise the ERROR condition.
STRINGRANGE	Raised if the portion of a string extracted by the SUBSTR function does not lie completely within the source string. Standard action: For that portion of the substring which lies outside the source string a null string is returned. The null string is

Condition	Description

concatenated with that portion of the substring which lies within the source string.

Example:

DECLARE   S CHARACTER(4)
              INITIAL('TEST'),
              S1 CHARACTER(4);

S1 = SUBSTR(S, 3, 4) ;
S1 contains 'ST'

S1 = SUBSTR(S, 0, 3) ;
S1 contains 'TE'

STRINGSIZE

Raised when a longer string is assigned to a shorter one. The rightmost characters or bits are discarded. Standard action: comment and continue.

SUBSCRIPTRANGE

Raised when a subscript is outside the declared bounds. Result is undefined. Standard action: raise the ERROR condition.

PICTURE AND FORMAT SPECIFICATIONS

I. PICTURE CHARACTERS

Character	Meaning

9

The associated position contains a decimal digit.

Example: If A=51 and is edited with a picture of '999' it will appear as 051

V

The associated position contains decimal point scaling. It does not specify appearance of the point.

Example: If A=51.1 and is edited with a picture of '999V9' it will appear as 0511

K

The associated position indicates the beginning of the exponent.

Example: If A=53.1 and is edited with a picture of '999K99' it will appear as 53102

E

The associated position will contain the letter E indicating the beginning of the exponent.

Character	Meaning

Example: If A=53.1 and is edited with a picture of '999E99' it will appear as 531E02

.   The associated position will contain the character **.**

Example: If A=53.1 and is edited with a picture of '999V.9' it will appear as 053.1

Z   The associated position will be made blank if it contains a leading zero. Otherwise, it contains the digit.

Example: If A=53.1 and is edited with a picture of 'Z99V.99' it will appear as 53.10

B   The associated position will contain a blank.

Example: If A=53.1 and is edited with a picture of 'B999V.99' it will appear as 053.1

Y   The associated position will be made blank if it contains a zero, leading or otherwise.

−   The associated field will contain a minus sign if the number is negative and will be made blank otherwise. If there are two or more consecutive minus signs, the minus sign will drift.

Example: If A=−53.1 and is edited with a picture of '−9999V9' it will appear as −00531

If the picture is '− − − −9V9' it will appear as −531

+   The associated field will contain a plus sign if the number is positive and will be made blank otherwise. If there are two or more

Character	Meaning

consecutive plus signs, the plus sign will drift.

Example: If A=53.1 and is edited with a picture of '+9999V99' it will appear as +005310

If the picture is '+++99V9' it will appear as +531

S — The associated field will contain a plus sign or minus sign depending on the value of the number. If there are two or more consecutive "S" the sign will drift.

Example: If A=−5.2 and B=71 and they are edited with a picture of 'S999V.99' they will appear as −005.20 and +071.00 If they are edited with a picture of 'SS99V.9' they will appear as −05.2 and +71.0

$ — The associated position will contain a $. If there are two or more consecutive "$" the sign will drift.

Example: If A=106.75 and is edited with a picture of '$9999V.99' it will appear as $0106.75 If it is edited with a picture of '$$$99V.99' it will appear as $106.75

, — The associated position will contain a comma.

Example: If A=102791 and is edited with a picture of '999,999.' It will appear as 102,791.

CR — The associated two positions will contain the letters "CR" if the number is negative

Character	Meaning
	and two blanks otherwise. CR must appear to the right of all the digits.
	Example: If A=−5.35 and is edited with a picture of '$999V.99BCR' it will appear as $005.35 CR
DB	The same as for CR except that DB will appear.
A	The associated position may contain an alphabetic character or a blank.
	Example: If A='THE COMPUTER' and is edited with a picture of 'AAAAAAAAAAAA' it will appear as THE COMPUTER
X	The associated position may contain any alphabetic character, any digit, or a blank.
	Example: If A='THE COMPUTER' and B=663 and they are both edited with a picture of 'XXXXXXXXXXX' they will appear as THE COMPUTER and 663

II. FORMAT SPECIFICATIONS

Specification		Meaning
A or A(w)	Input:	Treat the next w characters as alphabetic (character string) data. W must be specified.
	Output:	Treat the corresponding data item as a

Specification	Meaning
	character string of length $\underline{w}$, extending it on the right with blanks or truncating from the right if necessary. If $\underline{w}$ is not specified it is taken as the current length of the item.
	Example: If X = 'CAT' and is edited with A or A(3) it will appear as CAT; edited with A(1) it will appear as C; and edited with A(5) it will appear as CATbb.
B or B($\underline{w}$)	Input: Read a bit string from the next $\underline{w}$-character field. The string need not fill the field. $\underline{W}$ must be specified.
	Output: Treat the corresponding data item as a bit string of length $\underline{w}$, extending it on the right with blanks or truncating from the right if necessary. If $\underline{w}$ is not specified it is taken as the current length of the item.
C($\underline{spec}$) or C($\underline{spec}$, $\underline{spec}$)	Input or Output: Read or write a complex numeric data item. Each $\underline{spec}$ is one of the specifications F, E, or P. If two specifications are used the first applies to the real part of the item; the second to the imaginary part. If only one specification is used it applies to both parts.
E($\underline{w}$, $\underline{d}$) or E($\underline{w}$, $\underline{d}$, $\underline{s}$)	Input: Read a floating-point number from the next $\underline{w}$-character field. The number need not fill the field. The rightmost $\underline{d}$ digits are assumed to follow the decimal point unless an explicit decimal point appears elsewhere in the field.
	Output: Write a floating-point number in the next $\underline{w}$-character field. $\underline{S}$ is the number of significant digits to be written; $\underline{d}$ is the number of digits to be written following the

Specification		Meaning

decimal point. The number is rounded to $\underline{d}$ digits following the decimal point. If $\underline{s}$ is omitted it is taken to be $\underline{d}+1$. W must be greater than $\underline{d}+5$. If $\underline{d} \leq 0$ the decimal point will not appear.

Example: If A=123.45 and is edited with E(10,4) it will appear as 1.2345E+02; edited with E(10,2,4) it will appear as 12.34E+01.

F($\underline{w}$) or
F($\underline{w}$, $\underline{d}$) or
F($\underline{w}$, $\underline{d}$, $\underline{p}$)

Input: Read a fixed-point number from the next $\underline{w}$-character field. The number need not fill the field. The rightmost $\underline{d}$ digits are assumed to follow the decimal point unless an explicit decimal point appears elsewhere in the field.

Output: Write a fixed-point number in the next $\underline{w}$-character field. If p is specified the number will be scaled by multiplying by 10^p before writing. If $\underline{p}$ and/or $\underline{d}$ are omitted they are assumed to be 0. If $\underline{d} \leq$ or is omitted the point will not appear. Otherwise, the number is rounded to $\underline{d}$ digits following the decimal point.

Example: If A = −1.23 and is edited with F(2) it will appear as −1; edited with F(3, 0) it will appear as −1.; edited with F(5,−1,3) it will appear as −1230

P'specs'

Input or Output

Specs comprise a string of picture characters as shown in Part I of this appendix.

Specification		Meaning
R(label)	Input or Output	Transfer the editing function to the FORMAT statement at label.
X($\underline{w}$)	Input:	Ignore the next $\underline{w}$ characters.
	Output:	Insert $\underline{w}$ blanks into the output stream.

ANSWERS TO EXERCISES

CHAPTER 1

1.1 The identifiers are

A_B	VARIABLE
TIME	S360
$_AMOUNT	X1Y2
IBM	

The non-identifiers are

A*B	ACCOUNT-NUMBER
PL/I	(TEMP)

1.2

Expression	PL/I Equivalent
x^3	X**3
$(x-1)(x+1)$	$(X-1)*(X+1)$
$x^2 + 2x + 1$	X**2 + 2*X + 1, or, preferably X*(X + 2) + 1
$\sqrt{a^2 + b^2}$	SQRT(A**2 + B**2)
$\dfrac{a + b + c}{3}$	(A + B + C)/3

1.3

```
EX1_3:    PROCEDURE OPTIONS (MAIN) ;

          /* SOLUTION TO EXERCISE 1.3 */

          DECLARE ( A, B, C ) FLOAT ;
          GET LIST( A, B ) ;
          C = SQRT ( A**2 + B**2 ) ;
          PUT LIST( A, B, C ) ;
     END EX1_3 ;
```

1.4

```
EX1_4:    PROCEDURE OPTIONS (MAIN) ;

          /* SOLUTION TO EXERCISE 1.4 */

          DECLARE ( GROSS, TAX, NET ) FLOAT ;
          GET LIST( GROSS ) ;
          TAX = 0.22*GROSS ;
          NET = GROSS - TAX ;
          PUT LIST( GROSS, TAX, NET ) ;
     END EX1_4 ;
```

1.5   The answers may differ because the fractions used cannot be exactly represented in the computer. Errors due to this fact are discussed more fully in Chapter 4.

1.6

```
EX1_6: PROCEDURE OPTIONS (MAIN) ;
       /* SOLUTION TO EXERCISE 1.6 */

       DECLARE (A, B, C, ROOT1, ROOT2) FLOAT ;
       GET LIST(A, B, C) ;

       ROOT1 = (-B + SQRT(B**2 - 4*A*C)) / (2*A) ;
       ROOT2 = (-B - SQRT(B**2 - 4*A*C)) / (2*A) ;

       PUT LIST(A, B, C, ROOT1, ROOT2) ;

    END EX1_6 ;
```

1.7

```
EX1_7: PROCEDURE OPTIONS (MAIN) ;
       /* SOLUTION TO EXERCISE 1.7 */
       DECLARE (P,I,N,RESULT) FLOAT ;

       GET LIST (P, I, N) ;
       RESULT = P*(1+I)**N ;
       PUT LIST  (RESULT) ;

END EX1_7 :
```

ANSWERS TO EXERCISES - CHAPTER 2

2.1   The use of the variable DISC makes it unnecessary to evaluate the expression $B^{**}2 - 4^*A^*C$ more than once, with the result that the program will execute faster. Also, the identifier DISC helps to clarify what the program is doing in the statements where roots are computed, i.e., computing the discriminant.

2.2

$$1) \quad R = 3$$
$$R = 2$$
$$R = 1$$
$$2) \quad R = 1$$
$$R = 2$$
$$R = 1$$

2.3

```
EX2_3:     PROCEDURE OPTIONS (MAIN) ;

           /* SOLUTION TO EXERCISE 2.3 */

           DECLARE ( S1, S2, S3,     /* SIDES OF TRIANGLE */
                     TYPE ) FLOAT ; /* RELATION OF SIDES */
START:     TYPE = 0 ;
           GET LIST( S1, S2, S3 ) ;

           /* S1, S2, AND S3 FORM A TRIANGLE IF EACH IS
           LESS THAN THE SUM OF THE OTHER TWO. IS THIS
           THE CASE -- */

           IF (S1+S2>S3) & ( S2+S3>S1) & (S1+S3>S2) THEN
              /* THEY FORM A TRIANGLE */
              TYPE = 1 ;

           ELSE  /* THIS COULD BE TERMINAL CASE */
                 IF S1+S2+S3=0 THEN GO TO STOP ;
                 ELSE GO TO PRINT ; /* NO TRIANGLE */

           /* IS TRIANGLE ISOSCELES -- */

           IF (S1=S2) | (S1=S3) | (S2=S3) THEN
              /* TRIANGLE IS ISOSCELES */
              TYPE = 2 ;

           /* IS TRIANGLE EQUILATERAL -- */

           IF (S1=S2) & (S1=S3) THEN
              /* TRIANGLE IS EQUILATERAL */
              TYPE = 3 ;

PRINT:     /* PRINT RESULTS */
           PUT LIST( S1, S2, S3, TYPE ) ;

           GO TO START ;
STOP:      END EX2_3 ;
```

2.4

```
EX2_4:     PROCEDURE OPTIONS (MAIN) ;

           /* SOLUTION TO EXERCISE 2.4 */

           DECLARE ( S1, S2, S3,    /* THE THREE SIDES */
                     LONG,          /* LONGEST SIDE */
                     TYPE ) FLOAT ; /* RELATION OF SIDES */

START:     TYPE = 0 ;
           GET LIST( S1, S2, S3 ) ;

           /* DO WE HAVE A TRIANGLE -- */

           IF (S1+S2>S3) & (S2+S3>S1) & (S1+S3>S2) THEN
              /* WE HAVE A TRIANGLE */
              TYPE = 1 ;

           ELSE   /* THIS COULD BE TERMINAL CASE */
                  IF S1+S2+S3=0 THEN GO TO STOP ;
                  ELSE GO TO PRINT ;

           /* IS TRIANGLE ISOSCELES -- */

           IF (S1=S2) | (S1=S3) | (S2=S3) THEN
              /* TRIANGLE IS ISOSCELES */
              TYPE = 2 ;

           /* IS IT A RIGHT TRIANGLE -- */

           /* FIND LONGEST SIDE */
           LONG = S1 ;
           IF S2>LONG THEN LONG = S2 ;
           IF S3>LONG THEN LONG = S3 ;

           /* SEE IF PYTHAGOREAN THEOREM HOLDS */
           IF (S1**2+S2**2+S3**2-LONG**2) =LONG**2 THEN
              /* IT DOES */
              DO ;
                 TYPE = TYPE + 3 ;
                 GO TO PRINT ; /* CAN'T BE EQUILATERAL */
              END ;

           /* IS TRIANGLE EQUILATERAL -- */

           IF (S1=S2) & (S1=S3) THEN
              /* TRIANGLE IS EQUILATERAL */
              TYPE = 3 ;

PRINT:     /* PRINT RESULTS */
           PUT LIST( S1, S2, S3, TYPE ) ;

           GO TO START ;
STOP:    END EX2_4 ;
```

2.5 Yes, A = B = C is a legal PL/I statement. It is an assignment statement; the variable A will receive the value 1 or 0 depending on whether B and C are or are not equal, respectively. The first = is thus an assignment operator, and the second = is a relational operator. The difference in meaning is determined from the context. The statement could perhaps be clarified by writing it as

$$A = (B=C) ;$$

ANSWERS TO EXERCISES - CHAPTER 3

3.1   A: −99999 to 99999 in steps of 1
       B: −99999 to 99999 in steps of 0.00001 to 1, depending on its value. There will always be five significant digits because the decimal·point "floats."
       C: −999.99 to 999.99 in steps of 0.01
       D: −7 to 7 in steps of 1. The largest magnitude expressible in three binary digits is 111, or 7 decimal.

3.2

Constant	Attributes	Notes
123	FIXED DECIMAL(3,0)	
'CAT'	CHARACTER(3)	
'''CAUSE'	CHARACTER(6)	The first character is a quote mark; the second through sixth are the letters.
−3.75	FIXED DECIMAL(3,2)	Neither the minus sign nor the decimal point counts as a digit.
0.03	FIXED DECIMAL(3,2)	The leading zero is significant to the precision of the number.
.03	FIXED DECIMAL(2,2)	

278

3.3 As a general rule, it is a good idea to organize IF statements so that the conditions most likely to be true are tested first. Testing a condition takes time; if the condition is not true, the time is wasted.

3.4 1, −2, 3, −4, 5, −6, 7, −8, 9, −10

ANSWERS TO EXERCISES - CHAPTER 4

4.1 The number of elements in an array is the product of the number of elements in each dimension. Hence, the array NAME(9, 0:9, 0:9, 0:9) has 9x10x10x10 = 9000 elements.

4.2 The sum of the elements in array A, i.e., SUM1 will be high by a factor of ten since each element of A is added into the sum ten times instead of just once, so the program is not correct. Because of the extra additions, the program is inefficient as well. The statement at S1 should be moved to follow the statement at L1. Such as:

```
EX4_2:  PROCEDURE OPTIONS (MAIN) ;
            /* SOLUTION TO EXERCISE 4.2
               EFFICIENT USE OF DO LOOPS. */

            DECLARE (A(10), B(10,10), I, J, SUM1, SUM2)
                                    FIXED ;

            GET LIST (A, B) ;

            SUM1, SUM2 = 0 ;
L1:         DO I = 1 BY 1 TO 10 ;
S1:            SUM1 = SUM1 + A(I) ;
L2:            DO J = 1 BY 1 TO 10 ;
S2:               SUM2 = SUM2 + B(I,J) ;
            END L2 ;
         END L1 ;

            PUT LIST (SUM1, SUM2) ;

         END EX4_2 ;
```

4.3

```
EX4_3:     PROCEDURE OPTIONS (MAIN) ;

           /* SOLUTION TO EXERCISE 4.3 -
              FIND LARGEST VALUE IN ARRAY */

           DECLARE  ( A(20), LARGE ) FIXED DECIMAL(5,2),
                      I  FIXED BINARY ;

START:     /* READ THE NUMBERS */
           GET LIST( A ) ;

           /* INITIALIZE 'LARGE' */
           LARGE = A(1) ;

           /* FIND LARGEST NUMBER */
           DO I = 2 BY 1 TO 20 ;
              IF A(I)>LARGE THEN LARGE = A(I) ;
           END ;

           /* PRINT RESULTS */
           PUT LIST( A, LARGE ) ;

           GO TO START;
        END EX4_3 ;
```

```
EX4_4:    PROCEDURE OPTIONS (MAIN) ;
            /* SOLUTION TO EXERCISE 4.4

              MATRIX MULTIPLICATION */

          DECLARE   ( A, B, C )(15,15) FLOAT,
                    ( I, J, K )          FIXED BINARY,
                    SUM   FLOAT ;

          /* READ VALUES FOR MATRICES 'A' AND 'B' */
          GET LIST( A, B ) ;

          /* FORM PRODUCT IN 'C' */

          DO I = 1 BY 1 TO 15 ;

            DO J = 1 BY 1 TO 15 ;

              SUM = 0 ;

              DO K = 1 BY 1 TO 15 ;

                SUM = SUM + A (I,K)*B (K,J) ;

              END

              C (I,J) = SUM ;

            END ·
          END ;

          /* PRINT RESULTS */
          PUT LIST( A, B, C ) ;
        END EX4_4 ;
```

```
EX4_5:      PROCEDURE OPTIONS (MAIN) ;

            /* SOLUTION TO EXERCISE 4.5 */

            DECLARE  LETTERS(15)       CHARACTER(1),
                     ( POSITION(0:15), I ) FIXED ;

START:      /* INITIALIZATION */
            POSITION = 0 ;
            /* READ CHARACTERS INTO 'LETTERS' */
            GET LIST( LETTERS ) ;

            /* SCAN FOR 'Q' */

            DO I = 1 BY 1 TO 15 ;
               IF LETTERS(I)='Q' THEN
                  DO ;
                     /* UPDATE COUNT OF 'Q'S */
                     POSITION(0) = POSITION(0) + 1 ;

                     /* ADD LATEST POSITION OF OCCURRENCE
                        TO NEXT ELEMENT OF LIST */
                     POSITION( POSITION(0) ) = I ;
                  END ;
            END ;

            /* PRINT RESULTS */
            PUT LIST( LETTERS, POSITION ) ;

            GO TO START ;
         END EX4_5 ;
```

```
EX4_6:    PROCEDURE OPTIONS (MAIN) ;

          /* SOLUTION TO EXERCISE 4.6 */

          DECLARE ( LETTERS(15), KEY ) CHARACTER(1),
                  ( POSITION(0:15), I ) FIXED ;

          /* INITIALIZATION */
START:    POSITION = 0 ;
          GET LIST( KEY ) ;

          /* READ CHARACTERS INTO 'LETTERS' */
          GET LIST( LETTERS ) ;

          /* SCAN FOR KEY */

          DO I = 1 BY 1 TO 15 ;
             IF LETTERS(I)=KEY THEN
                DO ;
                    /* UPDATE COUNT OF APPEARANCES
                       OF KEY CHARACTER */
                    POSITION(0) = POSITION(0) + 1 ;

                    /* RECORD THE POSITION OF ITS LATEST
                       APPEARANCE IN THE NEXT VACANT
                       ELEMENT OF 'POSITION' */
                    POSITION( POSITION(0) ) = I ;
                END ;
          END ;

          /* PRINT RESULTS */
          PUT LIST( KEY, LETTERS, POSITION ) ;

          GO TO START ;
       END EX4_6 ;
```

4.7

```
EX4_7:     PROCEDURE OPTIONS (MAIN) ;

               /* SOLUTION TO EXERCISE 4.7 */

               DECLARE  I FIXED,
                          ( A(10), TEMP ) FLOAT ;

START:         /* READ IN THE NUMBERS TO BE SORTED */
               GET LIST( A ) ;

               /* PRINT THE ORIGINAL LIST */
               PUT LIST( A ) ;

SORT:          /* SORT THE NUMBERS INTO ASCENDING ORDER */
               DO I = 2 BY 1 TO 10 ;
                  IF A(I-1)>A(I) THEN
                      DO ;
                          /* TRANSPOSE THE NUMBERS */
                          TEMP = A(I) ;
                          A(I) = A(I-1) ;
                          A(I-1) = TEMP ;
                          GO TO SORT ;
                      END ;
               END ;

               /* PRINT THE SORTED LIST */
               PUT LIST( A ) ;

               /* REVERSE THE ARRAY */
               DO I = 1 BY 1 TO 5 ;
                  TEMP= A(I) ;
                  A(I) = A(11-I) ;
                  A(11-I) = TEMP ;
               END ;

               /* PRINT THE NEW LIST */
               PUT LIST( A ) ;

               GO TO START ;
           END EX4_7 ;
```

```
EX4_8:     PROCEDURE OPTIONS (MAIN) ;

               /* SOLUTION TO EXERCISE 4.8 */

               DECLARE ( X, TX ) FLOAT ;

               DO X = -3 BY 0.5 TO 3 ;

                   /* ESTABLISH DENOMINATOR */
                   TX = X**2 - 1 ;

                   IF TX=0 THEN /* DO NOT DIVIDE */
                       PUT LIST( 'X = ', X,
                                   ' CAUSES DIVISION BY ZERO.' ) ;
                   ELSE PUT LIST( X, X/TX ) ;
               END ;
           END EX4_8 ;
```

4.9

```
EX4_9:    PROCEDURE OPTIONS (MAIN) ;

          /* SOLUTION TO EXERCISE 4.9 */

          DECLARE (KEYZIP (10),
                   ZIP)            CHARACTER (5),

                  (NAME(10,20),
                   ADDRESS(10,20),
                   NAM,
                   ADD)           CHARACTER (25) VARYING ;

          DECLARE IK (10)         FIXED INITIAL ((10) 0),
                  (I,J)           FIXED ;

                                  /* READ IN 10 KEY ZIP CODES */
          GET LIST (KEYZIP) ;

LOOP:     GET LIST (ZIP, NAM, ADD) ;
          IF ZIP = '00000' THEN GO TO PRINT ;  /* LAST ITEM */

          DO I = 1 TO 10 ;
             IF ZIP ¬= KEYZIP(I) THEN GO TO CHECK ;
             IF IK(I) = 20 THEN GO TO LOOP ;
             IK(I) = IK(I) + 1 ;
             NAME    (I,IK(I)) = NAM ;     /* SAVE NAME   */
             ADDRESS(I,IK(I)) = ADD ;      /* AND ADDRESS */
             GO TO LOOP ;
CHECK:    END ;
          GO TO LOOP ;

PRINT:    DO I = 1 TO 10 ;
             PUT LIST ('FOR ZIP CODE ', KEYZIP(I)) ;
             DO J = 1 TO IK(I) ;
                PUT LIST (NAME(I,J), ADDRESS(I,J)) ;
             END ;
          END ;

          END EX4_9 ;
```

4.10

```
EX4_10: PROCEDURE OPTIONS (MAIN);

  /* SOLUTION TO EXERCISE 4.10 */

  DECLARE (KEYZIP(10),ZIP) CHAR (5);

  DECLARE ( NAME(10,20),
            ADDRESS(10,20),
            NAM, ADD)  CHARACTER (25) VARYING ;

  DECLARE IK(10) FIXED INITIAL ((10)0) ;
  DECLARE (I,J) FIXED ;

  /* READ IN THE TEN KEY ZIP CODES */
  GET LIST (KEYZIP);

  /* READ THE SUBSCRIPTION LIST */
  GET LIST (ZIP,NAM,ADD) ;
  DO WHILE (ZIP ¬= '00000');
    DO I = 1 TO 10;
      IF ZIP = KEYZIP(I)
        THEN DO;
          J, IK(I) = IK(I) + 1;
          IF J > 20
            THEN PUT EDIT ('TABLE FULL FOR ZIP CODE ',
                ZIP) (A) ;
            ELSE DO;
              NAME(I,J) = NAM;
              ADDRESS(I,J) = ADD;
              END;
          I = 9999;  /* FORCE END OF DO-LOOP */
          END;
      END;
  GET LIST (ZIP,NAM,ADD);
  END;

  /* PRINT OUT A TABLE OF SUBSCRIBERS */
  DO I = 1 TO 10;
    PUT LIST ('FOR ZIP CODE',KEYZIP(I)) ;
    DO J = 1 TO IK(I);
      PUT LIST (NAME(I,J),ADDRESS(I,J)) ;
      END;
    END;

  END EX4_10 ;
```

4.11

```
EX4_11: PROCEDURE OPTIONS (MAIN);

  /* SOLUTION TO EXERCISE 4.11 */

  DECLARE (A(10), TEMP) FLOAT ;
  DECLARE (I, IMIN, J) FIXED ;

  /* READ IN THE NUMBERS TO BE SORTED */
  GET LIST (A);

  /* PRINT THE ORIGINAL LIST */
  PUT LIST (A) ;

  /* SORT THE NUMBERS INTO ASCENDING ORDER */
  DO I = 1 TO 9;
    TEMP = A(I);
    IMIN = I;
    DO J = I+1 TO 10;
      IF A(J) < TEMP
        THEN DO;
          TEMP = A(J);
          IMIN = J;
          END;
      END;
    TEMP = A(I);
    A(I) = A(IMIN);
    A(IMIN) = TEMP;
    END;

  /* PRINT THE SORTED LIST */
  PUT LIST (A) ;

  /* REVERSE THE ARRAY */
  DO I = 1 TO 5;
    TEMP = A(I);
    A(I) = A(11-I);
    A(11-I) = TEMP;
    END;

  /* PRINT THE NEW LIST */
  PUT LIST (A) ;

  END EX4_11 ;
```

5.1

```
EX5_1:    PROCEDURE OPTIONS (MAIN) ;

          /* SOLUTION TO EXERCISE 5.1 */

          DECLARE 1 JOB_ACCOUNT,
                  2 ACCOUNT_NUMBER   FIXED,
                  2 FUNDS            FIXED(8,2),
                  2 TIME,
                   3 COMPILE         FLOAT,
                   3 EXECUTE         FLOAT,
                  2 RATE             FIXED(5,2) ;

START:    GET LIST( JOB_ACCOUNT ) ;
          FUNDS = FUNDS - RATE*(EXECUTE + 0.5*COMPILE) ;

          PUT LIST( JOB_ACCOUNT ) ;

          GO TO START ;
          END EX5_1 ;
```

5.2   A.S.T will be assigned the value of B.S.T . In order to modify A.V.W
      the statement must be A.V = B, BY NAME ;

```
EX5_3:     PROCEDURE OPTIONS (MAIN) ;

           /* SOLUTION TO EXERCISE 5.3 */

           DECLARE 1 BOOKS,
                   2 FICTION,
                   (3 NOVELS(275),
                    3 SHORT_STORIES(200)) CHARACTER(10),
                   2 NON_FICTION,
                   (3 BIOGRAPHY(125),
                    3 DOCUMENTARY(70),
                    3 GEN_REFERENCE(100)) CHARACTER(10) ;

           DECLARE TITLE CHARACTER(20) ;

START:     GET LIST( TITLE ) ;

           IF TITLE='FICTION' THEN
              PUT LIST( FICTION ) ;
           ELSE
           IF TITLE='NONFICTION' THEN
              PUT LIST( NON_FICTION ) ;
           ELSE
           IF TITLE='NOVELS' THEN
              PUT LIST( NOVELS ) ;
           ELSE
           IF TITLE='SHORT STORIES' THEN
              PUT LIST( SHORT_STORIES ) ;
           ELSE
           IF TITLE='BIOGRAPHY' THEN
              PUT LIST( BIOGRAPHY ) ;
           ELSE
           IF TITLE='DOCUMENTARY' THEN
              PUT LIST( DOCUMENTARY ) ;
           ELSE
           IF TITLE='REFERENCE' THEN
              PUT LIST( GEN_REFERENCE ) ;
           GO TO START ;

       END EX5_3 ;
```

5.4

```
EX5_4: PROCEDURE OPTIONS (MAIN);

  /* SOLUTION TO EXERCISE 5.4 */

  DECLARE 1 SUBSCRIPTION,
            2 ZIP CHARACTER (5),
            2 PERSON,
             (3 NAME,
              3 ADDRESS) CHARACTER (25) VARYING;

  DECLARE 1 MAGAZINE (10),
            2 ZIP CHARACTER (5),
            2 PERSON (20),
             (3 NAME,
              3 ADDRESS) CHARACTER (25) VARYING,
            2 POINTER FIXED INITIAL ((10) 0);

  DECLARE (I, J) FIXED ;

  /* READ IN THE 10 KEY ZIP CODES */
  GET LIST (MAGAZINE.ZIP);

  /* READ IN THE SUBSCRIPTION LIST */
  GET LIST (SUBSCRIPTION) ;
  DO WHILE (SUBSCRIPTION.ZIP ¬= '00000');
    DO I = 1 TO 10;
      IF SUBSCRIPTION.ZIP = MAGAZINE.ZIP(I)
        THEN DO;
          J, POINTER(I) = POINTER(I) + 1;
          IF J > 20
            THEN PUT LIST ('TABLE FULL FOR ZIP CODE',
                   MAGAZINE.ZIP(I)) ;
            ELSE DO;
              MAGAZINE(I).PERSON(J) = SUBSCRIPTION.PERSON;
              I = 9999;     /* FORCE DO-LOOP TO END */
              END;
          END;
      END;
    GET LIST (SUBSCRIPTION);
    END;

  /* PRINT OUT MAGAZINE LIST */
  DO I = 1 TO 10;
    PUT LIST ('FOR ZIP CODE',MAGAZINE.ZIP(I)) ;
    DO J = 1 TO POINTER(I) ;
      PUT LIST (MAGAZINE(I).PERSON(J)) ;
      END;
    END;
  END EX5_4;
```

6.1 The ways in which a value can be assigned to a character string variable are

1. By direct assignment (assignment statement)
2. By the INITIAL attribute
3. By a GET statement
4. By a PUT statement with the STRING option

6.2

```
EX6_2:     PROCEDURE OPTIONS (MAIN) ;

               /* SOLUTION TO EXERCISE 6.2 */

               DECLARE (TYPE, SIDE1, SIDE2, SIDE3) FLOAT ;

START:         GET LIST(SIDE1, SIDE2, SIDE3) ;
               IF SIDE1=0 THEN GO TO DONE ;

               /* ASSUME TRIANGLE IS NEITHER ISOSCELES NOR
                  EQUILATERAL. */
               TYPE = 0 ;

               /* SET TYPE TO 1 IF NECESSARY. */
               IF (SIDE1=SIDE2) |
                  (SIDE1=SIDE3) |
                  (SIDE2=SIDE3)
                  THEN TYPE = 1 ;

               /* PRINT DATA AND RESULTS */
               PUT DATA(SIDE1, SIDE2, SIDE3, TYPE) ;
               GO TO START ; /* PROCESS NEXT CASE. */
DONE:      END EX6_2 ;
```

6.3 Data-directed input would be awkward in Example No. 23 because the data items on the input file must be fully qualified. This requirement would make the data extremely difficult to prepare. There would be no particular disadvantage to using data-directed output.

6.4 Data-directed output would be particularly useful in Example No. 14, because the output would be easily readable, e.g.,

$$NAME(1,2,3,4) = JOHN JONES$$

which indicates quite clearly that the name John Jones is associated with extension 1234. The results might be further clarified if the array had been named EXTENSION instead of NAME.

6.5

```
EX6_5:     PROCEDURE OPTIONS (MAIN) ;

           /* SOLUTION TO EXERCISE 6.5 */

           DECLARE   A1(10)    FIXED(10),
                     A2(10)    FLOAT(5),
                     KEY       CHARACTER(1),
                     I         FIXED ;

START:     /* READ THE FIRST CHARACTER */
           GET EDIT( KEY ) ( A(1) ) COPY ;

START2:    IF KEY='A' THEN
               GET EDIT( (A1(I)  DO I = 2,4,6,8,10) )
                       ( 5 F(10) ) COPY ;
           ELSE IF KEY='B' THEN
               GET EDIT( A1 ) ( 10 F(5) ) COPY ;

           ELSE IF KEY='C' THEN
               GET EDIT( A2 ) ( 10 F(5,2) ) COPY ;

           ELSE IF KEY='D' THEN
               DO ;
                   GET EDIT( KEY ) ( X(50), A(1) ) COPY ;
                   GO TO START2 ;
               END ;

           ELSE IF KEY='E' THEN GO TO STOP ;
           GO TO START ;

STOP:    END EX6_5 ;
```

6.6 Three lines will be printed: the value of X will appear on the first; SKIP(2) causes a double-space; the format repeats in order to print the value of Y (on the third line). At this point the list is exhausted and transmission stops and the SKIP(2) phrase is not encountered and therefore has no effect.

6.7

```
EX6_7: PROCEDURE OPTIONS (MAIN);

/* SOLUTION TO EXERCISE 6.7 */

DCL (DAY_OF_WEEK,#DAYS_IN_MONTH,I,J,K) FIXED;
DCL CALANDER (42) FIXED;

GET LIST (DAY_OF_WEEK,#DAYS_IN_MONTH);
IF DAY_OF_WEEK>=1 & DAY_OF_WEEK<=7
   & #DAYS_IN_MONTH>=28 & #DAYS_IN_MONTH<=31
  THEN DO;
    CALANDER = 0;   /* INITIALIZE TO ZERO'S */
    J = 0;
    DO I = DAY_OF_WEEK TO DAY_OF_WEEK+#DAYS_IN_MONTH-1;
      CALANDER(I),J = J + 1;
      END;

    /* PRINT THE CALANDER FOR THIS MONTH */
    DO I = 0 TO 5;    /* WEEK OF MONTH */
      PUT SKIP;
      DO J = 1 TO 7;    /* DAY OF WEEK */
        K = CALANDER(7*I+J);
        IF K>0
          THEN PUT EDIT (K) (X(2),F(2));
          ELSE PUT EDIT ('   ') (A);
        END;
      END;
    END;
  ELSE DO;
    PUT EDIT ('INPUT DATA OUT OF RANGE') (A) SKIP;
    PUT DATA (DAY_OF_WEEK,#DAYS_IN_MONTH) SKIP;
    END;
END EX6_7 ;
```

```
EX6_8: PROCEDURE OPTIONS (MAIN);

  /* SOLUTION TO EXERCISE 6.8 */

  /* THIS PROGRAM READS IN A NUMBER CORRESPONDING TO
     THE DAY OF THE WEEK THAT NEW YEAR'S DAY FALLS ON
     (WHERE 1 = SUNDAY).  USING THIS INFORMATION, THE
     PROGRAM PRINTS OUT A CALANDER FOR THE YEAR. */

  DCL (MOD,LENGTH) BUILTIN;

  DCL #DAYS_IN_MONTH (0:12) BINARY FIXED
      INITIAL (0,31,28,31,30,31,30,31,31,30,31,30,31);

  DCL MONTH (12) CHAR (9) VAR INIT ('JANUARY','FEBRUARY',
      'MARCH','APRIL','MAY','JUNE','JULY','AUGUST',
      'SEPTEMBER','OCTOBER','NOVEMBER','DECEMBER');

  DCL (IMONTH,DAY_OF_WEEK,I,J,K) BINARY FIXED;
  DCL CALANDER (42) BINARY FIXED;

  GET LIST (DAY_OF_WEEK);

  IF DAY_OF_WEEK>=1 & DAY_OF_WEEK<=7
    THEN DO IMONTH = 1 TO 12;    /* MONTH OF YEAR */
      DAY_OF_WEEK = DAY_OF_WEEK + #DAYS_IN_MONTH(IMONTH-1);
      DAY_OF_WEEK = MOD(DAY_OF_WEEK,7);
      IF DAY_OF_WEEK = 0
        THEN DAY_OF_WEEK = 7;

    CALANDER = 0;    /* INITIALIZE TO ZERO'S */
    J = 0;

    DO I = DAY_OF_WEEK TO DAY_OF_WEEK
       + #DAYS_IN_MONTH(IMONTH) - 1;
      CALANDER(I),J = J + 1;
      END;

    /* PRINT THE CALANDER FOR THIS MONTH */

    I = 15 - (LENGTH(MONTH(IMONTH))/2);
    PUT EDIT (MONTH(IMONTH)) (X(I),A) SKIP (3);
    DO I = 0 TO 5;     /* WEEK OF MONTH */
      PUT SKIP;
      DO J = 1 TO 7;    /* DAY OF WEEK */
        K = CALANDER(7*I+J);
        IF K>0
          THEN PUT EDIT (K) (X(2),F(2));
          ELSE PUT EDIT ('   ') (A);
        END;
      END;
    END;
```

295

```
         END;
    ELSE DO;
       PUT EDIT ('INPUT DATA OUT OF RANGE') (A) SKIP;
       PUT DATA (DAY_OF_WEEK) SKIP;
       END;
END EX6_8;


6.9


EX6_9: PROCEDURE OPTIONS(MAIN) ;

       /* SOLUTION OT EXERCISE 6.9   */

       DECLARE #DAYS (12) FIXED
                    INITIAL(31,28,31,30,31,30,31,31,
                             30,31,30,31) ;
       DECLARE FRIDAY13 FIXED INITIAL(0) ;
       DECLARE (I,DAY) FIXED ;

       GET LIST (DAY);       /* STARTING DAY FOR YEAR */
       IF DAY >=1 & DAY <= 7
          THEN DO ;
             DO I = 1 TO 12 ;
               IF DAY=1 THEN FRIDAY13=FRIDAY13+1 ;
               DAY =  MOD(#DAYS(I) +DAY,7) ;
             END ;
             PUT LIST (' # FRIDAY 13THS IN YEAR  = ',
                        FRIDAY13) ;
             END ;
          ELSE PUT LIST ('STARTING DAY IS OUT OF RANGE')
    END EX6_9 ;
```

7.2   (Includes solution to 7.1)

```
EX7_1:    PROCEDURE OPTIONS (MAIN) ;

          /* SOLUTION TO EXERCISE 7.1 */


MMULT:    PROCEDURE ( A, B, C ) ;

          DECLARE   ( A, B, C ) (15,15) FLOAT,
                    ( I, J, K ) FIXED BINARY,
                    SUM FLOAT ;

          DO I = 1 TO 15 ;
             DO J = 1 TO 15 ;

                SUM = 0 ;

                DO K = 1 TO 15 ;
                   SUM = SUM + A(I,K)*B(K,J) ;
                END ;

                C(I,J) = SUM ;

             END ;
          END ;

          RETURN ;

       END MMULT ;

          DECLARE   ( X, Y, Z ) (15,15) FLOAT ;
          DECLARE MMULT ENTRY( (*,*)FLOAT, (*,*)FLOAT,
                               (*,*)FLOAT ) ;

START:    GET LIST( X, Y ) ;
          CALL MMULT( X, Y, Z ) ;
          PUT EDIT( ((X(I,J) DO J = 1 TO 15) DO I = 1 TO 15) )
                  (PAGE, 15( 15 F(15,6), SKIP) )
                 ( ((Y(I,J) DO J = 1 TO 15) DO I = 1 TO 15) )
                  (PAGE, 15( 15 F(15,6), SKIP) )
                 ( ((Z(I,J) DO J = 1 TO 15) DO I = 1 TO 15) )
                  (PAGE, 15( 15 F(15,6), SKIP) ) ;

          GO TO START ;

       END EX7_1 ;
```

7.3 The non-recursive function shown below with a driver program is much more efficient than the recursive function shown on page 163, because it will execute much faster; for each multiplication in the following function, the recursive function uses one multiplication and one procedure call.

```
EX7_3:    PROCEDURE OPTIONS (MAIN) ;

              /* SOLUTION TO EXERCISE 7.3 */


FACT: PROCEDURE( N ) RETURNS( FIXED ) ;

              /* SOLUTION TO EXERCISE 7.3 -
                 NON-RECURSIVE FACTORIAL */

          DECLARE ( N, I, F ) FIXED ;

          F = 1 ;

          DO I = 2 TO N ;
             F = F*I ;
          END ;

          RETURN( F ) ;

      END FACT ;


          DECLARE FACT ENTRY( FIXED )  RETURNS( FIXED ) ;

          DO I = 1 TO 6 ;
             PUT SKIP LIST( FACT(I) ) ;
          END ;

      END EX7_3 ;
```

```
EX7_4:     PROCEDURE OPTIONS (MAIN) ;

           /* SOLUTION TO EXERCISE 7.4 */


POLY: PROCEDURE( A, N, X ) RETURNS( FLOAT ) ;

           DECLARE   A(0:20) FLOAT, /* COEFFICIENTS */
                     N FIXED, /* DEGREE OF POLYNOMIAL */
                     X FLOAT,  /* VALUE OF VARIABLE */
                     I FIXED,

                     ( VAL,        /* EVALUATED POLYNOMIAL */
                       TX ) FLOAT ;

           VAL = A(0) ; /* INITIALIZE VALUE */
           TX = 1 ;      /* 'TX' AVOIDS EXPONENTIATION */

           DO I = 1 TO N ;

              TX = TX*X ; /* NEXT POWER OF X   */

              /* ADD NEXT TERM */
              VAL = VAL + A(I)*TX ;

           END ;

           RETURN( VAL ) ;

        END POLY ;


               DECLARE   ( X(0:20), Y ) FLOAT,
                         ( N, I ) FIXED ;

               DECLARE   POLY ENTRY( (*)FLOAT, FIXED, FLOAT )
                         RETURNS( FLOAT ) ;

START:         GET LIST( N, (X(I) DO I = 0 TO N) ) COPY ;

               DO Y = 0 BY .1 TO 1 ;
                  PUT EDIT( POLY( X, N, Y ) )
                          ( SKIP(2), E(16,8) ) ;
               END ;

               GO TO START ;

            END EX7_4 ;
```

299

7.5

```
EX7_5:   PROCEDURE OPTIONS (MAIN) ;

           /* SOLUTION TO EXERCISE 7.5 */


SORT: PROCEDURE( RECORD ) ;

           /* SORT DATA RECORDS IN AN
              ARRAY OF STRUCTURES. */

           DECLARE 1 RECORD(100),
                     2 NAME,
                     (3 LAST,
                      3 FIRST) CHARACTER(12),
                      3 MIDDLE CHARACTER(2),
                     2 NUMBER  FIXED,
                         /* 'NUMBER' IS THE SORT KEY */
                     (2 OLD_BAL,
                      2 SER_CHG,
                      2 NEW_BAL) FLOAT,

                     1 TEMP, /* TEMP STORAGE FOR SORT */
                      2 T1,
                      (3 T2,
                       3 T3) CHARACTER(12),
                       3 T4  CHARACTER(2),
                      2 T5    FIXED,
                      (2 T6,
                       2 T7,
                       2 T8)   FLOAT,
                      (I, K) FIXED ;

               DO K = 100 BY -1 TO 2 ;
                  DO I = 2 BY 1 TO K ;
                     IF NUMBER(I)<NUMBER(I-1) THEN
                        DO ;

                           /* TRANSPOSE RECORDS */
                           TEMP = RECORD(I) ;
                           RECORD(I) = RECORD(I-1) ;
                           RECORD(I-1) = TEMP ;

                        END ;
                  END ;
               END ;
               RETURN ;
```

```
END SORT ;

        DECLARE   1 ACCOUNT(100),
                  2 NAME,
                  (3 LAST,
                   3 FIRST) CHARACTER(12),
                   3 MID    CHARACTER(2),
                  2 NO       FIXED,
                  (2 OLD,
                   2 SER,
                   2 NEW)    FLOAT ;

    GET LIST( ACCOUNT ) ;

    CALL SORT( ACCOUNT ) ;

    PUT PAGE ;
    DO I = 1 TO 100 ;
        PUT SKIP LIST( NO(I), LAST(I), OLD(I),
                       SER(I), NEW(I) ) ;
    END ;

END EX7_5 ;
```

7.6

```
EX7_6: PROCEDURE OPTIONS (MAIN);

/* SOLUTION TO EXERCISE 7.6 */

DCL (INPUT_1,INPUT_2) FIXED;

GET LIST (INPUT_1,INPUT_2);
CALL PRINT_MONTH(INPUT_1,INPUT_2);


PRINT_MONTH: PROCEDURE (DAY_OF_WEEK,#DAYS_IN_MONTH);

  DCL (DAY_OF_WEEK,#DAYS_IN_MONTH,I,J,K) FIXED;
  DCL CALANDER (42) FIXED;

  IF DAY_OF_WEEK>=1 & DAY_OF_WEEK<=7
     & #DAYS_IN_MONTH>=28 & #DAYS_IN_MONTH<=31
    THEN DO;
      CALANDER = 0;   /* INITIALIZE TO ZERO'S */
      J = 0;
      DO I = DAY_OF_WEEK TO DAY_OF_WEEK+#DAYS_IN_MONTH-1;
        CALANDER(I),J = J + 1;
        END;

      /* PRINT THE CALANDER FOR THIS MONTH */
      DO I = 0 TO 5;    /* WEEK OF MONTH */
        PUT SKIP;
        DO J = 1 TO 7;    /* DAY OF WEEK */
          K = CALANDER(7*I+J);
          IF K>0
            THEN PUT EDIT (K)  (X(2),F(2));
            ELSE PUT EDIT ('    ') (A);
          END;
        END;
      END;
    ELSE DO;
      PUT EDIT ('INPUT DATA OUT OF RANGE') (A) SKIP;
      PUT DATA (DAY_OF_WEEK,#DAYS_IN_MONTH) SKIP;
      END;
  END PRINT_MONTH;


  END EX7_6 ;
```

```
EX7_7: PROCEDURE OPTIONS (MAIN);

/* SOLUTION TO EXERCISE 7.7 */

/* THIS PROGRAM READS IN A NUMBER CORRESPONDING TO
   THE DAY OF THE WEEK THAT NEW YEAR'S DAY FALLS ON
   (WHERE 1 = SUNDAY).  USING THIS INFORMATION, THE
   PROGRAM PRINTS OUT A CALANDER FOR THE YEAR. */

DCL (MOD,LENGTH) BUILTIN;
DCL #DAYS_IN_MONTH (0:12) FIXED
    INITIAL (0,31,28,31,30,31,30,31,31,30,31,30,31);
DCL MONTH (12) CHAR (9) VAR INIT ('JANUARY','FEBRUARY',
    'MARCH','APRIL','MAY','JUNE','JULY','AUGUST',
    'SEPTEMBER','OCTOBER','NOVEMBER','DECEMBER');
DCL (IMONTH,DAY_OF_WEEK,I) FIXED;

GET LIST (DAY_OF_WEEK);
DO IMONTH = 1 TO 12;     /* MONTH OF YEAR */
   DAY_OF_WEEK = DAY_OF_WEEK + #DAYS_IN_MONTH(IMONTH-1);
   DAY_OF_WEEK = MOD(DAY_OF_WEEK,7);
   IF DAY_OF_WEEK = 0
     THEN DAY_OF_WEEK = 7;

   /* PRINT THE CALANDER FOR THIS MONTH */
   I = 15 - (LENGTH(MONTH(IMONTH))/2);
   PUT EDIT (MONTH(IMONTH)) (X(I),A) SKIP (3);
   CALL PRINT_MONTH(DAY_OF_WEEK,#DAYS_IN_MONTH(IMONTH));
   END;

PRINT_MONTH: PROCEDURE (DAY_OF_WEEK,#DAYS_IN_MONTH);

   DCL (DAY_OF_WEEK,#DAYS_IN_MONTH,I,J,K) FIXED;
   DCL CALANDER (42) FIXED;

   IF DAY_OF_WEEK>=1 & DAY_OF_WEEK<=7
      & #DAYS_IN_MONTH>=28 & #DAYS_IN_MONTH<=31
     THEN DO;
       CALANDER = 0;    /* INITIALIZE TO ZERO'S */
       J = 0;
       DO I = DAY_OF_WEEK TO DAY_OF_WEEK+#DAYS_IN_MONTH-1;
         CALANDER(I),J = J + 1;
         END;
```

```
       /* PRINT THE CALANDER FOR THIS MONTH */
       DO I = 0 TO 5;      /* WEEK OF MONTH */
         PUT SKIP;
         DO J = 1 TO 7;      /* DAY OF WEEK */
           K = CALANDER(7*I+J);
           IF K>0
             THEN PUT EDIT (K) (X(2),F(2));
             ELSE PUT EDIT ('    ') (A);
           END;
         END;
       END;
     ELSE DO;
       PUT EDIT ('INPUT DATA OUT OF RANGE') (A) SKIP;
       PUT DATA (DAY_OF_WEEK,#DAYS_IN_MONTH) SKIP;
       END;
  END PRINT_MONTH;


  END EX7_7 ;


7.8


EX7_8: PROCEDURE (DAY_OF_WEEK)  RETURNS(FIXED) ;

/* SOLUTION TO EXERCISE 7.8 */

/* A MONTH CONTAINS A FRIDAY THE THIRTEENTH IF
   (AND ONLY IF) THE MONTH STARTS ON A SUNDAY. */

DCL MOD BUILTIN;
DCL #DAYS_IN_MONTH (0:12) FIXED
    INITIAL (0,31,28,31,30,31,30,31,31,30,31,30,31);
DCL (IMONTH,DAY_OF_WEEK) FIXED;
DCL K13 FIXED INITIAL (0); /* FRIDAY THE 13TH COUNTER */


DO IMONTH = 1 TO 12;     /* MONTH OF YEAR */
  DAY_OF_WEEK = DAY_OF_WEEK + #DAYS_IN_MONTH(IMONTH-1);
  DAY_OF_WEEK = MOD(DAY_OF_WEEK,7);
  IF DAY_OF_WEEK = 0
    THEN DAY_OF_WEEK = 7;
    ELSE IF DAY_OF_WEEK = 1 /* MONTH STARTS ON SUNDAY */
      THEN K13 = K13 + 1;    /* INCREMENT COUNTER */
  END;

  RETURN (K13) ;

END EX7_8 ;
```

8.1

```
EX 8_1:    PROCEDURE OPTIONS (MAIN) ;
           /* SOLUTION TO EXERCISE 8.1 */


MMULT:     PROCEDURE( A, B, C, N ) ;

           DECLARE   ( A, B, C ) (N,N) FLOAT,
                     ( I, J, K, N ) FIXED,
                     SUM FLOAT ;

           DO I = 1 TO N ;
             DO J = 1 TO N ;

               SUM = 0 ;

               DO K = 1 TO N ;
                  SUM = SUM +  A(I,K)*B(K,J) ;
               END ;

               C(I,J) = SUM ;

             END ;

           END ;

         END MMULT ;

           DECLARE MMULT ENTRY( (*,*) FLOAT, (*,*) FLOAT,
                                (*,*) FLOAT, FIXED) ;

           DECLARE N FIXED ;

START:     GET LIST (N) ;

B:         BEGIN ;

               DECLARE ( X, Y, Z ) (N,N) FLOAT ;

               GET LIST( X, Y ) ;

               CALL MMULT ( X, Y, Z, N ) ;
```

```
PUT EDIT( ((X(I,J) DO J = 1 TO N) DO I = 1 TO N) )
         (PAGE, (N) ( (N) E(15,6), SKIP) )
       ( ((Y(I,J) DO J = 1 TO N) DO I = 1 TO N) )
         (PAGE, (N) ( (N) E(15,6), SKIP) )
       ( ((Z(I,J) DO J = 1 TO N) DO I = 1 TO N) )
         (PAGE, (N) ( (N) E(15,6), SKIP) ) ;

END ;

GO TO START ;

END EX8_1 ;
```

ANSWERS TO EXERCISES - CHAPTER 9

9.1   In P1, the effective on-unit for OVERFLOW at the time the
statement at X is executed is GO TO Z. The first on-unit, GO TO
Y, is overridden by the second one, GO TO Z, in the outer block.
The on-unit in the BEGIN block is stacked on the latter unit; the
first REVERT statement re-establishes GO TO Z. The second
REVERT statement has no effect: only those conditions enabled
within a block may be REVERTed within that block.

In P2, the effective on-unit for OVERFLOW at the time the
statement at X is executed is GO TO Y. The on-unit established in
the BEGIN block is active only while execution is in the block.

9.2

```
EX9_2: PROCEDURE OPTIONS (MAIN);

  /* SOLUTION TO EXERCISE 9.2 */

  DECLARE (KEYZIP(10),ZIP) CHAR (5);

  DCL (NAME(10,20),ADDRESS(10,20),NAM,ADD) CHAR (25) VAR;

  DCL IK(10) FIXED INITIAL ((10)0);
  DCL (I,J) FIXED;

  ON ENDFILE (SYSIN)
    BEGIN;
      /* PRINT OUT A TABLE OF SUBSCRIBERS */

      DO I = 1 TO 10;
        PUT LIST ('FOR ZIP CODE',KEYZIP(I)) SKIP (3);
        PUT SKIP;
        DO J = 1 TO IK(I);
          PUT LIST (NAME(I,J),ADDRESS(I,J)) SKIP;
          END;
        END;
      STOP;
      END;

  /* READ IN THE TEN KEY ZIP CODES */
  GET LIST (KEYZIP);

  /* READ THE SUBSCRIPTION LIST */
  DO WHILE ('1'B);
    GET LIST (ZIP,NAM,ADD);
    DO I = 1 TO 10;
      IF ZIP = KEYZIP(I)
        THEN DO;
          J, IK(I) = IK(I) + 1;
          IF J > 20
            THEN PUT EDIT ('TABLE FULL FOR ZIP CODE ',
                ZIP) (A) SKIP;
            ELSE DO;
              NAME(I,J) = NAM;
              ADDRESS(I,J) = ADD;
              END;
          I = 9999;   /* FORCE END OF DO-LOOP */
          END;
      END;
    END;

  END EX9_2;
```

10.1

```
EX 10_1:   PROCEDURE OPTIONS (MAIN) ;

           /* SOLUTION TO EXERCISE 10.1 -
              REVERSE A CHARACTER STRING */

           DECLARE   STRING      CHARACTER(20) VARYING,
                     TEMP        CHARACTER(1),
                     ( I, CHARS ) FIXED ;

START:     /* READ STRING */
           GET LIST( STRING ) ;

           /* PRINT INPUT STRING */
           PUT SKIP(2) LIST( STRING ) ;

           /* REVERSE THE STRING */

           CHARS = LENGTH( STRING ) ;

           DO I = CHARS/2 BY -1 TO 1 ;

              TEMP = SUBSTR( STRING,I,1 ) ;

              SUBSTR( STRING,I,1 ) =
                  SUBSTR( STRING,CHARS+1-I,1 ) ;

              SUBSTR( STRING,CHARS+1-I,1 ) = TEMP ;

           END ;

           /* PRINT RESULTS */
           PUT SKIP LIST( STRING ) ;

           GO TO START ;
       END EX10_1 ;
```

10.2

```
EX10_2:    PROCEDURE OPTIONS (MAIN) ;

           /* SOLUTION TO EXERCISE 10.2 -
              PRINT FIRST NONBLANK CHARACTER */

           DECLARE   STRING   CHARACTER(100) VARYING,
                     I         FIXED ;

START:     /* READ STRING */
           GET LIST( STRING ) ;

           /* FIND FIRST NONBLANK CHARACTER */
           DO I = 1 BY 1 TO LENGTH (STRING)
                WHILE( SUBSTR ( STRING,I,1 ) = ' ' )
           END ;
           IF I > LENGTH (STRING) THEN GO TO START ;

           /* PRINT ORIGINAL STRING AND RESULTS */
           PUT SKIP LIST( STRING ) ;
           PUT SKIP LIST( SUBSTR ( STRING,I,1 ) ) ;

           GO TO START ;
        END EX10_2 ;
```

10.3

```
EX 10_3:   PROCEDURE OPTIONS (MAIN) ;

           /* SOLUTION TO EXERCISE 10.3 -
              DELETE BLANKS FROM A STRING */

           DECLARE   TEXT   CHARACTER (200) VARYING,
                     POS    FIXED ;

           ON ENDFILE (SYSIN) GO TO EOJ ;

START:     /* READ STRING */
           GET LIST ( TEXT ) COPY ;

           /* DELETE BLANKS */

           POS = INDEX( TEXT,' ' ) ;

           DO WHILE ( (POS¬=0) ) ;

              IF POS >= LENGTH (TEXT)
                 THEN DO ;
                      TEXT = SUBSTR( TEXT,1,POS-1 ) ;
                      GO TO PRINT ;
                      END ;

              TEXT = SUBSTR( TEXT,1,POS-1 ) ||
                     SUBSTR( TEXT, POS+1 ) ;


              POS = INDEX( TEXT,' ' ) ;

           END ;

           /* PRINT RESULTS */
PRINT:     PUT LIST( TEXT ) ;

           GO TO START ;
EOJ:       END EX10_3 ;
```

10.4

```
EX10_4: PROCEDURE OPTIONS (MAIN);

  /* SOLUTION TO EXERCISE 10.4 */

  DCL (LENGTH,SUBSTR,INDEX,MAX,MIN) BUILTIN;
  DECLARE (TEXT,WORD) CHARACTER (200) VARYING;
  DCL P FIXED;

  /* READ STRING */
  GET LIST (TEXT) COPY;

DO WHILE (LENGTH(TEXT) > 0);
  /* GET THE FIRST (OR NEXT) WORD */
  DO P = 1 TO LENGTH(TEXT)
      WHILE (INDEX('.,; ',SUBSTR(TEXT,P,1))=0);
    END;
  P = MIN(P,LENGTH(TEXT));
  WORD = SUBSTR(TEXT,1,MAX(P,2)-1);
  /* IS FIRST CHARACTER 'A'? */
  IF SUBSTR(WORD,1,1) = 'A'
    THEN PUT LIST (WORD) SKIP;
  IF P >= LENGTH(TEXT)
    THEN TEXT = '';
    ELSE TEXT = SUBSTR(TEXT,P+1);
  END;
END EX10_4;
```

10.5

```
EX10_5:     PROCEDURE OPTIONS (MAIN) ;

            /* SOLUTION TO EXERCISE 10.5 */

            DECLARE   TEXT   CHARACTER(200) VARYING,
                      CHAR   CHARACTER(1),
                      (SENT,   /* NO. OF SENTENCES */
                      WORDS,  /* NO. OF WORDS */
                      LETTERS)   FIXED ;

START:      /* INITIALIZE AND READ TEXT */
            SENT, WORDS, LETTERS = 0 ;
            GET LIST( TEXT ) ;

            /* EXAMINE TEXT FOR WORDS AND SENTENCES, AND
               COUNT LETTERS IN THE PROCESS */

            DO I = 1 BY 1 TO LENGTH( TEXT ) ;
               CHAR = SUBSTR( TEXT, I, 1 ) ;
               IF CHAR='.' THEN
                   DO ;
                       /* A PERIOD ENDS A WORD AND A SENT. */
                       WORDS = WORDS + 1 ;
                       SENT = SENT + 1 ;
                   END ;
               ELSE IF CHAR=' ' THEN WORDS = WORDS + 1 ;
               ELSE   LETTERS = LETTERS + 1 ;

               /* NOTE THE ASSUMPTION THAT A CHARACTER IS
                  CONSIDERED TO BE A LETTER IF IT IS NOT
                  A PERIOD OR A BLANK. */

            END ;

            /* PRINT RESULTS */
            PUT SKIP EDIT( 'SENTENCES =', SENT,
                           'WORDS/SENTENCE =', WORDS/SENT,
                           'LETTERS/WORD =', LETTERS/WORDS )
                          ( X(10), A, F(4) ) ;
            GO TO START ;
         END EX10_5 ;
```

10.6

```
EX10_6: PROCEDURE OPTIONS (MAIN);

  /* SOLUTION TO EXERCISE 10.6 */

  DCL (SUBSTR,INDEX,LENGTH,VERIFY) BUILTIN;
  DECLARE (ENG,WORD) CHARACTER (200) VARYING,
          PIG CHARACTER (400) VARYING,
          (FIRST,    /* FIRST CHARACTER IN A WORD */
           LAST,     /* LAST CHARACTER IN A WORD */
           VOL,      /* POSITION IN WORD OF A VOWEL */
           LW) FIXED;  /* LENGTH OF A WORD */

  DCL FLAG BIT (1);   /* '.,;' IN WORD */

  ON ENDFILE (SYSIN)
    STOP;

  DO WHILE ('1'B);
    GET LIST (ENG) COPY;
    PIG = '';
    FIRST = 0;

    /* LOOP FOR CONVERTING WORDS */
    DO WHILE (FIRST < LENGTH(ENG));
      /* FIND FIRST NON-BLANK CHARACTER */
      FIRST = VERIFY(ENG,' ');

      /* FIND NEXT BLANK CHARACTER -- END OF A WORD */
      LW = INDEX(SUBSTR(ENG,FIRST),' ');

      IF LW = 0
        THEN LW = LENGTH(ENG) + 1 - FIRST;
        ELSE LW = LW - 1;
      /* LW = NUMBER OF CHARACTERS IN A WORD */
      LAST = FIRST + LW;

      /* PUT THESE CHARACTERS INTO WORD */
      WORD = SUBSTR(ENG,FIRST,LW);

      /* CHECK LAST CHARACTER IN WORD FOR PUNCTUATION */
      IF INDEX('.,;',SUBSTR(WORD,LW,1)) ¬= 0
        THEN DO;
          FLAG = '1'B;
          LW = LW - 1;
          END;
        ELSE FLAG = '0'B;
```

```
          /* FIND FIRST VOWEL IN WORD */
          VOL = VERIFY(WORD,'BCDFGHJKLMNPQRSTVWXYZ');

          /* CONVERT WORD TO PIG LATIN */
          PIG = PIG || SUBSTR(WORD,VOL,LW-VOL+1)
                    || SUBSTR(WORD,1,VOL-1) || 'AY';

          IF FLAG
            THEN PIG = PIG || SUBSTR(WORD,LW+1);
          PIG = PIG || ' ';
          IF LAST > LENGTH(ENG)
          THEN ENG = '';
          ELSE ENG = SUBSTR(ENG,LAST);
        END;

     PUT SKIP LIST (PIG);
     END;

END EX10_6;
```

ANSWERS TO EXERCISES - CHAPTER 11

11.1

```
EX11_1: PROCEDURE OPTIONS (MAIN);

   /* SOLUTION TO EXERCISE 11.1 */

   DECLARE (SAVE,CHECK) FILE RECORD;

   DCL 1 SAVING,
         (2 NAME,
          2 ADDRESS) CHARACTER (20),
          2 ACCT_NO FIXED,
          2 BALANCE FLOAT;

   DCL 1 CHECKING,
         (2 NAME,
          2 ADDRESS) CHARACTER (20),
          2 ACCT_NO FIXED,
          2 BALANCE FLOAT;

   DCL (SAVE_EOF_FLAG,CHECK_EOF_FLAG) BIT (1);
```

```
     ON ENDFILE (SAVE)
        BEGIN;
          SAVING.NAME = (20) 'Z';
          SAVE_EOF_FLAG = '1'B;
          END;

     ON ENDFILE (CHECK)
        BEGIN;
          CHECKING.NAME = (20) 'Z';
          CHECK_EOF_FLAG = '1'B;
          END;

R1: FORMAT (SKIP,A);

   SAVE_EOF_FLAG, CHECK_EOF_FLAG = '0'B;

   READ FILE (SAVE) INTO (SAVING);
   READ FILE (CHECK) INTO (CHECKING);

   DO WHILE (¬(SAVE_EOF_FLAG & CHECK_EOF_FLAG));
     IF SAVING.NAME < CHECKING.NAME
       THEN DO;
         PUT EDIT (SAVING.NAME,SAVING.ADDRESS) (R(R1));
         READ FILE (SAVE) INTO (SAVING);
         END;
       ELSE DO;
         PUT EDIT (CHECKING.NAME,CHECKING.ADDRESS) (R(R1));
         IF SAVING.NAME = CHECKING.NAME
           THEN READ FILE (SAVE) INTO (SAVING);
         READ FILE (CHECK) INTO (CHECKING);
         END;
     PUT SKIP (2);
     END;
   END EX11_1;


11.2


EX11_2: PROCEDURE OPTIONS (MAIN) ;
       /* SOLUTION TO EXERCISE 11.2  */
       /* EDIT TEXT                  */

       DECLARE TEXT FILE RECORD ;
       DECLARE RECORD CHARACTER (100) ;
       DECLARE POSITION FIXED ;    /* KEY FOR UPDATING */
       DECLARE OLD_STRING  CHARACTER (100) VARYING ;
       DECLARE NEW_STRING  CHARACTER (100) VARYING ;
       DECLARE (I, J) FIXED ;
       DECLARE KEY_FLAG BIT (1) ;
```

```
ON ENDFILE (SYSIN)
      BEGIN ;
      CLOSE FILE (TEXT) ;
      OPEN FILE (TEXT) SEQUENTIAL ;
      DO I = 0 TO 99 ;
        READ FILE (TEXT) INTO (RECORD) ;
        PUT LIST (I,RECORD ) SKIP ;
      END ;
      STOP ;
      END ;

ON KEY (TEXT)
    BEGIN ;
    PUT EDIT ('*** KEY<',POSITION,'> NOT FOUND' )
             (A, F(5), A) SKIP ;
    KEY_FLAG = '1'B ;
    END ;

OPEN FILE (TEXT) UPDATE DIRECT ;
KEY_FLAG = '0'B ;

DO WHILE ('1'B) ;
  GET LIST (POSITION, OLD_STRING, NEW_STRING) SKIP;
  READ FILE (TEXT) INTO (RECORD) KEY (POSITION) ;
  IF KEY_FLAG
    THEN KEY_FLAG = '0'B ;
    ELSE DO ;
         I = INDEX (RECORD, OLD_STRING) ;
         IF I > 0
           THEN DO ;
                L = LENGTH(OLD_STRING) ;
                RECORD = SUBSTR(RECORD,1,I-1) ||
                     NEW_STRING ||
                     SUBSTR(RECORD,I+L) ;
                REWRITE FILE(TEXT) FROM (RECORD)
                     KEY (POSITION) ;
                END ;
           ELSE DO ;
                PUT EDIT ('*** <', OLD_STRING,
                     '> NOT FOUND') (A) SKIP ;
                END ;
         END ;
  END ;
END EX11_2 ;
```

11.3

```
EX11_3: PROCEDURE OPTIONS(MAIN) ;

        /* SOLUTION TO EXERCISE 11.3
              PROCESS A FILE WITH A MIXTURE OF DATA TYPES */

           DECLARE 1 CASH BASED (P),
                       2 TRANSACTION  CHARACTER(8),
                       2 AMOUNT        FLOAT,

                     1 CREDIT BASED (P),
                       2 TRANSACTION  CHARACTER(8),
                       2 CUSTOMER,
                       3 NAME         CHARACTER(30),
                       3 STREET       CHARACTER(30),
                       3 CITY         CHARACTER(25),
                       3 STATE        CHARACTER(15),
                       2 AMOUNT        FLOAT,

                     1 INV  BASED (I),
                       2 TRANSACTION  CHARACTER(8),
                       2 CUSTOMER,
                       3 NAME         CHARACTER(30),
                       3 STREET       CHARACTER(30),
                       3 CITY         CHARACTER(25),
                       3 STATE        CHARACTER(15),
                       2 AMOUNT        FLOAT,

                     (PURCH,
                      INVOICE) FILE SEQUENTIAL RECORD,
                     (CREDITAMT, CASHAMT)   FLOAT INITIAL (0) ;

        ON ENDFILE (PURCH)
                BEGIN ;
                PUT DATA (CREDITAMT, CASHAMT) SKIP ;
                STOP ;
                END ;

        DO WHILE ('1'B) ;
          READ FILE (PURCH) SET (P) ;
          IF CASH.TRANSACTION = 'CASH'
             THEN CASHAMT = CASHAMT+CASH.AMOUNT ;
             ELSE DO ;
                 CREDITAMT = CREDITAMT + CREDIT.AMOUNT ;
                 LOCATE INV SET (I) FILE (INVOICE) ;
                 INV = CREDIT ;
                 END ;
        END ;

        END EX11_3 ;
```

11.4

```
EX11_4:   PROCEDURE OPTIONS (MAIN) ;

              /*   SOLUTION TO EXERCISE 11.4
                   READ SOCIAL SECURITY NUMBERS AND PRINT
                   EMPLOYEE RECORD ACCESSED FROM DIRECT
                   ACCESS FILE.
                   NOTE:
                   THE DECLARE STATEMENT FOR 'FILENAME' IS
                   NOT ADEQUATE FOR ALL IMPLEMENTATIONS OF
                   PL/I.   ADDITIONAL INFORMATION MAY BE
                   REQUIRED BY THE OPERATING SYSTEM.   */

              DECLARE  1 EMPLOYEE,
                         2 NAME,
                          3 LAST        CHARACTER(15),
                          3 FIRST       CHARACTER(10),
                         2 SOCIAL_SECURITY  FIXED DECIMAL(9),
                          /* USED AS RECORD KEY */
                         2 DEPARTMENT  FIXED DECIMAL(3),
                         2 RATE_OF_PAY,
                          3 REGULAR     FLOAT,
                          3 OVERTIME    FLOAT,
                         2 DATE_OF_LAST_REVIEW CHARACTER(6) ;

              DECLARE  EMPLFIL  RECORD DIRECT KEYED INPUT ;

              DO WHILE ('1'B) ;
              GET LIST (SOCIAL_SECURITY) ;

              /* ACCESS EMPLOYEE'S RECORD FROM DIRECT ACCESS
                 FILE. */
              READ FILE( EMPLFIL ) INTO( EMPLOYEE )
                                   KEY( SOCIAL_SECURITY ) ;

              /* PRINT RECORD */
              PUT LIST( EMPLOYEE ) SKIP ;

              END ;

          END EX11_4 ;
```

11.5

```
EX11_5:   PROCEDURE OPTIONS (MAIN) ;

               /*   SOLUTION TO EXERCISE 11.5
                    CREATE DIRECT ACCESS FILE FOR USE BY
                    EXAMPLE NO. 5.1
                    NOTE:
                    THE DECLARE STATEMENT FOR 'FILENAME' IS
                    NOT ADEQUATE FOR ALL IMPLEMENTATIONS OF
                    PL/I.   ADDITIONAL INFORMATION MAY BE
                    REQUIRED BY THE OPERATING SYSTEM.    */

               DECLARE   1 EMPLOYEE,
                           2 NAME,
                            3 LAST        CHARACTER(15),
                            3 FIRST       CHARACTER(10),
                           2 SOCIAL_SECURITY FIXED DECIMAL(9),
                            /* USED AS RECORD KEY */
                           2 DEPARTMENT  FIXED DECIMAL(3),
                           2 RATE_OF_PAY,
                            3 REGULAR     FLOAT,
                            3 OVERTIME    FLOAT,
                           2 DATE_OF_LAST_REVIEW CHARACTER(6) ;

               DECLARE  EMPLFIL   RECORD DIRECT KEYED OUTPUT ;

               DO WHILE ('1'B) ;
               GET LIST( EMPLOYEE ) ;

               /* PLACE RECORD IN DIRECT ACCESS FILE. */
               WRITE FILE( EMPLFIL ) FROM( EMPLOYEE )
                                     KEYFROM( SOCIAL_SECURITY ) ;

               END ;

         END EX11_5 ;
```

12.1

```
EX12_1: PROCEDURE OPTIONS (MAIN);

  /* SOLUTION TO EXERCISE 12.1 */

  DCL NULL BUILTIN;
  DCL P POINTER ;

  DECLARE 1 PASSENGER BASED (P),
            2 NAME CHARACTER (20),
            2 SEAT CHARACTER (3),
            2 MENU CHARACTER (40),
            2 LINK OFFSET (DAY);

  DCL (FLIGHT,LAST,TEST,PREV) POINTER;
  DCL PERSON CHAR (20), FUNCTION CHAR (6);
  DCL FOUND_FLAG BIT (1);

  DCL COUNT FIXED;      /* NUMBER OF 'REGULAR' MEALS */

  ON ENDFILE (SYSIN)
    BEGIN;
      TEST = FLIGHT;
      COUNT = 0;
      DO WHILE (TEST ¬= NULL);
        IF TEST->MENU = 'REGULAR'
          THEN COUNT = COUNT + 1;
          ELSE PUT LIST (TEST->MENU) SKIP;
        TEST = TEST->LINK;
        END;
      PUT EDIT ('REGULAR MEALS: ',COUNT) (A,F(5)) SKIP;
      STOP;
      END;

  FLIGHT = NULL;

  /* MAIN LOOP FOR PASSENGER PROCEESING */

  DO WHILE ('1'B);
    GET EDIT (FUNCTION) (SKIP,A(6));

    IF FUNCTION = 'ADD'
      THEN DO;  /* ADD A NEW PASSENGER */
        ALLOCATE PASSENGER ;
        GET EDIT (NAME,SEAT,MENU) (SKIP,A(20),A(3),A(40));
        IF FLIGHT = NULL
```

```
      THEN FLIGHT = P;
      ELSE LAST->LINK = P;
   P->LINK = NULL;
   LAST = P;
   END;

ELSE IF FUNCTION = 'CANCEL'
    THEN DO;  /* CANCEL A PASSENGER */
      GET EDIT (PERSON) (SKIP,A(20));
      /* NAME TO BE CANCELLED */
      PREV = NULL;
      TEST = FLIGHT;
      FOUND_FLAG = '0'B;
      /* GO THROUGH LIST TO FIND PERSON */
      DO WHILE (TEST ¬= NULL);
        IF TEST->NAME = PERSON
          THEN DO;  /* PERSON FOUND */
            FOUND_FLAG = '1'B;
            IF PREV = NULL
              THEN FLIGHT = TEST->LINK;
              ELSE PREV->LINK = TEST->LINK;
            IF TEST = LAST
              THEN LAST = PREV;
            FREE TEST->PASSENGER ;
            TEST = NULL;
            END;
          ELSE DO;
            PREV = TEST;
            TEST = TEST->LINK;
            END;
        END;
      IF ¬ FOUND_FLAG
        THEN PUT SKIP EDIT ('NOT ON FLIGHT: ',
            PERSON) (A);
      END;
    ELSE PUT SKIP EDIT ('ILLEGAL FUNCTION: ',
        FUNCTION) (A);
  END;

END EX12_1;
```

12.2   By keeping a pointer to the last passenger in the list we avoid the
       need to search the list to find the last passenger each time we want
       to add a passenger. As the list gets longer, such searches would
       require increasingly more time.

```
EX12_3: PROCEDURE OPTIONS (MAIN);

   /* SOLUTION TO EXERCISE 12.3 */

   DCL NULL BUILTIN;
   DCL (P,RES) POINTER;
   DECLARE 1 PASSENGER BASED (P),
             2 NAME CHARACTER (20),
             2 SEAT CHARACTER (3),
             2 MENU CHARACTER (40),
             2 LINK OFFSET (DAY);

   DECLARE 1 RESERVATION BASED (RES),
             2 FLIGHT OFFSET (DAY),
             2 LAST OFFSET (DAY),
             2 DAY AREA;

   DCL TEST OFFSET (DAY);
   DCL PO POINTER;
   DCL PERSON CHAR (20), FUNCTION CHAR (6);
   DCL FUTURE FILE RECORD ;    /* THIS DECLARE MAY NOT BE
                                  ADEQUATE FOR SOME COMPILERS */
   DCL (DAYNO,OLD_DAYNO) FIXED;   /* NUMBER OF DAY */


   ON KEY (FUTURE)
     BEGIN;
       PUT EDIT ('INCORRECT DAY NUMBER:',DAYNO)
           (A,F(5)) SKIP;
       FUNCTION = 'ON KEY';     /* STOP FURTHER PROCESSING */
       END;

   ON ENDFILE (FUTURE)
     SIGNAL ENDFILE (SYSIN);

   ON ENDFILE (SYSIN)
     BEGIN;
       CLOSE FILE (FUTURE);
       OPEN FILE (FUTURE) SEQUENTIAL ;

       ON ENDFILE (FUTURE)
         BEGIN;
           CLOSE FILE (FUTURE);
           STOP;
           END;
```

```
   DO WHILE ('1'B);
     READ FILE (FUTURE) INTO (RESERVATION);
     PUT EDIT ('--- FLIGHT LIST ---') (A) SKIP (2);
     TEST = FLIGHT;
     DO WHILE (TEST ¬= NULL);
       PUT EDIT (TEST->NAME) (A) SKIP;
       TEST = TEST->LINK;
       END;
     END;
   END;

ALLOCATE RESERVATION;
OPEN FILE (FUTURE) UPDATE DIRECT;
OLD_DAYNO = C;

DO WHILE ('1'B);
  GET EDIT (DAYNO,FUNCTION) (SKIP,F(3),A(6));
  IF OLD_DAYNO ¬= DAYNO
    THEN DO;

      /* UPDATE FUTURE FILE IF NECESSARY */

      IF OLD_DAYNO > 0
        THEN REWRITE FILE (FUTURE) FROM (RESERVATION)
            KEY (OLD_DAYNO);
      READ FILE (FUTURE) INTO (RESERVATION) KEY (DAYNO);
      OLD_DAYNO = DAYNO;
      END;

  IF FUNCTION = 'ADD'
    THEN CALL ADD ;
    ELSE IF FUNCTION = 'CANCEL'
      THEN CALL CANCEL ;

      ELSE IF FUNCTION = 'NEXT'
        THEN DO;
          /* UPDATE LIST FOR THIS DAY'S FLIGHTS */
          REWRITE FILE (FUTURE) FROM (RESERVATION)
              KEY (DAYNO);
          OLD_DAYNO = 0;
          END;
        ELSE PUT EDIT ('UNKNOWN FUNCTION: ',
            FUNCTION) (A) SKIP;
  END;
```

```
ADD: PROCEDURE ;
    /* ADD A PASSENGER TO THE LIST */
    ALLOCATE PASSENGER IN (DAY) ;
    P->LINK = NULL;
    GET EDIT (NAME,SEAT,MENU) (A(20),A(3),A(40)) SKIP;
    IF FLIGHT = NULL
      THEN FLIGHT = P;
      ELSE LAST->LINK = P;
    LAST = P;
  END ADD ;

  CANCEL: PROCEDURE ;
      /* DELETE A PASSENGER FROM THE LIST */
      GET EDIT (PERSON) (SKIP,A(20)) ;
      IF FLIGHT ¬= NULL
        THEN DO;
          PO = NULL;
          TEST = FLIGHT;
          DO WHILE (TEST ¬= NULL) ;
            IF TEST->NAME = PERSON
              THEN DO;  /* DELETE */
                IF TEST = FLIGHT
                  THEN FLIGHT = FLIGHT->LINK;
                  ELSE PO->LINK = TEST->LINK;
                IF TEST = LAST
                  THEN LAST = PO;
                FREE TEST->PASSENGER;
                TEST, PO = NULL;
                END;
              ELSE DO;  /* CHAIN */
                PO = TEST;
                TEST = TEST->LINK;
                END;
            END;
          IF PO ¬= NULL
            THEN PUT SKIP EDIT ('NOT ON FLIGHT: ',
                PERSON) (A);
          END;
        ELSE PUT SKIP EDIT ('FLIGHT EMPTY') (A);
    END CANCEL ;

END EX12_3;
```

```
EX 12_4: PROCEDURE OPTIONS (MAIN);

  /* SOLUTION TO EXERCISE 12.4 */

  DCL NULL BUILTIN;

  DCL (P,Q,R) POINTER;

  DCL 1 PERSON BASED (P),
        (2 NAME,
         2 ADDRESS) CHARACTER (20),
         2 LINK POINTER;

  DCL START POINTER;  /* POINTER TO FIRST PERSON */

  DCL (NAME,ADDRESS) CHAR (20);

  ON ENDFILE (SYSIN)
    BEGIN;
      P = START;
      DO WHILE (P ¬= NULL);
        PUT EDIT (P->PERSON.NAME,P->PERSON.ADDRESS)
            (A(20),X(3),A(20)) SKIP;
        P = P->PERSON.LINK;
        END;
      STOP;
      END;

  START = NULL;

  /* MAIN LOOP FOR READING NAMES */

  DO WHILE ('1'B);
    GET EDIT (NAME,ADDRESS) (A(20)) SKIP;

    /* ALLOCATE STORAGE FOR A PERSON */
    ALLOCATE PERSON;
    P->PERSON.NAME = NAME;
    P->PERSON.ADDRESS = ADDRESS;
    P->PERSON.LINK = NULL;

  IF START = NULL   /* LIST IS EMPTY */
    THEN START = P;
    ELSE DO;        /* CHAIN THROUGH THE LIST */
      Q = START;
      R = NULL;
      DO WHILE (Q ¬= NULL);
```

```
            IF Q->PERSON.NAME < NAME
               THEN DO:
                  R = Q;
                  Q = Q->PERSON.LINK;
                  END;
               ELSE Q = NULL;
            END;
         IF R = NULL
            THEN DO;
               /* PUT PERSON AT BEGINNING OF LIST */
               P->PERSON.LINK = START;
               START = P;
               END;
            ELSE DO;
               /* PUT PERSON AT MIDDLE OF LIST */
               P->PERSON.LINK = R->PERSON.LINK;
               R->PERSON.LINK = P;
               END;
         END;
   END;

END EX12_4;
```

INDEX

A

Abbreviations for keywords, 252–253
Accuracy, 11, 92
ALLOCATE statement, 228–229, 231, 242, 246
  areas, 242
  SET option, 246
ALLOCATION function, 261
Allocation of storage, 166–168, 170, 171, 227–232, 242, 246
AREA, 242
  assignment, 245
  condition, 246, 262
  size, 242
Arguments, 14, 145
  arrays, 160–161
  structures, 161
  to functions, 14–15, 145
  to subroutines, 148
Arithmetic:
  constants, 10–11, 51, 53
  data, 50–57
  expressions, 7–10, 125, 151
  functions, 14–15, 254–256

Arithmetic (*cont.*):
  operators, 8, 250–251
   strength, 9
  variables, 12, 49–56
Array:
  arguments, 160–161
  assignment, 77
  declarations, 71–72
  elements, 69
  expressions, 77–78, 89–90
  functions, 258–259
  I/O, 78, 132, 212
  multi-dimensional, 76
  parameters, 145
  of pointers, 238
  of structures, 99–100
Assignment:
  area, 245
  arithmetic, 12
  array, 77
  BY NAME, 105–106
  label, 65
  locator, 232
  multiple, 13
  string, 190–194
  structures, 102

Assignment operator, 12, 29, 250
Assignment statement, 5, 12–13
Attributes:
  AREA, 242
  arithmetic, 50–57
  AUTOMATIC, 229–230
  base, 53
  BASED, 215–219, 231, 242
  BINARY, 53
  BIT, 62–63
  CHARACTER, 59
  COMPLEX, 67
  CONTROLLED, 228–230, 246
  conversion, 114, 128–129, 207–208, 211
  DECIMAL, 53–54
  default, 55
  dimension, 70, 76
  DIRECT, 219, 225
  ENTRY, 158, 160, 163
  EXTERNAL, 156, 157, 166
  factoring, 15, 50
  FILE, 202
  FIXED, 51–52
  FLOAT, 53
  INITIAL, 66–67, 73–74, 78
  INPUT, 204
  KEYED, 219
  LABEL, 65–66
  length, 59, 62, 67
  OFFSET, 243
  OUTPUT, 204
  PICTURE, 55–57, 61–62
  POINTER, 232, 246
  precision, 51
  PRINT, 203
  REAL, 67
  RECORD, 211
  RECURSIVE, 163
  RETURNS, 161, 162
  scale, 53
  scope, 156, 166, 170

Attributes (*cont.*):
  SEQUENTIAL, 219
  STATIC, 227
  STREAM, 211
  UPDATE, 223
  VARYING, 60, 61, 63, 198
AUTOMATIC attribute (*see* Attributes, AUTOMATIC)

B

Base attribute (*see* Attributes, base)
BASED attribute (*see* Attributes, BASED)
Based variable, 215–219, 231
  allocation, 231, 242
BEGIN:
  block, 165, 167, 170
  statement (*see* Statements, BEGIN)
BINARY attribute (*see* Attributes, BINARY)
Binary point, 53, 67
BIT attribute (*see* Attributes, BIT)
Bit string data, 62–63, 190
Blank:
  in character strings, 58
  padding, 192
Block:
  BEGIN, 165
  procedure, 165
Blocking factor, 214
Boolean algebra, 45
Boolean variables, 64
Buffer, 207–209
Built-in functions, 14–15, 254
BY, 81, 90
BY NAME option, 105–106

C

CALL statement (*see* Statements, CALL)
Chained list, 233

CHARACTER attribute (*see* Attributes, CHARACTER)

Character sets, 248–251

Character string data, 57–62, 190–193

  input/output, 113, 115, 117, 118, 122, 137, 138

  manipulation, 190–199

CHECK condition, 186–188

CLOSE statement (*see* Statements, CLOSE)

COLUMN, 132

Comment, 4

Comparison operators, 28–29, 250

Compilation, 18–19

  of BEGIN blocks, 167

  of procedures, 145

Compiler, 18

COMPLEX attribute (*see* Attributes, COMPLEX)

COMPLEX function, 254

Concatenation, 197-198

Conditions, 262–265

  causes, 176

  disabled, 181, 183

  enabled, 181

  prefix, 181, 182

  programmer-defined, 184

  response, 176–177

Constants:

  arithmetic, 10–11, 51, 53

  bit, 62

  character string, 57–58

  label, 65

CONTROLLED attribute (*see* Attributes, CONTROLLED)

Control variable, 81, 90

  value at exit from loop, 83

CONVERSION condition, 128, 263

Conversion of data, 114–115, 128, 160

COPY option, 129

D

Data:

  arithmetic, 50–57

  attributes, 49

  bits, 62–63

  character, 57–62

  conversion, 114–115, 128, 160, 211

  forms, 113, 211

  homogeneous, 70, 96

  label, 65–66

  locator, 231, 234, 243

  non-homogeneous, 96

  non-numeric, 190

  offset, 243

  pointer, 231, 242

  string, 49, 57–62

  transmission, 208

Data-directed I/O, 115–116

  contents of list, 127

  data conversion, 128

  data representation, 113

  termination, 115, 116

Debugging, 44, 84, 172, 176, 184

DECIMAL attribute (*see* Attributes, DECIMAL)

Decimal point, 55, 56, 67

Decision:

  block, 27

  statement, 28

Declaration, 19

  of parameters, 145

  procedure, 144, 154, 158–159

DECLARE statement, 4, 15, 50

  for area, 242

  for arrays, 71–72

  with ENTRY, 158, 160, 163

  with EXTERNAL, 156, 157, 166

  for files, 202

  with INITIAL, 66

  with LABEL, 65

  with PICTURE, 55–56, 61–62

DECLARE statement (*cont.*):
  with RETURNS, 161, 162
  for storage allocation, 227, 228, 231
  for string data, 59, 62
  for structures, 98
Diagnostic facilities:
  CHECK condition, 186–188, 264
  ON statement, 177–178, 184
  SIGNAL statement, 183, 184
Dimension attribute, 70, 76, 99, 100–101
Direct-access file, 219–225
  characteristics, 219, 222
DIRECT attribute (*see* Attributes, DIRECT)
Disabled conditions, 181, 182
DO:
  group, 41–44
  in I/O list, 134
  loop, 79–88, 90
  statement, 41–43, 81–88
    nested, 86
Drifting characters, 123, 267–268

E

Edit-directed I/O, 116–126
  contents of list, 127
  data conversion, 128
  data representation, 113
  termination, 126
Editing specifications (*see* Format phrases)
Efficiency:
  of execution, 22, 54, 57, 79, 87, 211, 214
  of input/output, 212, 214
  of storage usage, 170, 230
Elementary level, 97, 98
ELSE, 33–41
Enabled conditions, 181
ENDFILE condition, 176, 185–186, 263
End of file, 176, 185–186, 208

END statement (*see* Statements, END
ENTRY attribute (*see* Attributes, ENTRY)
Errors:
  program, 172, 184, 186
  roundoff, 93
Execution:
  sequence, 20, 24, 81, 145, 155, 168–169
  termination, 25, 27
Expressions:
  as arguments, 151
  arithmetic, 7–10
  array, 76–77, 78
  in formats, 125
  logical, 29, 45–46
    value, 45–46
  structure, 102
EXTERNAL attribute (*see* Attributes, EXTERNAL)
External devices, 111
  direct-access, 219
  sequential, 219
  speed, 211
External procedures, 158

F

File, 202–207
  attributes:
    DIRECT, 219, 225
    INPUT, 204
    KEYED, 219
    OUTPUT, 204
    PRINT, 203
    RECORD, 211
    SEQUENTIAL, 219
    STREAM, 211
  closing, 204
  data representation, 113
  definition, 111
  direct-access, 219, 225
  opening, 204

File, attributes (*cont.*):
  sequential, 219
  standard, 111, 185, 202
FILE attribute (*see* Attributes, FILE)
FIXED attribute (*see* Attributes, FIXED)
FIXEDOVERFLOW condition, 176, 178–180, 263
Fixed-point data, 51–52
FLOAT attribute (*see* Attributes, FLOAT)
Floating-point data, 53
Flow chart, 20, 21, 23, 26, 32, 33, 37, 38–39
Format phrases, 118–120, 122–123, 130, 132, 269–272
FORMAT statement (*see* Statements, FORMAT)
FREE, 228, 235
FROM clause, 212, 223
Function:
  built-in, 14–15, 195, 198, 254–261
  procedure, 148, 150

G

GET statement, 5, 110–112
  with COPY option, 129
  with FILE option, 203
  with STRING option, 137–138
Global identifiers, 156, 165
GO TO statement, 25, 79, 83, 84
  eliminating, 84

I

Identifiers, 6
  global, 156, 165
  local, 156, 165
  redefinition, 154, 169
  scope, 155-156, 166, 170

IF statement, 28–43, 63
  nested, 43
INDEX function, 198, 256
Indexing, 73
Information retrieval, 108, 198
INITIAL attribute (*see* Attribute, INITIAL)
Inner loop, 86–87
IN option, 242
INPUT attribute (*see* Attributes, INPUT)
Integer, 10, 51
Internal:
  identifiers, 165
  procedures, 158
Inter-record gap, 209–210, 215
Interrupts, 176
  processing, 181
  standard action, 176, 180, 262–265
INTO option, 211, 216, 221
I/O:
  of arrays, 78, 132
  device, 111
  efficiency, 212, 214
  list, 113, 127
  statements (*see* Statements, GET; Statements, PUT; Statements, READ; Statements, WRITE)
  stream, 126, 211
  termination, 114, 115, 116, 125–126, 208–209
Iteration, 79

K

Key, record, 219
Key clause, 221, 225
KEYED attribute (*see* Attributes, KEYED)
KEYFROM option, 221
KEY option, 221, 225
Keywords, 7
  abbreviations, 252–253

L

Label, statement, 24–25
LABEL attribute (*see* Attributes,
    LABEL)
Label data, 65–66
LENGTH function, 60, 61, 63, 256
Level, elementary, 97, 98
Level number, 98, 99
LINE:
  format phrase, 132
  option, 130
Linked list, 233
List, I/O, 113, 127
  contents, 127
List (array), 69
List-directed I/O, 111–115
  contents of list, 127
  data conversion, 114, 128–130
  data representation, 113
  termination, 114
Local identifiers, 156, 165
LOCATE statement (*see* Statements,
    LOCATE)
Locator qualifier, 233, 234, 251
Locator variable, 232, 243
  OFFSET, 243
  POINTER, 232, 243
Logical:
  construction, 32–33, 44–45
  errors, 44, 172, 186
  expressions, 31, 45–46
  operators, 29
    strength, 31
  record, 214
  sequence, 20
  statement, 20
Loop, 79–88
  characteristics, 82–83
  nested, 86

M

MAIN option, 142, 158
Main procedure, 142

N

Null:
  on-unit, 180
  statement, 40
  string, 58
NULL, 233

O

Object program, 18
OFFSET attribute (*see* Attributes,
    OFFSET)
ON statement (*see* Statements, ON)
On-unit, 176–177
  canceling, 180
  null, 180
  overriding, 178–179
  redefinition, 178–179
  stacking, 180
OPEN statement (*see* Statements,
    OPEN)
Operands, 7
Operating system, 176, 181
Operators, 250–251
  arithmetic, 8
    strength, 9
  assignment, 12, 29, 250
  comparison, 28
  locator, 234
  logical, 29
    strength, 31
  relational, 28
  string, 194, 197
Output (*see* I/O)
OUTPUT attribute (*see* Attributes,
    OUTPUT)

OVERFLOW condition, 176, 183, 263

P

Padding, 192
PAGE:
  format phrase, 132
  option, 130
Parameters, 145
  arrays, 145
  name, 147
  structures, 152–153
  value, 147
Physical record, 209, 211
PICTURE, 266–269
  attribute, 55–57, 61–62
    for arithmetic data, 55–57
    for character data, 61–62
  specification characters, 122–123
    drifting, 123
PL/C, 16, 67, 140, 163, 225, 246, 250, 259
POINTER attribute (see Attributes, POINTER)
Pointer variables, 215, 231–232, 246
Precision:
  attribute, 51
  of data, 11
Prefixes, 181–182
PRINT attribute (see Attribute, PRINT)
Procedures, 142
  arguments, 145
  declaration, 144, 145, 158–159
  external, 158
  function, 148, 150
  internal, 158
  main, 142
  nesting, 157–158

Procedures (cont.):
  parameters, 147, 148
  recursive, 163
  subroutine, 148
PROCEDURE statement, 4, 145
  with MAIN option, 142, 158
Program, 1
  main, 142
  object, 18
  phases, 18–19
  source, 18
  structure, 19–20
  subprogram (see Procedures)
Program library, 162
Programmer-defined, conditions, 184
Progress block, 27
Pseudo-variable, 196
PUT statement, 5, 111–112
  with FILE option, 203
  with LINE option, 130
  with PAGE option, 130
  with SKIP option, 130
  with STRING option, 137–138

Q

Qualification operator:
  for locator data, 233, 251
  for structure data, 101, 251
Qualified names, 101, 102
  expressions, 102
  in I/O , 116
  offset, 243
  pointer, 234

R

READ statement (see Statements, READ)

REAL attribute (*see* Attributes, REAL)

Recommended practices:
  buffering, 207–209
  DO-WHILE, 84
  indentation:
    DO, 44
    structures, 99
  labeling DO loops, 80
  loops, construction, 86
  minimizing roundoff error, 93
  PICTURE effect on execution, 57
  use of CHECK, 162, 186–188
  use of ENTRY and RETURNS, 160–161

Record:
  keys, 219–220
  logical, 214
  physical, 209, 211

RECORD attribute (*see* Attributes, RECORD)

RECURSIVE attribute (*see* Attributes, RECURSIVE)

Relational operators, 28, 250–251

Remote format specifications, 139–140

Repetitive specifications, 132–133

Replication factor:
  in constants, 56–57, 58, 62
  in formats, 125

RETURNS attribute (*see* Attributes, RETURNS)

RETURN statement (*see* Statements, RETURN)

REVERT statement (*see* Statements, REVERT)

REWRITE statement (*see* Statements, REWRITE)

Roundoff error, 93

Row major order, 78

S

Scale attribute (*see* Attribute, scale)

Scientific notation, 10–11

Scope:
  of group, 44
  of identifiers, 155–156, 166, 170
  of loop, 88
  of prefixes, 181–182

Search argument, 198

SEQUENTIAL attribute (*see* Attributes, SEQUENTIAL)

Sequential file, 219
  characteristics, 219

SET option:
  ALLOCATION statement, 246
  READ statement, 217

SIGNAL statement (*see* Statements, SIGNAL)

SKIP:
  format phrase, 132
  option, 130

Source program, 18

Specification characters (*see* PICTURE)

Standard file, 111, 185, 202

Statement labels, 24–25

Statements:
  ALLOCATE, 228–229, 231, 242, 246
  assignment, 5, 12–13
  BEGIN, 165
  CALL, 148
  CLOSE, 204, 206
  DECLARE, 4, 15, 50
  DO, 41–43, 81–88
  END, 6, 20, 43, 79, 80
  executable, 19
  FORMAT, 139
  FREE, 228, 235

Statements (*cont.*):
  GET, 5, 110–112
  GO TO, 25, 79, 83, 84
  IF, 28–43, 63
  LOCATE, 217
  null, 40
  ON, 177, 184
  OPEN, 204, 206
    with TITLE option, 206
  PROCEDURE, 4, 145
  PUT, 5, 110–112
  READ, 211
    with KEY, 221
    with SET, 217
  RETURN, 144, 149–150
  REVERT, 180
  REWRITE, 223–225
  SIGNAL, 183, 184
  STOP, 28
  transfer, 25, 28
  WRITE, 212
    with KEYFROM, 221
STATIC attribute (*see* Attributes,
    STATIC)
STOP statement (*see* Statements,
    STOP)
Storage allocation, 166–168, 170,
    171, 227–232, 242, 246
Storage classes:
  automatic, 229–230
  based, 231, 242
  controlled, 228–230, 246
  static, 227, 230
STREAM attribute (*see* Attribute,
    STREAM)
Stream I/O, 126
String:
  assignment, 190–194
  bit, 62–63
  character, 57–62, 190

String (*cont.*):
  destination, 193
  null, 58
  source, 193
STRING option, 137–138
STRINGRANGE condition, 195,
    264
STRINGSIZE, 265
Structure assignment, 102
  BY NAME option, 105–106
Structured programming, 25, 84–85,
    172–175, 184, 185–186
Structures, 96
  arrays, 99–100
  declaration, 98
  expressions, 102
  major, 101
  minor, 101
  as parameters, 152–153
Subprogram, 142
Subroutine, 142
Subroutine, procedure, 148
SUBSCRIPTRANGE condition,
    176, 182, 265
Subscripts, 71
  bounds, 71–72
  in I/O list, 133
  number, 76
SUBSTR function, 194–195
  as pseudo-variable, 196
Substring, 194
SYSIN, 185
SYSPRINT, 185
SYSTEM, on-unit, 180

T

Tables (arrays), 69
Termination:
  of execution, 25, 27

Termination (*cont.*):
  of I/O, 114, 115, 116, 125–126,
    208–209
Title option, 206
TO, 81, 90
Transfers:
  conditional, 28
  unconditional, 25

U

UNDERFLOW condition, 176, 264
UPDATE attribute (*see* Attributes,
    UPDATE)

V

Variables, 2
  arithmetic, 12, 49–56
  based, 215–219, 231

Variables (*cont.*):
  character string, 57, 59–62
  label, 65–66
  names, 6
  pointer, 215, 231–232
  pseudovariable, 196
  simple, 73
  subscripted, 73
VARYING attribute (*see* Attributes,
    VARYING)

W

WHILE, 81, 84, 90
WRITE statement (*see* Statements,
    WRITE)

Z

ZERODIVIDE condition, 176, 264
Zero suppression, 127